THE TALKING BOOK

ALLEN DWIGHT CALLAHAN

THE

Talking
Book

AFRICAN AMERICANS AND THE BIBLE

YALE UNIVERSITY PRESS   NEW HAVEN & LONDON

Published with assistance from the Annie Burr Lewis Fund and the Louis Stern
Memorial Fund.

Set in Scala and Scala Sans by Duke & Company, Devon, Pennsylvania.
Printed in the United States of America.

Library of Congress Cataloging-in-Publication Data
Callahan, Allen Dwight.
   The talking book : African Americans and the Bible / Allen Dwight Callahan.
      p.   cm.
   Includes bibliographical references and index.
   ISBN-13: 978-0-300-10936-8 (cloth : alk. paper)
   ISBN-10: 0-300-10936-9 (cloth : alk. paper)
      1. Bible—Black interpretations—History. 2. Bible—Criticism, interpretation, etc.
3. Afrocentrism—Religious aspects—Christianity—History. 4. African Americans—
Religion. I. Title.
   BS521.2.C35 2006
   220.089′96073—dc22   2006006464

A catalogue record for this book is available from the British Library.

The paper in this book meets the guidelines for permanence and durability of the Committee on Production Guidelines for Book Longevity of the Council on Library Resources.

10 9 8 7 6 5 4 3 2 1

To my mother, Olivia Estes—my first librarian, who taught me how to hear the books talk

Above this firmament of your Scripture I believe that there are other waters, immortal and kept safe from earthly corruption. They are the peoples of your city, your angels, on high above the firmament. Let them glorify your name and sing your praises, for they have no need to look up to this firmament of ours or read its text to know your word. For ever they gaze upon your face and there, without the aid of syllables inscribed in time, they read what your eternal will decrees. They read your will: they choose it to be theirs: they cherish it. They read it without ceasing and what they read never passes away. For it is your own unchanging purpose that they read, choosing to make it their own and cherishing it for themselves. The book they read shall not be closed. For them the scroll shall not be furled. For you yourself are their book and you forever are.

—*Augustine,* Confessions

CONTENTS

ACKNOWLEDGMENTS

MUCH OF WHAT IS GOOD in this volume devolves from the good graces of others. Abraham Smith of the Perkins School of Theology at Southern Methodist University and Hugh Paige of the University of Notre Dame reviewed an earlier, vastly inferior draft of this work and were nonetheless graciously supportive. A. G. Miller of Oberlin College provided me with photocopies of Theophilus Gould Steward's *The End of the World* and some helpful pointers on the historiography of African-American religion. Randall Burkett of Emory University, Professors Harvey Cox and Jon Levenson of the Harvard Divinity School, and Professor Anthony Pinn of Rice University carefully reviewed chapters in draft and proposed important suggestions and corrections. I have learned much from each of these kind and learned colleagues. In addition, portions of this manuscript have benefited from the editorial attentions of Missy Daniel at *Religion and Ethics Newsweekly;* her red pen has spared the reader much unhappy prose. I am grateful to my research associate in the early phase of this work, Irene Monroe, for her thoughtfulness, candor, wit, and energy. I am indebted to John Wright of the University of Minnesota for sharing so generously with me his time, his texts, and his encyclopedic command of African-American literature. And I am pleased to acknowledge here Lara Heimert and her colleagues at Yale University Press for finding merit in this book that, judging from my sheaf of rejection letters, others did not.

Finally, I owe an inestimable debt of gratitude to my friend and literary agent, Donald Cutler, without whose counsel, encouragement, unerring sense of literary style, and seemingly boundless patience this volume would never have come to press.

Some of the thoughts and a few of the words in this work first appeared in others. I anticipated what I have written here about the Apostle Paul in an article that appeared in a collection of essays on slavery and biblical interpretation. The chapter on Exile elaborates on thinking reflected in essays I wrote treating the biblical figures Nehemiah and Ezekiel and in a lecture on the biblical imagery of Babylon that I delivered in Cuba in the summer of 2001. I developed the chapter entitled "Emmanuel" from a lecture I presented several years ago in Brazil reviewing African-American interpretations of the figure of Jesus. In that summary review I said little about Hip-Hop and "Gansta" Rap, cultural forces of which I was then only dimly aware.

I have ranged freely through several academic disciplines in this book. The result may be, in the words of Augustine, too much for some and too little for others. No doubt specialists in the various fields into which I have wandered will be dismayed if not displeased, at least occasionally if not repeatedly. Though I write as a generalist with some claim to expertise in biblical studies, Americanists and ethnomusicologists, art historians and literary critics may read me as a dilettante. So be it. The French psychoanalyst Jacques Lacan once wrote in defense of his own eclectic method, "Whoever is functioning at the level of the pursuit of truth can completely make do without the advice of the specialist." I cannot be as dismissive as Lacan: I invite the reader to refer to the notes throughout this work citing my interest in, and dependence upon, "the advice of the specialist." But for whatever truth I have attained or failed to attain in this pursuit, I am fully and solely responsible.

PROLOGUE

AFRICAN AMERICANS ARE THE children of slavery in America. And the Bible, as no other book, is the book of slavery's children.

The evidence is everywhere in African-American culture. In black churches, of course, where preaching is a venerable art form with all the virtuosity and inventiveness of jazz, a sermon not based on a biblical text is unthinkable. The Bible's impact on the African-American imagination also has been broad and varied in the arts. Negro spirituals, that great corpus of African-American sacred music, are shot through with biblical allusions, and the genre of African-American music called "gospel" takes its name from its obsession with biblical stories from the life of Jesus.

Yet biblical phrases and motifs have been manifest in African-American life far beyond the boundaries that moderns have marked off with the word *religion*. In traditional parlance still used in some African-American churches, what preachers do with the Bible in their sermons is spoken of as "taking a text." American slaves and their descendants have taken the texts of the Bible in every sense of the word: embraced them, endured them, seized them, stolen them, caught them, and captured them. African-American politicians have always flavored their rhetoric with scriptural allusions. Traditional African-American folk medicine, called variously "conjure," "roots," or "hoodoo," bases many of its incantations on biblical texts and figures. Whether as slaves absconding from plantations, terrorized sharecroppers in flight from Jim Crow, or Civil Rights activists protesting discrimination and disenfranchisement, African Americans have spoken of escape from oppression as an Exodus and their goal of a better life as the Promised Land. In the 1930s, littérateurs of the Harlem Renaissance brought black biblical folklore to American belles lettres. Biblical interpretation is a veritable subgenre in the Hip-Hop music of African-American urban youth, and the figure of Jesus inhabits what poet Sonia Sanchez has called "a theological space" in which young black people identify with his biblical words and deeds.

The Bible has been available to African Americans as no other literature. "Biblical imagery was used because it was at hand," writes historian of religion Charles Long. "It was adapted to and invested with the experience of the slave." In so doing, the slaves took in hand what was at hand and impressed it into the service of forming the collective imagination, the cultural task of any people if they are to survive. As literary critic and novelist Albert Murray put it, "People live in terms of images which represent the fundamental conceptions embodied in their rituals and myths. In the absence of adequate images they live in terms of such compelling images (and hence rituals and myths) as are abroad at the time." For, continues Murray, echoing the dictum from the book of Proverbs, "Where there is no adequate vision the people perish." In the Bible, slavery's children found "such compelling images" to live by, that they might not perish in the howling wilderness of America.

American slaves did not read the Bible through, or even over and against, the traditions they brought with them from West Africa: they read the Bible as a text into which these traditions were woven. The characters and events of the Bible became the functional equivalent of the ancestors and heroes long celebrated in West Africa. The many ancestral and natural spirits were subsumed in the Holy Spirit, and the mighty acts of God supplanted ancient tales of martial valor. Biblical patriarchs and heroes now sat on the stools of the esteemed ancestors of ages past.

Biblical imagery was also the idiom for remnants of traditional West African material culture. The themes of much of African-American folk sculpture, especially gravestones and other funereal monuments, are biblical: the iconic patterns and techniques of sacred ornamentation, however, are African. West African traditions of ornamented textiles lived on in the work of slave seamstresses in America, who decorated their patchwork quilts with appliqué figures from the Bible instead of the symbols and icons of ancient myths that their African ancestors had wrought in cloth with the same techniques.

As modernity's most thoroughly humiliated people, small wonder that African Americans have taken the texts of the Bible so eagerly and earnestly. Slavery's children entered history from below: from their straitened vantage they came to see in the holy scriptures that God grants victory to the unlikeliest people—people like themselves—and by the unlikeliest means. The Bible privileges those without privilege and honors those without honor. And so there is a special affinity between the Bible and the rankest of its readership's rank and file. Its accounts of the exaltation of the humble and humbling of the high and mighty have appealed to people in the humblest of circumstances.

The special relation between the Bible and common people inheres in the peculiar protagonists, unlikely heroes, and reversals of fortune that punctuate its pages. The Bible is one of the few books of world literature that looks at life "from below." It is replete with upsets that flout the rules of power, privilege, and prestige. Several stories in the book of Genesis challenge the ancient custom of primogeniture: the second child, the also-ran of the family, gets what was intended for the firstborn son. The prominence if not dominance of women in stories of Abraham, Isaac, and Jacob qualify the ancient rule of men over women—stories that, to compound the irony, scholars call "Patriarchal narratives." In the story of the Exodus runaway slaves stage a spectacular escape, the military might of an empire and their deep-seated fear of freedom notwithstanding. The early legends of Israel's monarchy still carry traditions that are stridently antimonarchical, and Israel's greatest king is a former shepherd boy moonlighting as a musician who becomes by turns a mercenary, a murderer, and a Peeping Tom. His dynasty is a disaster, and the nation over which his troubled descendants rule is eventually overrun by a succession of foreign empires even as it collapses from the force of its internal corruption. The insightful national pundits who saw it all coming—the prophets—go unheeded, and their oracles, gathered at the end of the Old Testament, become ancient Israel's dustbin of history.

The biblical penchant for bringing peripheral people to the center of history continues *con brio* in the New Testament. The Savior of the world hails from the jerkwater of Nazareth with a band of country bumpkins in tow. A few of those bumpkins go on to be the leaders of the early church. The Apostle Paul boasts that most of the people in the churches he counseled at Corinth had no pretensions to noble birth or bearing: nevertheless they shall be judges in a divine tribunal at the end of the age. Later in a theological tour de force, Paul writes to these congregations that his hardships, rejection, and failure only confirm his exalted vocation as an apostle. And in the last book of the Bible, the book of Revelation, the high and the mighty are incinerated in the fires of divine judgment, and God sets up the victims of injustice as rulers over a new heaven and a new earth. From Genesis to Revelation, from the beginning of the Bible to the end, the losers ultimately become the winners.

African slaves and their descendants discerned something in the Bible that was neither at the center of their ancestral cultures nor in evidence in their hostile American home: a warrant for justice in this world. They found woven in the texts of the Bible a crimson thread of divine justice antithetical to the injustice they had come to know all too well. African Americans began to trace that thread in the last quarter of the eighteenth century, at the very moment the Founding Fathers of the new nation were reaching the conclusion that the rights to life, liberty, and the pursuit of happiness did not extend to slaves.

African-Americans were taking texts of the Bible and reaching their own conclusions. The God of holy scripture had made slaves no less than their masters in the divine image and likeness. The Apostle Paul had declared that master and slave were equal in God's sight. And in the book of Exodus God had freed the ancient Hebrews from bondage in Egypt: the liberation of slaves had been God's will. These were ideas at least as revolutionary as any Jeffersonian proposition. In the scriptures they found a God that "sits high and looks low," as a traditional African-American prayer puts it; that the humble are exalted and exalted humbled; that the judgment of God would be the justice of the slave. From the periphery of a hostile world, slavery's children found that justice at the center of the Bible.

CHAPTER ONE

The Talking Book

And I longed to read my Bible,
For precious words it said;
But when I begun to learn it,
Folks just shook their heads,

And said there was no use trying,
Oh! Chloe, you're too late;
But as I was rising sixty,
I had no time to wait.

So I got a pair of glasses,
And straight to work I went,
And never stopped til I could read
The hymns and Testament.

Then I got a little cabin—
A place to call my own—
And I felt as independent
As the queen upon her throne.

—*Frances Harper, "Learning to Read"*

HE WAS STYMIED. In the 1850s, William Brown Hodgson struggled to translate a manuscript written in Arabic script by a West African Muslim named London who was a slave on a Georgia plantation. The language corresponded to none of the dialects that the learned philologist knew. The letters formed the following mysterious sounds: "fas chapta o jon / inde be ginnen wasde wad / and wad was wid god / ande wad was god." Hodgson puzzled over the unintelligible text until, sounding it out phonetically, he realized that the lines of Arabic script were from neither an Arabic text nor an Arabic translation of an English text. London had used Arabic letters to transliterate a few sentences into what Hodgson called "the Negro Patois of English." Rendered in Standard English, the lines were not only clear but familiar: "The first chapter of John / In the beginning was the word / And the word was with God / And the word was God," the opening words of the Gospel of John in the New Testament.[1]

African Americans first encountered the Bible as strangers in a strange land of slavery, through the strange language of English letters, and by the strange religion of Evangelical Protestantism. It is at the collision of the Great Awakening and the Peculiar Institution in colonial America that African Americans became literate and, subsequently, literary.

London, an African in America and a slave, was a literate Muslim. Yet his very literacy bears testimony to his encounter with the Bible not as written text but as spoken word. Many African slaves were, like London, literate Muslims. Many others claimed ancestral faiths without Holy Writ. But even those African slaves who came to the New World as Christians had yet to read the Bible for themselves. Into what was to become Louisiana and Florida, Spanish ships brought many Catholic Angolan slaves: Catholicism had been the official religion of the Congo kingdom since the sixteenth century, when it had been adopted in the royal court after contacts with the Portuguese. Iberian Catholicism on both sides of the Atlantic had made its peace with slavery at least a century before its missionary success in the Congo. Catholic priests catechized illiterate African slaves in the Spanish colonies to accept their lot as God's will.

In the British colonies of mid-Atlantic North America, both the Puritans and the Anglicans made modest attempts to introduce slaves to Christianity throughout the seventeenth and eighteenth centuries. Some clergymen composed special catechisms of biblical phrases and doctrinal sentences that slaves could be taught to parrot in preparation for baptism. Puritan divine Cotton Mather reconciled himself to the wretchedness of the slave's life, provided that through baptism and religious instruction masters helped to secure for them a compensatory, beatific afterlife. "The State of your Negroes in this World, must be low, and mean, and abject; a State of Servitude. No Great Things in this World can be done for them. Something then, let there be done, towards their welfare in the World to Come." Mather also resolved, "A Catechism shall be got ready for them; first shorter, then Larger; Suited to their poor Capacities." Mather favored teaching slaves to read the Bible, but "Until that might be accomplished," he suggested that they "Learn by heart, certain Particular Verses of Scripture."[2]

But the master class in general and the Southern planter class in particular remained indifferent at best and often openly hostile to the religious instruction of slaves. Before the beginning of the eighteenth century, few slaves professed Christianity, and those who did often gained little more than a vague assurance of blessedness in the afterlife. The few words of scripture they learned were bowdlerized in catechetical instruction that urged them to accept slavery as divinely ordained, and those texts were heard but rarely read by the slave: many colonists and virtually all slaves were illiterate.

This status quo was challenged by Evangelicalism, that enthusiastic, intensely personal Protestantism that swept North America in waves of religious revival from the middle of the eighteenth century through the first half of the nineteenth. Evangelical preachers traveled through the colonies—and later the states and territories of the new nation—inviting their hearers to the remission of their sins based on the atoning power of Christ's death on the cross; they claimed for themselves and their hearers dramatic, direct access to God's grace. These preachers proclaimed a divine salvation needed by all and available to all, boldly pitching their Gospel in the public square. The sermons of these preachers were always evocative expositions of the Bible, for Evangelicals insisted that the complete script of salvation had been inscribed in the pages of holy scripture. The two essential tenets of Evangelicalism were the paramount authority of the Bible and direct personal experience of God.[3] Unmediated access to the Bible was an Evangelical imperative. Thus for Evangelicals, reading became a matter of religion. Leaders of the early-nineteenth-century American public school movement were Evangelical members of the clergy and the religious press readily published their advocacy.[4] Just as Evangelical religion required that one have the experience of saving faith for oneself, it required that one read that sacred script for oneself.

The open, public preaching of Evangelicals was inclusive in the extreme. The social unit of measurement for the Evangelical preacher was neither the church nor the chapel but the crowd: the bigger the crowd the better, for all needed to hear the message of eternal salvation. In the crowds that came to hear them, Evangelical preachers noted the sizeable presence of African slaves. Slaves in significant numbers came under the influence of Christianity in the British colonies and were thus introduced to the Bible through the mass Evangelicalism of the Great Awakening of the 1740s. Traveling through Hanover County, Virginia, the white Presbyterian Evangelist Samuel Davies reported in 1751, "There is a great number of Negroes in these Parts; and sometimes I see a 100 and more among my hearers."[5] In 1755 Davies reported, "Never have I been so struck with the appearance of an assembly as when I have glanced my eye to that part of the meeting house where they usually sit, with so many black countenances eagerly attentive to every word they hear, frequently bathed in tears." He observed that "some . . . negroes have been in great trouble about their souls; their hearts have been broken for sin; they have accepted Christ as their only Saviour; and are Christians indeed." Davies's testimony is echoed in the recollections of other Evangelical preachers as well.[6]

Evangelical Christianity was and remains a formidable force in African-American religion. This is not to suggest that anything like a majority of American slaves were Evangelical Christians or Christians of any kind. As late as the mid-nineteenth century Henry Highland Garnet, Frederick Douglass, Richard Allen, and the abolitionist firebrand David Walker all assert that "heathenism" was predominant in the slave community.[7] Nevertheless the impact of Protestant Evangelicalism on African-American culture and consciousness was profound and indelible. Black and white as well as rich and poor came together and commingled at the camp meetings in the enthusiasm of revivalist religion. This ecstatic, emotional leveling of otherwise ruthlessly rigid castes of the new American society brought the slaves into a community that approximated, albeit only for fleeting moments, spiritual equality. And as egalitarian relations became the proclaimed ideal if not the realized norm in Evangelical denominations, some slaves voted with their feet against those communions that discriminated against them. A Catholic priest complained that enforced segregation in his church had offended slaves and caused them to boycott Mass and take up reading the Protestant Bible.[8] It was in this spiritually charged ambient that African Americans began to hear the Bible speak to them.

READING, WRITING, AND RELIGION

This ambience marked the proselytizing efforts of the Baptists and Methodists. "The spread of Baptist and Methodist evangelicalism between 1770 and 1820," observes Albert Raboteau, "changed the religious complexion of the South by bringing unprecedented numbers of slaves into member- ship in the church and by introducing even larger numbers to at least the rudiments of Christianity."[9] And though Baptists and Methodists would later be divided over abolition, the aggressive proselytizing of these two denominations would reap a harvest of African-American souls. The Free Church polity, quasi-democratic governance, and disestablishmentarian ethos of the Baptists promised African Americans more opportunities for direct participation than any other denomination.[10]

Developments in the piety, practice, and polity of the Virginian Bap- tists is especially indicative of how Evangelicalism was transmogrified in the postrevolutionary South, where sporadic outbreaks of revivalist religion still occurred. The Baptists are especially important in the collec- tive religious history of African Americans because the denominational change of direction on the question of slavery is most starkly documented among them and because they were the most successful of all Evangelicals in converting African Americans. Or better put: African Americans were most successful at becoming Baptists.

The Anglican establishment persecuted Baptist Evangelists and as- sociated them with sedition and disorder. An anti-Baptist petition to the Virginia assembly of 1777 warned that "there have been nightly meetings of slaves to receive the instruction of these [Baptist] teachers without the consent of their masters, which have produced very bad consequences."[11] In the 1780s several Baptist leaders freed their slaves, and at the end of the decade the General Committee of Virginia Baptists issued an official condemnation of slavery, "a violent deprivation of the rights of nature."[12] But local Baptist associations repudiated the condemnation, arguing that slaveholding was a matter of individual Christian conscience, that slavery was beyond the jurisdiction of any religious society, and that the proper preoccupation of the church should be amelioration, not emancipation. Thus the Free Church polity, quasi-democratic governance, and disestab- lishmentarian ethos that black Baptists found so liberating contributed fundamentally to the demise of abolition among white Baptists in the South. By the beginning of the nineteenth century, the Baptists had traded their unvarnished revivalist manners, and the emancipationist sentiment that attended them, for respectability under the Southern slave regime.

The early decades of this period gave rise to a cadre of virtually independent black preachers who shepherded black congregations. Both ideologically and institutionally, blacks were implicitly establishing an island of autonomy in their own communities of faith, "in some cases without any active involvement of white missionaries or masters whatsoever."[13] Some white Evangelicals balked at the notion of a black pastorate: a Presbyterian leader advised his church that slave preachers "should never be taken from among themselves," because "the circumstances preclude them from the preparation and study which such a charge involves." But biblical literacy was so important to Evangelical religion that Evangelicals challenged antiliteracy slave codes by teaching converted slaves how to read. Following the Revolutionary War, Evangelical Christians established so-called Sabbath Schools for the instruction of African Americans in several states. At the same time, some leaders of the American Revolution championed universal literacy as a necessity for the advancement of democracy, and plans for the education of African Americans even accompanied emancipation in some postrevolutionary state actions.[14]

Thus at the end of the eighteenth century and the beginning of the nineteenth, African American Christians were fitfully consolidating their own leadership. This florescence of autonomy was accompanied by a restive, sometimes insurgent reinterpretation of Evangelical Christianity and with it Evangelical Christianity's Book. "Inevitably the slaves' Christianity contradicted that of their masters," observes Raboteau. "The division was deep; it extended to the fundamental interpretation of the Bible."[15]

Evangelicalism would make the Bible the most accessible literature in America. African-American Evangelicals would make it the most dangerous. In 1800 two slaves of Tom Prosser, Gabriel and his brother Martin, were the architects of an abortive uprising in Henrico County, Virginia, that was to be one of the largest slave revolts in American history. Gabriel and Martin recruited thousands of slaves at nocturnal prayer meetings with what one informant described as "an impassioned exposition of Scripture." The enslaved brothers preached that the Israelites were "a type of successful resistance to tyranny; and it was argued, that now, as then, God would stretch forth his arm to save, and would strengthen a hundred to overthrow a thousand."[16] Ben Woolfolk was a slave who actively participated in the conspiratorial meetings in which the brothers Gabriel and Martin Prosser organized the ill-fated revolt. Later captured, Woolfolk testified to his role and the role of others in the conspiracy.[17] In the transcript of his confession, Woolfolk recalls that he himself spoke at a meeting at which Gabriel, Gabriel's brother Martin, and other co-conspirators were present with arms. Woolfolk testified, "I told them that I had heard in the days of old, when the Israelites were in the service of king Pharaoh, they were taken from him by the power of God, and were carried away by Moses. God had blessed him with an angel to go with him, but that I could see nothing of that kind in these days." According to Woolfolk's testimony, Martin replied, "I read in my Bible where God says if we will worship Him we should have peace in all our land; five of you shall conquer an hundred, and a hundred a thousand of our enemies." The allusion is to a passage in the book of Leviticus: "If ye walk in my statutes, and keep my commandments, and do them . . . I will give peace in the land . . . five of you shall chase an hundred and an hundred of you shall put ten thousand to flight" (Lev. 26:3–8).

The African Church of Charleston, South Carolina, was a congregation of black Methodists founded in 1818 after several thousand blacks had withdrawn their memberships from white Methodist churches in Charleston following a dispute over a segregated burial ground. It became the venue of another abortive revolt that received inspiration from the Bible. An informant who betrayed the revolt alleged that Denmark Vesey, a charismatic class leader at the church, had inspired his fellow parishioners to violence by reading passages from the Bible.[18] In the transcript of the testimony of the slave informant named Rolla, the Exodus story figures prominently at a meeting of the co-conspirators at Vesey's home.

> That night at Vesey's we determined to have arms made, and each man put in 12½ cents toward that purpose. Though Vesey's room was full I did not know an individual there. At this meeting Vesey said we were to take the Guard-House Magazine to get arms; that we ought to rise up and fight against the whites for our liberties; he was the first to rise up and speak, and he *read to us from the Bible, how the Children of Israel were delivered out of Egypt from bondage.* He said that the rising would take place, last Sunday night week, (the 16th of June) and that Peter Poyas was one.[19]

After the plot had been uncovered and the conspirators arrested, a note inscribed with the following message would found in a trunk belonging to Peter Poyas: "Fear not, the Lord God that delivered Daniel is able to deliver us."[20]

At the trial of the co-conspirator Mingo a slave named William testi- fied, "At Mingo's house I took up the Bible and read two chapters from the prophet Tobit."[21] What it called in its table of contents the book of Tobit is numbered among "the Books called the Apocrypha," the traditional collection of fourteen books usually placed in the Bible between the Old and New Testaments. The Apocrypha's value had been disputed since the Reformation: Martin Luther had openly disdained them, translating them hastily and under protest, and the Westminster Confession of 1648 would ultimately pronounce them of no authority. Though surviving edi- tions from the 1630s lack them, the King James Version of 1611, the Bible of colonial American Protestants contained the Apocrypha: in 1615 Archbishop George Abbott forbade the printing of Bibles without them. The British and Foreign Bible Society would continue to follow that policy until 1826.[22] And so it is certain and unremarkable that the book of Tobit was in the Bible that Vesey and his co-conspirators read.

We do not know which two chapters of Tobit they read. But in the thirteenth chapter of the book they would have found these petitions in Tobit's prayer.

> If you turn to him with your whole heart, and with your whole mind, and deal uprightly before him, then will he turn unto you: Therefore see what he will do with you, and confess him with your whole mouth, and praise the Lord of might, and extol the everlasting King: in the land of my captivity do I praise him, and declare his might and majesty to a sinful nation. (13:6)

> Give praise to the Lord, for he is good: and praise the everlast- ing King, that his Tabernacle may be builded in thee again with joy: and let him make joyful there in thee, those that are cap- tives, and love in thee for ever those that are miserable. (13:10)

> O blessed are they which love thee, for they shall rejoice in thy peace: blessed are they which have been sorrowful for all thy scourges, for they shall rejoice for thee, when they have seen all thy glory, and shall be glad for ever. (13:14)

In chapter fourteen of the book, Tobit anticipates the fulfillment of Jonah's prophecy against Nineveh, a prophecy that was not fulfilled in the biblical book of Jonah. The aged Tobit instructs his son Tobias to take his family and leave Nineveh "because those things which the Prophet Jonah spake, shall surely come to pass" (14:8). Afterward, "God will have mercy on [our brethren] . . . and afterward they shall return from all places of their captivity, and build up Jerusalem gloriously" (14:5). The book concludes with Tobias dying after "he heard of the destruction of Nineveh . . . and before his death he rejoiced over Nineveh" (14:15). Nineveh, the evil capital of the Israelites' Assyrian conquerors, had escaped judgment in the book of Jonah: there the Ninevites repented of their evil in response to Jonah's preaching. Nineveh is finally destroyed for its iniquities in the book of Tobit. American slaves living in a land of captivity would have rejoiced to hear that the delayed justice due a wicked land would not be denied.

After Vesey's plot was exposed, he and 130 of his co-conspirators were arrested and tried. Thirty-seven, including Vesey himself, were executed. The African Church was razed, and new laws strictly proscribed reading, writing, preaching, and assembly of slaves. The consensus of the planter class was that unsupervised reading of the Bible among the slaves turned religion into rebellion. By permitting slave preachers unmediated access to the Bible, the Methodists were paying for a mistake that the established church was loath to make. An Episcopal minister commented with some satisfaction that such a plot could never have been hatched among black Episcopalians because in the Episcopal Church they "were not allowed to exhort or expound scriptures in words of their own . . . and to utter . . . whatever nonsense might happen into their minds."[23] Where slave religion was not repressed altogether, planters subsidized white missionaries to take the teeth out of Evangelical religion.

The master class would learn from the Christian slave revolts of the first third of the nineteenth century the incendiary potential of uncensored religious instruction in the slave quarters, and slave owners became even more determined to prevent the spread of literacy among slaves. Sanctions against teaching slaves to read and write were severe: slaves discovered caught writing or learning to write might have their fingers cut off.[24] As a young slave the great abolitionist orator Frederick Douglass frequently heard his mistress read the Bible aloud, and it was this experience, as he later wrote in his autobiography, that "roused in me the desire to learn."[25]

Later Douglass would complain that under the slave regime "men and women were obliged to hide in barns and woods and trees from professing Christians, in order to read the Holy Bible."[26] Though a few chosen domestic slaves might be taught to read along with the master's children and others might learn by stealth, the mass of slaves remained illiterate. And the Bible remained a closed book.

The reaction that followed in the wake of the Nat Turner rebellion in August 1831 was a veritable crackdown on African-American Christianity. Between 1830 and 1834 Virginia, North Carolina, South Carolina, Alabama, and Louisiana all enacted legislation making the education of slaves punishable by fine or imprisonment and completely prohibiting unsupervised slave gatherings and slave preaching.[27] During a legislative debate in South Carolina in 1834 that resulted in the passing of laws making it illegal to teach slaves to read and write, planter Whitemarsh Seabrook charged that anyone who wanted slaves to read the Bible belonged in "a room in the Lunatic Asylum."[28]

Some planters, of course, discouraged slave religion in any form: "My boss didn't allow us to got to church or pray or sing," reported one ex-slave. "If he caught us praying or singing, he whipped us. He didn't care much for nothing except farming."[29] Some slave masters preferred dissipation to piety as a better form of social control. Florida planter Zephaniah Kingsley, opposed to the religious instruction of his slaves, made it his policy to "never interfere in [the slaves'] connubial and domestic affairs" and "encouraged as much as possible dancing, merriment, and dress, for which Saturday afternoons and night, and Sunday morning were dedicated."[30] Visiting Saint Louis in 1818, John Mason Peck observed, "The negroes were accustomed to assemble in the pleasant afternoons of the Sabbath, dance, drink, and fight."[31]

Planters who preferred religion to revelry as a form of social control began to retain missionaries to their slaves who would indoctrinate them with biblical exhortations to submission. James L. Belin, a Methodist minister in Murrells Inlet, South Carolina, began his four decades of missionary labors among the slaves as early as 1819. In 1832, less than a year after the Nat Turner rebellion, the Episcopalian rice planters of Waccamaw, South Carolina, established their own mission to their slaves and retained a twenty-eight-year-old English cleric, Alexander Glennie, as an Episcopal missionary. Glennie rotated among the plantations so that he visited each one once or twice a month, and his slave congregations grew from 10 to 529 communicants in 1862. In his memoirs J. Motte Alston, patriarch of the Woodbourne plantation, described Glennie's activity: "The Reverend Alexander Glennie and his wife would come to us once every fortnight. He always came to dinner, after which he would teach the Negro children their catechism and preach to all of my Negroes at night. They always had a half-holiday on these occasions, so as to let them brush up and make a respectable appearance. It was a law that all should attend."[32]

A northern visitor described the Alston's family leading in daily devotions: "A signal from the mistress caused the sounding of a bell in the hall, and some ten or twelve men and women house-servants, of remarkably neat and tidy appearance . . . entered the apartment. They took a stand at the remote end of the room and our host, opening a large, well-worn family Bible, read the fifty-fourth chapter of Isaiah. Then, all kneeling, he made a short, extemporaneous petition, closing with the Lord's Prayer; all present, black as well as white, joining in it. Then Heber's beautiful hymn, 'From Greenland's Icy Mountains,' was sung; the Negroes, to my ear, making much better music than the whites."[33]

Slaves were rarely introduced to the Bible through the medium of the printed page. For many slaves biblical literacy began with spontaneous aural memorization and oral recall. Slaves mimicked what they heard in sermons from white preachers and readers, and in repeating what they heard they often improvised on it. J. Motte Alston remarked on his slaves' capacity for remembering scripture recited by Glennie: "It was quite wonderful what retentive memories [the slaves] had, for few could read. The minister would always read the evening services of the Episcopal Book of Common Prayer and always, too, the same Psalter so as to enable the congregation to respond, which they did most accurately and devoutly." A Northern visitor at Glennie's chapel in All Souls Parish, Georgia, reported, "The congregation responded and sang the Te deum with Mr. Glennie. Some had books and could read, but as all could not, he would read two lines of a hymn and then they would all sing and so on." Glennie delivered his sermons in catechetical form, he first posing the question, the congregation then providing the "scripted" answer. Glennie may have developed this form of preaching to evoke a worship experience more stirring than that of conventional Anglican liturgy, but the liturgical form was also shaped by the exigencies of illiterate worship.[34]

Elizabeth Botume was among the abolitionists, missionaries, teachers, and journalists called Gideon's Band that accompanied Yankee soldiers who occupied South Carolina's Sea Islands during the Civil War. At Christmas the slaves on Hilton Head Island invited her to preach for them. After her sermon, of which, she was convinced, her audience "understood very little," the congregation engaged in a rousing chorus of "Joy to the World" followed by extemporaneous prayers. Botume reported that in the prayers each of the slaves "tried to introduce, in his uncouth phraseology, some of the passages of Scripture he had heard read."[35] Harriet Ware, another abolitionist member of Gideon's Band, described the worship meetings of the slaves there in which "at regular intervals one hears the elder 'deaconing' a hymnbook hymn, which is sung two lines at a time."[36] The practice of lead singers "lining" or singing the first two verses of a hymn in advance of the rest of the congregation suited illiterate worshippers.

The practice of starting a song with several leading lines that in turn elicit a choral response was an oral pattern that approximated traditional forms of West African musical composition. African-American singers plied this ancestral musical form in setting biblical phrases and stories to spontaneously improvised songs raised in worship. It was through the human voice, then, and not the printed page, that the Bible came to inhabit the slave's inner world. The slaves' Bible became musical, even as the slaves' music became biblical. Through the peculiar liturgies of the Peculiar Institution, slaves could become biblically articulate without the benefit of letters. "No one on the place was taught to read or write," recalled former slave Silas Jackson. "On Sunday the slaves who wanted to worship would gather at one of the large cabins with one of the overseers present and have their church, after which the overseer would talk. . . . No one read the Bible. Sandy Jasper, Mr. Ashbie's coachman, was the preacher. He would go to the white Baptist church on Sunday with family and would be better informed because he heard the white preacher." James Smith of Bowie County, Texas, recalled that his master would allow his slaves to hold church services on Wednesday nights, Sunday mornings, and Sunday nights, and "would read the Negro parson a chapter in the Bible, select his text, and give him some instructions about handling the text."[37]

Even with these liturgical devices to accommodate them, slaves were not content with illiterate worship in a religion of the Book. In the contradiction between American Evangelicalism's imperative of literacy and American slavery's imperative of illiteracy, African Americans confronted the Bible as a book both opened and closed. As the Word of God it spoke to them, but as a written text it greeted its illiterate black readers with silence. Early African-American literature is marked by the appearance of the silent page, what literary critic Henry Louis Gates, Jr., in a classic analysis has identified as the trope of the Talking Book.[38]

The first occurrence of the Talking Book is the memoir of freed African slave James Albert Ukawsaw Gronniosaw, *A Narrative of the Most Remarkable Particulars in the Life of James Albert Ukawsaw Gronniosaw, an African Prince, as Related by Himself* (1772). As the young victim of Dutch slavers, Gronniosaw recalls his initial experience with the literacy of his captors.

> [My master] used to read prayers in public to the ship's crew every Sabbath day; and when I first saw him read, I was never so surprised in my life, as when I saw the book talk to my master, for I thought it did, as I observed him to look upon it, and move his lips. I wished it would do so with me. As soon as my master was done reading, I followed him to the place where he put the book, being mightily delighted with it, and when nobody saw me, I opened it, and put my ear down close upon it, in great hopes that it would say something to me; but I was very sorry, and greatly disappointed, when I found that it would not speak. This thought immediately presented itself to me, that every body and every thing despised me because I was black.[39]

The sons of his master read to him from the Bible as they sought to convince the slave convert John Jea that he was still a slave in spite of his conversion. After they left him, Jea writes, "I took the book, and held it up to my ears, to try whether the book would talk to me or not, but it proved to be all in vain, for I could not hear it speak one word." "The book," Jea laments, "would not talk to me."[40] The trope also appears in the autobiographical account of Nigerian seaman, ex-slave, and abolitionist Olaudah Equiano, *The Interesting Narrative of the Life of Olaudah Equiano, or Gustavus Vassa, the African, Written by Himself,* published in 1789. As a captive slave on a voyage from Barbados to Virginia, Equiano tells of his amazement regarding the European practice of reading; "I had often seen my master . . . employed in reading; and I had a great curiosity to talk to the books, as I thought [he] did; and so to learn how all things had a beginning: for that purpose I have often taken up a book, and have talked to it, and then put my ears to it, when alone, in hopes it would answer me; and I have been very much concerned when I found it remained silent."[41] Equiano's signed portrait published in his *Narrative* shows him with the Bible resting in his lap. He commends himself to his readers as a reader of the Talking Book, and the Book itself is depicted in his possession and poised to "speak," that is, as open to him as to his readers.

THE SPIRIT AND THE LETTER

Some slaves became preachers in spite of illiteracy, and their rhetorical prowess came to be the stuff of legend. A former slave recounted the following story he had heard about an illiterate slave preacher.

> We all went to church every Sunday. We would go to the white folks' church in the morning and to our church in the evening. Bill McWilliams, Old Master's oldest boy, didn't take much stock in church. He owned a nigger named Bird, who preached for us. Bill said, "Bird, you can't preach, you can't read. How'n hell can you get a text out of the Bible when you can't even read? How'n hell can a man preach that don't know nothing?" Bird told him the Lord had called him to preach and He'd put the things in his mouth that he ought to say. One night Bill went to church, and Bird preached the hair-raisingest sermon you ever heard. Bill told him all right to go and preach, and he gave Bird a horse and set him free to go anywhere he wanted to and preach.[42]

Nevertheless, the vocation of the slave preacher often gave rise to an urgent desire for literacy. After his conversion, the slave Peter Randolph "became impressed that I was called of God to preach to the other slaves . . . but then I could not read the Bible, and I thought I could never preach unless I learned to read the Bible."[43] Preachers are prominent among the earliest literate slaves. Several claimed to have acquired literacy by the grace of Providence alone. The highest aspiration of African slave John Jea was to read the Bible for himself in English and Dutch, the languages of eighteenth-century Dutch New York. Jea realized his aspiration, as he would later recount in his memoirs, with supernatural help.

> Thus my eyes were opened at the end of six weeks, while I was praying, in the place where I slept. Although the place was as dark as a dungeon, I awoke, as the Scripture saith, and found it illuminated with the light of the glory of God, and the angel standing by me, with the large book open, which was the Holy Bible. And said unto me, "Thou hast desired to read and understand this book, and to speak the language of it both in English and in Dutch. I will therefore teach thee, and now read," and then he taught me to read the first chapter of the gospel according to St. John. And when I had read the whole chapter, the angel and the book were both gone in the twinkling of an eye, which astonished me very much, for the place was dark immediately; being about four o'clock in the morning in the winter season. After my astonishment had a little subsided, I began to think whether it was a fact that an angel had taught me to read, or only a dream.[44]

Jea speaks of his miraculous literacy in words borrowed from the Apostle Peter's miraculous jailbreak in the twelfth chapter of the book of Acts: "And behold, the angel of the Lord cane upon him, and a light shined in the prison: and he smote Peter on his side, and raised him up, saying, Arise up quickly. And his chains fell off from his hands. And the angel said, Gird thyself, and bind on thy sandals. And so he did. And he saith unto him, Cast thy garment about thee, and follow me. And he went out, and followed him; and wist not that it was true which was done by the angel; but thought he saw a vision" (Acts 12:7–9). "Like Peter in prison," Jea was rescued from a dark prison by an angel, and miraculously liberated from illiteracy.[45] Even his account of that liberation is couched in the words of the Book. The limit of Jea's miraculous literacy was as remarkable as the literacy itself; he insisted that God had opened for him only one book, the Bible. "From that hour, in which the Lord taught me to read, until the present," he claims, "I have not been able to read any book, nor any reading whatever, but such as contain the word of God."[46]

African-American claims to miraculous literacy continued into the nineteenth century. George Washington Dupree, slave to a Baptist preacher

in Gallatin County, Kentucky, desired to become a preacher after his conversion at fifteen in 1842, but his illiteracy, so he thought, rendered that
vocation out of the question. After hearing "old Father David Woods" read
the New Testament one rainy evening, Dupree picked up Father Woods's
Bible and, driven by sheer desire, began to read the first three chapters
of the Gospel of John.[47]

Shaker Eldress and visionary Rebecca Cox Jackson, a free black woman
who established and led a Shaker sisterhood in Philadelphia in 1857, was
illiterate until well into adulthood. Born in 1795, she testified in her memoirs that her "great desire to read the Bible" was frustrated by her literate
brother's refusal to teach her to read and by his unsatisfactory services
as her amanuensis. After theological conflict had alienated her from her
family, she received divine assurance that "the time will come when you
can write." Shortly thereafter, while she worked as a dressmaker, "This
word was spoken in my mind":

> "Who learned the first man on earth?" "Why, God." "He is
> unchangeable, and if He learned the first man to read, He
> can learn you." I laid down my dress, picked up my Bible, ran
> upstairs, opened it, and kneeled down with it pressed to my
> breast, prayed earnestly to Almighty God if it was consistent
> with His holy will, to learn me to read His holy word. And
> when I looked on the word, I began to read. And when I found
> I was reading, I was frightened—then I could not read one
> word. I closed my eyes again in prayer and opened my eyes,
> began to read.

"So I done," Cox writes, "until I read the chapter. . . . So I tried, took my
Bible daily and praying and read until I could read anywhere."[48]

Miraculous literacy notwithstanding, most slaves came to read and
write by more conventional means. Though white women and children
were among the first grammar school teachers of some slaves, more often
slaves acquired literacy from other slaves.[49] "We had a nice big church just
for the colored people," recalled former slave Virginia Harris. "It was a
Baptist church and the pastor's name was Austin Butler. He was a man
with learning. . . . At Sunday school the pastor tried to learn us our A, B, C.
He done that because he was the only one that had anything."[50] "If there
happened to be a church located on or near the master's plantation,"

recounted former slave James Smith, "[he] would allow the slaves to be called together there on special occasions and instructed by a minister. If there chanced to be among the slaves a man of their own race who could read and write, he generally preached and would, at times and places unknown to the master, call his fellow slaves together and hold religious services with them. It was to such leaders as these that the slaves owed much of their religious instructions."[51]

Booker T. Washington observed that after Emancipation the ability to read continued to be correlated with the preaching vocation, but for reasons more human than divine. Preaching, he noted, "was an easy way to make a living." Washington illustrates the point with the tale "of a coloured man in Alabama, who, one hot day in July, while he was at work in a cotton-field, suddenly stopped, and, looking toward the skies, said: 'O Lawd, de cotton am so grassy, de work am so hard, and the sun am so hot dat I b'lieve dis darky am called to preach!'" Hewing wood and drawing water was still the lot of slavery's children after freedom came, and some sought to escape the drudgery by flight to the pulpit. Literacy would furnish that escape. "In the earlier days of freedom," writes Washington, "almost every coloured man who learned to read would receive a 'call to preach' within a few days after he began reading." Growing up in West Virginia during Reconstruction, Washington witnessed many men receive "the call," a dramatic affair often attended by conniptions and catatonic fits that recurred until the preacher-to-be accepted his new vocation. "In my youth," Washington confesses tongue-in-cheek, "I had a fear that when I had learned to read and write well I would receive one of these 'calls'; but, for some reason, my call never came."[52]

And though literate preachers illumined the path to literacy for many African Americans before and after Emancipation, literate slaves most often recalled that older slave women had taught them to read and write. These senior slaves presided over their young charges in impromptu, sometimes clandestine, classrooms in the house and in the field. We encounter the recurring figure of the literate "aunt" in former slave Susan Castle's reminiscence: "Some of the slaves on Master Thomas' place knowed how to read. Aunt Vic was one of the readers what read the Bible."[53] Former slave Charlotte Brooks remembered her secret instruction by "Aunt Jane" Lee, a Virginia slave who managed to learn how to read before being sold to a master in Louisiana. Brooks testified that Jane Lee "was the cause of so many on our plantation getting religion . . . it was Aunt Jane's praying and singing them old Virginia hymns that helped me so much. . . . She could read right good in the Bible and the hymnbook, and she would read to me one or two hymns at a time. I remember she read to me about Daniel in the lion's den and about the king having the three Hebrew children cast in the fiery furnace. O, how Aunt Jane used to love to read about the Hebrew children!"[54]

"A PLACE TO CALL MY OWN"

The legacy of the denial of literacy, and the African-American denial of that denial, is related in testimonies from the oral history of former slaves. They remembered the occasional ridicule by their masters for the ignorance of letters that the master class had imposed on them. A Virginia planter's supercilious daughter recalled the Bible "reading" of a slave woman named Deborah.

> As Aunt Deborah talked, her eyes were fixed covetously upon an old pair of spectacles which lay on the table. "Would you like to have those spectacles, mammy?" said Dorothy. "Thankee, honey, dey's je' what yo' mammay want; now I specs I kin read meh Bible." We handed her an open Bible, and the delighted old woman, with the book upside down, mumbled over and over again, "In meh father's house are many mansions." Then, when encouraged to read more, she began to move up and down, swaying from side to side, shouting fashion, her beaming black face bent over the book, and half said, half chanted, "I thank de Lord, he took meh feet out'n de miry clay, long wid Mary, Shadrach, an' 'Bednego." She evidently thought she was reading and 't would have been folly indeed to enlighten such blissful ignorance.[55]

Aunt Deborah rhapsodizes with a mélange of biblical allusions that suggest familiarity with the text, their confused admixture notwithstanding. For the slaves, biblical revelation could be summarized by this paradox: the Bible was a closed book that the illiterate read to learn its hidden contents by heart. Though unlettered, some slaves apprehended the spirit of the law they found in the inaccessible letters of the Book.

"We are by no means, as it is said of the Jews, 'people of the Book,'" novelist Ralph Ellison once observed. "Our expression has been oral as against literary."[56] So wrote the man who, in the age of Charlie Christian and Charlie Parker, forewent a career as a jazz musician and went on to write the Great American Novel. The ambivalent memory of African-American illiteracy is most lucid where African-American literature is most profound. In Toni Morrison's novel *Song of Solomon*, Macon Dead is directed to the names of his children by a steadfast exercise of biblical irrationality. The father, bitterly grieving the death of his wife in childbirth, insists it is fitting that the name for the newborn girl that he has selected by blind bibliomancy is the name of Pilate, the man who officiated at Jesus's execution. Though he "could not read a word," Macon Dead copies the name Pilate from the Bible and hands it to the midwife. When the horrified midwife tries to consign to the flames the slip of paper on which the baby's name is written, Macon Dead refuses: "It come from the Bible," he demands, putting the slip of paper back into the Book, "It stays in the Bible."[57] In another of Morrison's novels, *Beloved*, the character Denver speaks of her long-departed father, who could "count on paper and figure." It was Denver's father who, through his command of letters, had managed to win freedom for himself and his mother, Grandma. Grandma is a powerful lay preacher with extraordinary spiritual insight but nevertheless regrets her own illiteracy and "wished she could read the Bible like real preachers."[58]

If the genres of poetry and autobiographical narrative are the beginnings of African-American literature, even African-American literature does not properly begin with writing. It begins with religion, the Evangelical religion of slaves who heard the text of the Bible speak to them and made of its letters a sacred quest. The Bible was the chief goal of literacy for African Americans, for whom religion was both opportunity and mandate to acquire letters. The slave poet Jupiter Hammond exhorted his audience of fellow slaves to acquire literacy and devote themselves to reading the Bible, for in its sacred oracles they would discover comforting revelation "for such ignorant creatures as we." In 1787 Hammond, then seventy years old, put the matter this way: "If there was no Bible, it would not matter whether you could read or not."[59] In his recollection of the droves of newly freed slaves that thronged day schools, night schools, and Sunday schools across the South after the end of the Civil War, Booker T. Washington noted, "The great ambition of the older people was to try to learn to read the Bible before they died. With this end in view, men and women who were fifty and seventy-five years old would be found in night-schools." Adults of all ages filled the oversubscribed schoolrooms beyond capacity, and aspiring students were turned away for want of a place to stand. As Washington would later describe the experience, "It was a whole race of people trying to go to school."[60]

African Americans were learning en masse to read the Bible as a book both opened and closed. As the Word of God, it spoke to them with words that lent a new language to their dreams and their nightmares. As a written text, it greeted them with silence. But as they struggled to make the book talk to them, African Americans would make the Talking Book their own.

CHAPTER TWO

The Poison Book

The Bible is the graveyard of my poor people (the so-called Negroes) and I would like to dwell upon this book until I am sure that they understand that it is not quite as holy as they thought it was. I don't mean to say that there is no truth in it; certainly there is plenty of truth, if understood. Will you accept the understanding of it? The Bible charges all of its Great Prophets with evil, it makes God guilty of an act of adultery by charging Him with being the father of Mary's baby (Jesus), again it charges Noah and Lot with drunkenness, and Lot with getting children by his daughter. What a Poison Book.

—*Elijah Muhammad,* Message to the Blackman in America

IN NEW YORK CITY IN 1849, Frederick Douglass and the Presbyterian minister Henry Highland Garnet engaged in public debate over a campaign to solicit funds to provide Bibles for slaves in the South. Their confrontation was a rematch of sorts. The two had first debated in Buffalo, New York, in 1843. At that time the fiery and learned Garnet, whom Douglass described as "the most intellectual and moral colored man in our country," was advocating armed resistance to slavery.[1] Douglass, then an abolitionist in the mold of William Lloyd Garrison and so a pacifist, led the reasoned opposition in favor of "moral suasion." The convention put Garnet's proposal to a vote: Douglass and his partisans carried the day—by a single ballot.

Six years later, Douglass and Garnet were on opposite sides of the proposal to fund contraband Bibles for Southern slaves. This time the exchange was vitriolic: the abolitionist journal the *North Star* reported that Garnet described Douglass's scathing verbal attack as "poison from such a lofty place."[2] Douglass, acknowledged in his own time as the most eloquent man in America, denounced the plan with all the sound and fury his famed oratory could afford. He and other African-American leaders sympathetic to his opposition of the plan carried the debate, urging the capacity crowd at New York's Zion Church "not to give one cent toward this doubtful scheme."[3]

Douglass and Garnet were both African Americans. Both had escaped slavery from Maryland's Eastern Shore. But their respective experiences of slavery, literacy, and religion—and so their respective experiences of the Bible—were profoundly different, and those differences crystallized in diametrically opposed views of the Bible's liberating power. Garnet was descended from West African Mandinka and was proud of his pure-blood African heritage. His father had absconded from a Virginia plantation with his wife and children and fled to New York. As escaped slaves, the Garnets were in constant danger of being captured and reenslaved under the Fugitive Slave Law: young Henry carried a knife to defend himself from slave catchers as he walked through the streets of New York on his way to school. Later, as a student of Noyes Academy in Canaan, New Hampshire, Garnet fired a shotgun through the window of his dwelling to fend off irate townspeople who opposed the school's interracial policies. Son of a slave who had stolen his entire family out of bondage, formally educated in the North, duly ordained in a white denomination, and practiced in defending his freedom by force of arms, Garnet saw the liberating power of the Bible as self-evident. It was so for him: he assumed it would be so for slaves in the South who might manage to read or have read to them a contraband copy of the holy scriptures that he knew so well.

But Frederick Douglass knew better. Douglass stands as a brilliant exception to the iron rule that slaves are the silent partners in the business of history. Unlike most slaves under all slave regimes, we have his own words from his own hand. Douglass was a spectacular survivor forged in slavery's iron furnace. His long life and diverse personal experiences spanned the several dichotomies of the collective historical experience of African Americans: illiteracy and literacy, slavery and freedom, North and South, black (his slave mother) and white (his slave-master father), the United States before and after the Civil War. In Douglass we find both incarnation and synthesis of the forces that inform the African-American encounter with the Bible—the critical adoption of Evangelical religion, the relentless quest for literacy, and unflagging opposition to the slave regime in the South and those who colluded with it in the North.

Born of rape, bred in the slave quarters, and sold by his father, Douglass's early insistence on his humanity had been repeatedly rewarded with the lash, and his education had begun with clandestine snatches of letters. Only by Herculean effort had he taught himself to read as an adult, and only to discover what an anguished Abraham Lincoln would admit publicly in his Second Inaugural Address: that the abolitionists of the North and the planter class of the South read from the same Bible. Long before Lincoln, Douglass had learned that the Bible was the highest authority of American slavery and the strongest link in the chain of oppression and violence that warranted slavery as the sacred basis for the Christian culture of what would become the Confederacy. "I have met many religious colored people, at the South," Frederick Douglass wrote, "who are under the delusion that God requires them to submit to slavery and to wear chains with meekness and humility."[4] Bitter experience had taught Douglass and other slaves and former slaves that the master class of the United States bore a whip in one hand and a Bible in the other. It was this Bible that Garnet and his colleagues were now proposing to send to the South.

Other contemporary ex-slaves corroborated Douglass's testimony. The fugitive slave William Wells Brown bore witness to the currency of this perverse species of biblical religion.

> It was not uncommon in St. Louis to pass by an auction-stand, and behold a woman upon the auction-block, and hear the seller crying out, "How much is offered for this woman? She is a good cook, good washer, a good, obedient servant. She has got religion!" Why should this man tell the purchasers that she has got religion? I answer, because in Missouri, as far as I have any knowledge of slavery in the other states, the religious teaching consists in teaching the slave that he must never strike a white man; that God made him for a slave; and that, when whipped, he must not find fault for the Bible says, 'He that knoweth his master's will and doeth it not, shall be beaten with many stripes!' And slaveholders find such religion very profitable to them.[5]

It was on the basis of biblical claims that the erstwhile master of John Jea, a slave in eighteenth-century Dutch New York manumitted following his public confession of the Christian faith, sought to keep his former slave bound in both slavery and ignorance. "But my master strove to baffle me," Jea later wrote in his autobiography, "and to prevent me from understanding the Scriptures: so he used to tell me that there was a time to every purpose under the sun, to do all manner of work, that slaves were in duty bound to do whatever their masters commanded them, whether it as right or wrong; so that they must be obedient to a hard and spiteful master as to a good one."[6]

Douglass anticipated that the Bibles sent to the South would become raw material for proslavery propaganda. The master, holding the Bible and the whip, would now wield each in the service of the other. This biblical Christianity would be the only religion of the book that the slaves might know. It would be unlikely to nurture another Frederick Douglass. And Douglass could be certain that such religion would be unlikely to nurture a Henry Highland Garnet. Garnet, for his part, saw the critical spirit of the Bible as irrepressible: to make the Bible available to slaves in the South was tantamount to making a gift of the book of Southern Christianity that bore the seeds of the regime's undoing. No amount of proslavery propaganda, however lavishly laced with biblical proof texts, could indefinitely forestall those seeds coming to fruition in freedom for slavery's children. But Douglass knew intimately what Garnet's limited experience with slavery could not teach: that the justice of the Bible was not self-evident. Douglass had begun to learn the Bible as a slave, and he knew that some people reading the Bible under the slave regime remained tone-deaf to its message of justice.

In their 1849 New York debate, Douglass and Garnet tacitly agreed that Bible had been indispensable for the development of the religion of African-American Christians, and its lines and precepts fueled the abolitionist fire that burned in the breasts of both men. Even the U.S. Constitution ran a distant second to the Bible as the most powerful weapon in the ideological arsenal against slavery. It was on the basis of the Bible that Douglass had argued that American slavery was incompatible with the teachings of Jesus, and Garnet had cited the Apostle Paul's dictum that God "has made of one blood all nations" in support of the full humanity of African Americans. Both men enjoyed the precious competence of literacy that made its pages available to them. But whereas Garnet was convinced that the Bible would continue to aid and abet the abolitionist cause, Douglass knew that this powerful weapon had already fallen into the hands of the enemy.

Though African Americans early discerned a spirit of justice in the Bible, they discovered in the same moment that the letter of Holy Writ was sometimes at war with its spirit. The Bible is a book of contradictions. In its myth of origins and subsequent rules of gender relations, the Bible not only countenances but also authorizes the domination of man over woman. And yet these same scriptures have immortalized women as protagonists in a divine drama that runs from the Garden of Eden to the Garden of Gethsemane. Under the authority of Moses in the Old Testament and Paul in the New, the Bible sanctions slavery. The Bible's foundational narrative, however, is an account of the divine deliverance of slaves and the divine destruction of their masters. The Bible's regulations for the conduct of holy war give God's imprimatur to armed violence, genocide, and even the slaughter of noncombatants. Yet the most grandiose vision of global peace, heralding the abolition of weapons of mass destruction everywhere and for all time, comes from a prophetic oracle of the Bible. Its words adorn the United Nations building: "And they shall beat their swords into plowshares, and their spears into pruning hooks: nation shall not lift up sword against nation, neither shall they learn war any more." The words are the prophet Isaiah's: but the same oracle appears verbatim among the prophecies of Micah and Joel as well.

African Americans have held fast to the Bible only by holding fast to its contradictions. Indeed, the contradictions suited their condition, for African Americans themselves incarnated America's greatest contradiction. They were slaves in the land of the free. As slaves, they were at the same time persons and property. As people of African descent, they were heirs to a noble ancient history and an ignoble modern legacy. On the margins of American society, they remained at the center of its most bitter conflicts. Long after the fall of the slave regime, slavery's children bear the indelible marks of these contradictions.

Once the Bible began to speak to them, African Americans heard it saying some things that were hard for them to hear. It spoke with a voice that sometimes echoed their oppressors. The words of life could deal death, and its text could become noxious. The Talking Book was also a poison book. Toxic texts in the Old Testament seemed to condemn Africans and their descendants to slavery because they were Africans.

Toxic texts in the New Testament seemed to condemn Africans and their descendants to slavery because they were slaves.

THE CURSE

Phillis Wheatley, the first African-American woman to publish a book of poetry in English, reflected on her abduction from the land of her nativity in her poem, "On Being Brought from Africa to America."

> 'Twas mercy brought me from my Pagan land,
> Taught my benighted soul to understand
> That there's a God, that there's a Saviour too;
> Once I redemption neither sought nor knew.
> Some view our sable race with scornful eye,
> "Their color is a diabolic die."
> Remember, Christians, Negroes, black as Cain,
> May be refin'd, and join th'angelic train.[7]

The victim of a kidnapping celebrates as providential the crime perpetrated against her. We see here the beginnings of an apologia for the blight of African slavery on the Christian understanding of God's permissive will. Slavery backhandedly facilitated the conversion of Africans, dragging them bound and shackled into the light of the Christian Gospel. The distinctive African phenotype, the "diabolical die" that marked Africans as heathens destined for thralldom, was the blackness that, in the view of "some . . . with [a] scornful eye," marked Cain, the first fratricide. And here, the "scornful eye" is the poet's own.

This modern interpretation was of antique vintage. In early medieval commentary, the rabbis had speculated long ago that Cain had been made black by the back draft of soot from his unacceptable sacrifice.[8] In American religion, blackness itself would become a curse. In the scriptures of the Church of Latter-Day Saints, the curse of blackness would become canonical. The Book of Mormon declares, "[God] caused the cursing to come upon them [dark-skinned peoples], yea, even a sore cursing, because of their iniquity, . . . the Lord God did cause a skin of blackness to come upon them. Cursed shall be the seed of him that mixeth with their seed" (2 Nephi 5:21–23).

The effect of claiming that all Africans were the children of Cain was to claim every African was the seed of the first fratricide. This claim is "a stupid saying," writes the abolitionist clergyman James Pennington in 1843, "circulated by its framers without once recurring to the textbook fact, that Cain lived before the Deluge, and that all his posterity were swallowed up!" The flood that occurred later in the generation of Noah destroyed all life on the planet other than Noah's family and the menagerie that God had instructed him to preserve in the ark. "How then," demands Pennington, "can Cain have any posterity this side of the deluge? How could we have inherited his mark and curse? The supposition is false and absurd."[9]

African Americans reflected on the biblical account of the creation of the world and humankind as a vindication of their own world and humanity. All human beings, black and white, slave and free, were the descendants of Adam and Eve. The beginning of all stories, and all pedigrees, was to be found in the Garden of Eden and its first evicted tenants. In one African-American folktale, Adam requests that the Lord give him an extra measure of physical strength to overpower his contentious mate. God complies, and Adam literally beats the resentful but physically inferior Eve into submission. In a fit of pique Eve leaves the house and goes out to a cave between the roots of a tree in the apple orchard. There the Devil instructs Eve to ask the Almighty for the two keys, which, unbeknown to the Lord, lock the door to the kitchen and the bedroom in Eden. With these keys Eve then controls Adam's access to food and sex, and "that is the reason why the mens THINKS they is the boss and the women KNOWS they is the boss, because they got them two little keys to use in that sly women's way. Yes, forevermore and then some."[10]

Saint Augustine had taught Western civilization to read original sin in the book of Genesis, but their vernacular traditions suggest that African Americans never learned that lesson very well. So in the mid-twentieth century, the folk artist William Edmondson's sculpture *Eve* presents her dressed in a fig leaf, the hasty invention of wardrobe that she dons after eating the forbidden fruit. Edmondson's Eve boldly underscores her generative powers with her upheld breast, an ancient West African gesture used by a queen mother to remind others of her matriarchal authority. But unlike Michelangelo's portrait of Eve on the ceiling of the Sistine Chapel, the supporting characters of her cosmic tragedy do not linger on Edmondson's stage. She bears a fig leaf and her own breast, but no fruit. She is a solitary figure, without Adam, without the serpent, without the tree of the knowledge of good and evil. As Adam says of her in a pun on her name in Hebrew, *Ḥava,* and the Hebrew verb "to live," *ḥay,* she is the mother of all life.

Fathoming the relations between divinity and humanity, and focusing on the latter with the deity as ambivalent foil, was the predilection of African-American folklore. As a Southern African-American preacher explained in a folktale retelling the story of Cain's crime: "The first man what the Lord made, been named Adam. The first woman been named Eve. They had two children, Cain and Abel. The ma and the pa of them children was black, was colored folks." Cain, "a bad Negro, always shooting and cutting and gambling," kills his brother "in a dispute over the best watermelon patch." The Lord interrogates Cain about Abel's absence, to which Cain, "a sassy Negro," responds, "Am I my brother's keeper? I ain't got him in my pockets. I supposes he's off somewhere shooting craps." The Lord is angered by Cain's insolence, and frightens Cain by insistently restating the question "angry-like." Cain "got so scared that his hair stand straight and his face turn right pale—and sisters and brothers, there am what the first white man come from."[11] The folktale, of course, stands the conventional anti-African interpretation on its head. The first fratricide is not the occasion for the invention of blackness—a "diabolical die" applied to a protagonist presumed to be white. It is the occasion for the invention of whiteness.

Another Old Testament malediction against African people, however, proved even more resistant than Cain's mark. The book of Genesis reports that while Noah was in a drunken stupor, his son Ham "saw the nakedness of his father, and told his two brethren without" (9:22). The brothers Shem and Japheth back into their sleeping father's quarters and cover him unseen with a garment. On wakening, Noah becomes aware that Ham has seen his "nakedness" and, enraged, curses one of Ham's sons, Canaan: "Cursed be Canaan; a servant of servants shall he be unto his brethren" (9:25). On the slender thread of this obscure text exegetes spun out an interpretation claiming Ham's descendants as bearing an intergenerational curse of slavery. As early as ancient rabbinical commentary, Noah's son Ham and his progeny were condemned to slavery either because Ham had disrespected his drunken father or because he had copulated on the Ark when everyone else was proscribed from doing so.[12] These ancient and medieval interpretations would contribute to the biblical myth of Hamitic depravity punished by the sentence of slavery.

Because Ham and his progeny were identified with African peoples, the curse of perpetual servitude on his son Canaan was imputed as a biblical rationale for Africans enslavement in the Americas. The text became a favorite of antebellum Southern apologists. Speaking before the Mississippi Democratic State Convention in 1859, Jefferson Davis defended chattel slavery and the foreign slave trade as the "importation of the race of Ham," fulfillment of Africans' destiny to be "servants of servants."[13]

In his historical study of the respective lineages from the Hamitic line in the Bible, New England minister Hosea Easton contrasts the descendants of Ham and Japheth. Among the children of Ham Easton includes Assur, father of the Assyrians, "who probably founded the first government after the flood," the Egyptians, and the Carthaginians of North Africa. The members of the Hamitic line were distinguished throughout antiquity for their enlightened accomplishments in culture and commerce while the rest of the ancient world moved fitfully backward and forward by the force of arms. "The Egyptians alone," claimed Easton, "have done more to cultivate such improvements as comports to the happiness of mankind, than all the descendants of Japheth put together." People of African descent in America had a venerable lineage that long predated their descent into slavery. Indeed it was slavery that separated them from this glorious past, explains Easton: "In this country we behold the remnant of a once noble, but now heathenish people."[14]

Congregational minister and former slave James W. C. Pennington identified African Americans as the distant descendants of the amalgamated lines of Cush (Ethiopia) and Misraim (Egypt). He debunks the curse of Ham by pointing out that Canaan alone was cursed, and not the entire Hamitic line from which all Africans are descended. Writing in the third quarter of the nineteenth century, however, Episcopal priest James Theodore Holly grants that the Hamitic heir Canaan is under a curse and that modern history bears this out. But this very curse will be up-ended in a reversal at the end of the age: "The African race has been the servant of servants to their brethren of the other races during all the long and dreary ages of the Hebrew and Christian dispensations. And it is this service that they have so patiently rendered through blood and tears that shall finally obtain for them the noblest places of service in the Coming Kingdom."[15] In 1937 Holly's son, Alonzo Potter Burgess Holly, would argue in his book *God and the Negro* that the Negro was descended from Canaan. But Exodus

20:5 places a statute of limitations on divine punishment as only "unto the third and fourth generation." This meant that Noah's curse could not have been in effect for more than one hundred years and so had long been null and void millennia before American proslavery advocates claimed it as a proof text.[16]

THE MANDATE

Though the curse of Cain and the curse of Ham remained leitmotivs of proslavery propaganda, the Pauline letters figure more prominently than any other Christian scripture in the arguments of antebellum proslavery advocates. The verse "Slaves be obedient to yours masters," occurring in several places in the New Testament, is a text that appears in several biblical contexts.

> Servants, be obedient to them that are your masters according to the flesh, with fear and trembling, in singleness of your heart, as unto Christ. (Eph. 6:5)

> Servants, obey in all things your masters according to the flesh, not with eyeservice as menpleasers; but in singleness of heart, fearing God. (Col. 3:22)

> Let as many servants as are under the yoke count their own masters worthy of all honour, that the name of God be not blasphemed. (1 Tim. 6:1)

In American biblical interpretation this text came to be bigger than its several contexts because it served the slave regime in the theological ambience of Evangelicalism, the religious tradition shared by slave and master alike in the United States. As heirs of the Reformation, the ponderous persona of Paul gave weight to words that were welcome to a society that practiced slavery and valued biblical sanction for it. Thus Paul became, in the minds of both slave and master, the patron saint of the master class in the antebellum United States.

Jupiter Hammond, eighteenth-century slave poet and essayist, was the first African American to have his writings published in the United States. At age forty-nine on Christmas Day, 1760, he wrote "An Evening Thought: Salvation by Christ, with Penitential Cries" and in so doing became "the progenitor of African-American literature."[17] Born a slave and trained as a clerk and bookkeeper for his wealthy New England master, Hammond had become a Christian convert in the early years of the First Great Awakening. In his "Address to the Negroes of the City of New York" (1786), Hammond advises slaves to obey their masters, citing with approval Ephesians 6:5, which enjoins slaves to obey their masters as they would obey Christ. "Here is a plain command of God for us," exhorts Hammond, "to obey our masters. It may seem hard for us, if we think our masters wrong in holding us slaves, to obey in all things, but who of us dare dispute with God!" His counsel is pragmatic: "This should be done by us," he continues, "not only because God commands, but because our own peace and comfort depend upon it." Hammond's counsel is also qualified: slaves are to faithful carry out "all . . . lawful commands, and mind them [their masters] unless we are bid to do that which we know to be sin, or forbidden in God's word." Hammond concludes with an exhortation to New York's free blacks to abide by Paul's advice in 1 Timothy 2:2 "to lead quiet and peaceable lives in all Godliness and honesty."[18]

Proslavery apologists often referred to Paul's Epistle to Philemon, traditionally understood as a letter attending the return of a runaway slave, as a biblical sanction for slavery: indeed, the letter came to be called the "Pauline Mandate" for the return of fugitive slaves. Some slaves, for their part, found the mandate less than compelling. In 1833 Charles Colcock Jones, a white Presbyterian missionary to slaves, preached a sermon on the text in which he "insisted upon fidelity and obedience as Christian virtues in servants and upon the authority of Paul, [and] condemned the practice of running away." In response, "one half of [his] audience deliberately rose up and walked off with themselves."[19] The catechism was New World slavery's concession to Christianity. Throughout the seventeenth and eighteenth centuries both the Puritans and the Anglicans, the two predominant Christian communions in British North America, made modest attempts to introduce slaves to Christianity. In 1704 Elias Neau, a French Huguenot who had converted to Anglicanism, was appointed "catechist" for the church's missionary arm, the Society for the Propagation of the Gospel in Foreign Parts. Neau published a catechism for "instructing" slaves in the ways of the Bible.

Who gave you a master and a mistress?
God gave them to me.

> Who says that you must obey them?
> God says that I must.
> What book tells you these things?
> The Bible.[20]

Two years after the appearance of Neau's catechism, Puritan divine Cotton Mather published a catechetical pamphlet entitled *The Negro Christianized: An Essay to Excite and Assist the Good Work, the Instruction of Negro-Servants in Christianity* (1706). Among the select biblical verses that Mather included in his catechism were the Apostle Paul's several commands to slaves to obey their masters. The locus classicus was Ephesians 6:5, "Servants, be obedient to them that are your masters according to the flesh, with fear and trembling, in singleness of your heart, as unto Christ."[21]

Exhortations to servile obedience in the Pauline epistles would become the raw material for the catechesis of slaves in early-nineteenth-century plantation missions. "You ought to heared that preachin'," complained a former slave. "Obey your massa and missy, but nary a word about having a soul to save."[22] Frederick Douglass once quipped to the amusement of a British audience that this verse was the "Alpha and Omega, the beginning and the ending of the religious teaching received by the slaves in the United States."[23] For forty years until the outbreak of the Civil War, Episcopal missionary Alexander Glennie consistently preached a form of Pauline Christianity featuring this verse to his slave communicants.

> "Servants, be obedient to them that are your masters according
> to the flesh, with fear and trembling, in singleness of your
> heart, as unto Christ; not with eye service as men pleasers; but
> as the servants of Christ, doing the will of God from the heart:
> with good will doing service, as to the lord and not to men;
> knowing that whatsoever good thing any man doeth, the same
> shall he receive of the Lord, whether he be bond or free." This
> passage from the Bible shews to you, what God requires from
> you as servants; and there are many other passages which
> teach the same things. You should and remember these parts
> of the Bible, that you may be able "to do your duty in that state
> of life, unto which it has pleased God to call you." For although
> a bad servant may not wish to know what God requires of him,

yet a Christian servant will desire to know this, and to do his will in every thing.[24]

That the obedience of servants was Glennie's signal theme is reflected in ex-slave Mariah Heywood's terse summary of his preaching: "Parson Glennie come once a month to Sunnyside. Parson Glennie read, sing, pray. Tell us to obey Miss Minna."[25]

According to the testimony of slaves themselves, obedience was the first commandment of the Christianity preached to them. Talking to a government interviewer in 1938, ninety-year-old Sarah Fitzpatrick spoke of the religion of her masters: "White preacher he preach to the white folks and when he get through with them he preach to the niggers. Tell them to mind they master and behave theyself and they'll all go to heaven when they die. They come around and tell us to pray, get religion, that was on Sunday, but they'd beat the life out of you the next day if you didn't walk the chalk line. Our white folks made us go to church and Sunday School too. They made us read the Catechism. Guess the reason for that was, they thought it made us mind them better." In 1910 a former Alabama slave named Bill Pickens recalled the quality of preaching that he heard in the slave quarters: "I remember the old days how one of my master's slaves wanted to go to that church. 'You mind your business and hear the preacher what I send you,' master says. Once a month his preacher would come and talk to the colored folk. He'd tell them how they must obey their master and mistress and not steal any chickens. He wouldn't say much more than that. No real preaching."[26]

The grandmother of theologian and Christian mystic Howard Thurman was loath to hear the words of the Apostle Paul. The elderly woman allowed the young Thurman to read to her only, and on rare occasion, Paul's paean to love in 1 Corinthians 13. She later explained to Thurman,

> During the days of slavery, the master's minister would occasionally hold services for the slaves. Old man McGhee was so mean that he would not let a Negro minister preach to his slaves. Always the white minister used as his text something from Paul. At least three or four times a year he used as a text: 'Slaves, be obedient to them that are your masters . . . as unto Christ.' Then he would go on to show how it was God's will that we were slaves and how, if we were good and happy slaves,

God would bless us. I promised my Maker that if I ever learned to read and if freedom ever came, I would not read that part of the Bible.[27]

Nevertheless, some African Americans questioned the limited canon that this interpretation of Paul necessarily implies. They argued, in the words of Uncle Simon, the black preacher in William Wells Brown's antebellum novel *Clotel,* "thars more in de Bible den dat."[28] In a petition of 1774 to the Massachusetts House of Representatives, a group of colonial slaves enlist the words of Paul to argue against their status of perpetual servitude. It is slavery's conflict with Pauline commandments of family and communal life, they contend, that shows the institution to be inherently incompatible with Christianity.

Our lives are embittered to us . . . By our deplorable situation we are rendered incapable of shewing our obedience to Almighty God How can a slave perform the duties of husband to a wife or a parent to his child? How can a husband leave master to work and cleave to his wife How can the wife submit themselves to their husbands in all things How can the child obey their parents in all things? There is a great number of us sencear . . . members of the Church of Christ how can the master and the slave be said to fulfil the command Live in love let brotherly Love contuner [continue] and abound Beare ye one anothers Bordens How can the master be said to Bear my Borden when he Bears me down with the Have [heavy] chains of slavery and operson against my will and how can we fulfill our parte of duty to him whilst in this condition as we cannot searve our God as we ought in this situation.[29]

The petitioners claim that they cannot serve the Master because of their service to the masters, because in slavery they cannot obey the orders of the apostolic slave for Christ's sake, Paul. It is the Apostle who instructs believers to bear one another's burdens in Galatians 6:2 and enjoins the submission of wives to husbands and children to parents in Ephesians 5:22, 24, and Colossians 3:20. The patriarchal household was the norm for the master class of American colonial society, a norm as attractive to these slaves as it was unavailable to them. Parental control over children and a husband's exclusive sexual access to his own wife were troubled desiderata for black folks under the American slave regime. For the petitioners, Paul's commandments gave these desiderata the sanction of holy scripture.

Nineteenth-century revivalism "helped recast the Southern world view by increasingly grounding it in the Bible."[30] In the second quarter of the nineteenth century Southern whites, largely in response to the attacks by abolitionists, began to invoke the Scriptures in a systematic defense of slavery. Occasionally this biblical worldview required Southern biblical interpreters to make hash of the words of Jesus. And none of Jesus's words have been more influential—and more troublesome for the ideology of American slavery—than the Golden Rule: "Do unto others what you would have them do to you" (Matt. 7:12). Simple observance of this simple principle would have rendered American slavery impossible.

The Quakers—the only Christians to speak out consistently against slavery in the colonial era—made the Golden Rule the centerpiece of their condemnation of slavery.[31] In *A Caution and Warning to Great Britain and Her Colonies* (1766), Anthony Benezet recalled Quaker founder George Fox's message to the slaveholders of Barbados almost a century earlier: "Consider with yourselves if you were in the same condition as the blacks are, who came strangers to you and were sold to you as slaves; I say, if this should be the condition of you or yours, you would think it a hard measure, yea, and very great bondage and cruelty. And therefore consider seriously this, and do you for them as you would willingly have them do or any other do unto you were you in the like slavish condition, and bring them to know the Lord Christ."[32]

African Americans concurred with the plain-sense Quaker reading. Olaudah Equiano, recalling the kidnapping of his sister and himself from West Africa, pleaded: "O, ye nominal Christians! might not an African ask you, learned you this from your God? who says unto you, Do unto all men as you would men should do unto you. Is it not enough that we are torn from our country and friends to toil for your luxury and lust of gain? Must every tender feeling be likewise sacrificed to your avarice?"[33] And when mainline Protestant churches began their official assault on slavery, they followed the Quakers' precedent. At their Christmas Conference of 1784 the Methodists resolved that slavery was "contrary to the Golden Law of God on which hang on the Law and the Prophets."[34] The Presbyterian

General Assembly concluded its famous antislavery declaration of 1818 by quoting the Golden Rule.

Southern interpreters insisted, however, that the plain sense of the Golden Rule was plainly wrong. Writing for the South Carolina Baptist State Convention in 1822, Richard Furman brushed aside the Golden Rule's abolitionist implications. "Surely this rule is never to be urged against that order of things, which the Divine government has established," wrote Furman, "nor do our desires become a standard to us, under this rule, unless they have due regard to justice, propriety and the general good."[35] Writing for the *Southern Presbyterian Review* in July 1850, James Henley Thornwell echoed Furman's theme when he maintained that the Golden Rule only required that "we should treat our slaves as we feel that we ought to be treated if we were slaves ourselves."[36] Robert L. Dabney, another Southern Presbyterian, opined: "The rule of our conduct to our neighbor is not any desire which we might have, were we to change places, but it is that desire which we should, in that case, be morally entitled to have."[37] The Golden Rule obliged the master only to give to his slave "whatever was equitable, and due to one intelligent, social, immortal being, standing in such a relation to another."[38] In a letter to Francis Wayland, Richard Fuller insisted that Paul's exhortation to slaveholding Colossians to "give unto your servants that which is just and equal" was obviously a "special application" of the Golden Rule.[39]

African Americans sometimes summoned the words of the Lord to trump the words of the apostle. African American women pioneered a mode of public disputation in which they called Jesus to witness against the Bible itself. In the early nineteenth century, African Methodist Episcopal preacher Jarena Lee corroborates her contested call to preach with an appeal to the Gospel witness: "If the man may preach, because the Saviour died for him, why not the woman, seeing he died for her also? Is he not a whole Saviour, instead of a half one, as those who hold it wrong for a woman to preach, would seem to make it appear? Did not Mary first preach the risen Saviour, and is not the doctrine of the resurrection the very first climax of Christianity? Hangs not all our hope on this, as argued by St. Paul?"[40] The concluding rhetorical question is telling. Lee alludes to Paul's synopsis of the Gospel proclamation in 1 Corinthians 15:1–11, a resume of witnesses to the Resurrection into which he insinuates himself. But there are no women on Paul's witness list: Paul says nothing of the women who were by all other accounts the first to bear witness to the resurrection of Jesus. Lee has implicitly read against the grain of Paul's omission, in the last instance appealing to Paul's argument later in the same chapter 15 that the resurrection of Jesus is the basis of Christian hope: "And if Christ be not raised, your faith is vain; ye are yet in your sins. Then they also which are fallen asleep in Christ are perished. If in this life only we have hope in Christ, we are of all men most miserable" (15:17–19). Lee undermines the force of Paul's counsel to silence enjoined on the women of Corinth—the scriptural basis of the prohibition against women preachers—with Paul's insistence on the importance of the preaching of the resurrection. At the same time Lee includes the testimony of women to the resurrection precisely where Paul has failed to mention them in his list of witnesses in 1 Corinthians 15. Lee's reading of scripture subverts the silences of 1 Corinthians 14:33–36 and 15:1–11 with one deft stroke of interpretation.

Jarena Lee concludes the autobiographical account of her vocation as she has expressed it and defended it—with the words of Paul. Lee is finally confident in her calling because, she writes, "I have never found the Spirit to lead me contrary to the Scriptures of truth, as I understand them. 'For as many as are led by the Spirit of God are the sons of God.'"[41] Lee here quotes in the gender-exclusive parlance of the King James Version, Romans 8:14. Paul's declaration of the Spirit's victory over fear becomes Lee's declaration of the Spirit's victory over her fear of condemnation by the very words of him who wrote, "there is now no condemnation in Christ Jesus" (Rom. 5:1).

Orator and political philosopher Maria Stewart bucked the convention of female public silence to speak out against slavery and racial discrimination in the second quarter of the nineteenth century. Like Jarena Lee before her, Stewart too had initial misgivings about her vocation to proclaim what she called "the pure principals of religion." "I found that sin still lurked within; it was hard for me to renounce all for Christ, when I saw my earthly prospects blasted." And like Jarena Lee, she found solace in Paul's words from the Epistle to the Romans. "Thus ended these mighty conflicts, I received this heart-cheering promise, 'That neither death, nor life, nor principalities, nor powers, nor things present, nor things to come, should be able to separate me from the love of Christ Jesus, our Lord.'"[42]

Stewart's vocation as a lay preacher of Christian virtue met fierce resistance from men in the public square. The argument wielded by hostile interlocutors to silence her was biblical: Paul had said that women should be silent. Stewart's defense was itself biblical. She argues that the weightier matters of justice and mercy required as a moral imperative that she, though a woman, lift up her voice as a trumpet in Zion. "St. Paul declared that it is a shame for a woman to speak in public, yet our great High Priest and Advocate did not condemn the woman for a more notorious offence than this; neither will he condemn this worthless worm," Stewart insisted. Had not "Mary Magdalene first declare the resurrection of Christ from the dead?" When outraged white men insisted that Maria Stewart should not be speaking in public and cited Paul as sanctioning the silence of women, Stewart, as had Jarena Lee a half century earlier, cited the example of Mary Magdalene as the first preacher of the resurrection. Stewart's adversaries had quoted scripture against her; Stewart responded by quoting scripture against scripture, Jesus against Paul. "Did St. Paul but know of our wrongs and deprivations," Stewart argued, "I presume he would make no objections to our pleading in public for our rights."[43]

THE GOOD BOOK

African Americans found that the Bible had the power of curse and cure. Just as they would be emboldened by its promises, African Americans would remain marked by the legacy of the Bible's maledictions, which could be neither recalled nor revoked. In *The Fire Next Time . . .* , James Baldwin chronicles what he calls "the slow crumbling of my faith, the pulverization of my fortress." In this essay, at once an autobiography of his early life and obituary of his early vocation as a Holiness Pentecostal preacher, Baldwin shows himself to be American literature's most distinguished backslider. His adolescent crisis of faith was attended by a crisis of confidence in the Bible itself. "I realized," concluded the young Baldwin, "that the Bible had been written by white men. . . . I knew that according to many Christians, I was the descendent of Ham, who had been cursed, and that I was therefore predestined to be a slave. This had nothing to do with anything I was, or contained, or could become; my fate had been sealed forever, from the beginning of time. And it seemed, indeed, when one looked out over Christendom, that this was what Christendom effectively believed. It was certainly the way it behaved."[44] African Americans would continue to struggle, even in their own minds, with the ownership of the Bible that they shared with the master class. Alice Walker gives voice to this struggle in her novel *The Color Purple* through the dialogue between the protagonist Celie and her skeptical friend Shug.

> Then she tell me this old white man is the same God she used to see when she prayed. If you wait to find God in church, Celie, she say, that's who is bound to show up, cause that's where he live.
>
> How come? I ast.
>
> Cause that's the one that's in the white folks' white bible.
>
> Shug! I say. God wrote the bible, white folks had nothing to do with it.
>
> How come he look just like them, then? she say. Only bigger? And a heap more hair. How come the bible just like everything else they make, all about them doing one thing and another, and all the colored folks doing is gitting cursed?
>
> I never thought about that.[45]

If they were going to take their own share of the Bible, African Americans would have to counterinterpret the passages adduced as evidence of the biblical curses that black folks purportedly bore.

Ultimately African Americans embraced the Bible, a poison book, because it was so effective, in measured doses, as its own antidote. In the biblical book that bears his name, the prophet Jeremiah, declaring the failing health of the Israelite body politic, cries out in despair, "Is there no balm in Gilead; is there no physician there?" To this question the author of the Negro spiritual answers in the affirmative:

> There is a balm in Gilead
> To heal the sin-sick soul
> There is a balm in Gilead
> To make the wounded whole[46]

A biblical question has been inverted into a biblical answer: what was interrogative in the Bible has become declarative in the Negro spiritual. In this way the "black and unknown bards," as James Weldon Johnson called them, set a precedent for talking back to the Bible, using its own words to sharpen their pointed ripostes.

African Americans found the Bible to be both healing balm and poison book. They could not lay claim to the balm without braving the poison. The same book was both medicine and malediction. To afford themselves its healing properties, African Americans resolved to treat scripture with scripture, much like a homeopathic remedy; homeopathic medicine "uses a skillfully prepared or modified dosage of a disease in order to cure a disease."[47] Their cure for the toxicity of pernicious scripture was more scripture. The antidote to hostile texts of the Bible was more Bible, homeopathically administered to counteract the toxins of the text.

In America, the Bible would be at the same time gag order and preaching license. It would be the war cry of the pacifist and warrior's hymn of peace, and sacred scripture of both the Blue and the Gray. Illiterates would read its sacred letters; atheists would affirm its divine oracles; and sinners would celebrate its saints. As both curse and cure, slavery's children would distill antidotes for the toxic texts of the Bible and make those texts their own.

It remained, however, for them to make the Good Book a book that would truly be good for them.

CHAPTER THREE

The Good Book

Nigger never went to free school
Nor any other college
And all the white folks wonder where
That nigger got his knowledge
He chewed up all the Bible
And then spat out the Scripture
And when he 'gin to argue strong
He were a snortin' ripter.

—Southern folk song

IN 1837 THE FUGITIVE SLAVE Charles Ball described religion among the slaves this way. "The idea of revolution in the conditions of whites and blacks," he insisted, "is the corner-stone of the religion of the latter. . . . Heaven will be no heaven to him if he is not avenged of his enemies."[1] As one devout Christian slave opined, "Some folks say slaveholders may be good Christians, but I can't and won't believe it, nor do I think that a slaveholder can get to heaven. He may possibly get there, I don't know; but though I wish to get there myself, I don't want to have anything to do with slaveholders either here or in heaven."[2] Escaped slave Moses Roper reported in his autobiography that the slaves on his master's plantation, "thinking him [the master] a very bad example of what a professing Christian ought to be, would not join the connexion he belonged to, thinking they must be a very bad set of people."[3]

Of course, remedy inaccessible on earth would be forthcoming in heaven. A slave named Maurice, blinded by a blow to the head from his master's whip, recollected, "I feel great distress when I become blind . . . but then I went to seek the Lord; and ever since I know I see in the next world, I always have great satisfaction."[4] Heaven, however, was not only the place of remedy but also the place of redress. "There is . . . great consolation in knowing that God is just and will not let the oppressor of the weak, and the spoiler of the virtuous escape unpunished here and hereafter," declared ex-slave William Craft in 1860. "I believe a similar retribution to that which destroyed Sodom is hanging over the slaveholders."[5] The reference to Sodom—the iniquitous city that God destroys in the book of Genesis—suggests the inspiration of Craft's hope. The retribution he looked forward to was figured in the Bible.

The hypocrisy that provoked astonishment in some slaves provoked atheism in others. African Methodist Episcopal (AME) bishop Daniel Alexander Paine observed in the late 1830s that he knew slaves who refused to believe in the God of slaveholding Christians. "They hear their masters professing Christianity," Payne wrote, "they see their masters preaching the gospel; they hear these masters praying in their families, and they know that oppression and slavery are inconsistent with the Christian religion; therefore they scoff at religion itself—mock their masters and distrust both the goodness and justice of God. Yes, I have known them even to question his existence. I speak not of what others have told me, but of what I have both seen and heard from the slaves themselves."[6] Evangelical Christian slaves tacitly agreed with their atheist sisters and brothers in bondage that they would have a religion of justice or no religion at all. And they found the condemnation of the religion of their oppressors in the book their oppressors held to be sacred. Justice became a tenet of faith that even the otherwise faithless could hold with zeal. And so African Americans came to accept the Book of the religion while rejecting the religion of the Book.

Precisely because divine judgment eschewed the false and predictable categories of human preference—caste, color, and class—only those who met the rigorous criteria of righteousness would be allowed to enter the heavenly habitations. To walk the streets of the New Jerusalem, one had to be morally prepared. To catch a glimpse of the beatific vision as John does on Patmos in the book of Revelation, the singers of the Negro spirituals had to meet the requirements of Evangelical Christian deportment:

> I want to be ready
> I want to be ready
> I want to be ready
> To walk in Jerusalem jus' like John.[7]

The Negro spirituals are replete with anxiety about measuring up to the standards of the Last Judgment. The bards of the Negro spirituals looked toward the end of the age with certainty and anxiety. Divine judgment could even cleave through the faithful and drive a wedge between saints and sinners on the same pew. Though they singers expected that they would not fall under judgment, they apparently never expected that they could not. In the Negro spiritual "O Rocks Don't Fall on Me," the singer describes the pleading of sinners not to be buried in the rubble of judgment, but at the end of the song he takes up the very same plea himself.

In their hearts and beneath their breaths slaves cursed the house of bondage, and even these violent imprecations were in the language of the Bible. Governess Mary Livermore reports that Aggy, a mild-mannered slave cook, had watched helplessly as her master beat her daughter for some trifling offense. After the master was safely out of earshot, Livermore heard Aggy give voice to her outrage in the parlance of a biblical curse. "Thar's a day a-comin'! Thar's a day a-comin'! . . . I hear de rumblin' of de chariots! I see de flashin' ob de guns! White folks' blood is a-runnin' on de ground like a riber, an' de dead's heaped up dat high! . . . Oh, Lor'! hasten de day when de blows, an' de bruises, an' de aches, an' de pains, shall come to de white folks, an' de buzzards shall eat 'em as dey's dead in de streets. Oh, Lor'! roll on de chariots, an' gib de black people rest an' peace. Oh, Lor'! gib me de pleasure ob livin' till dat day, when I shall see white folks shot down like de wolves when dey come hongry out o' de woods!"[8] How often such imprecations were the *esprit d'escalier* of the slave quarters we will never know. As peons under Jim Crow, a later generation would give biblical expression to their resentment by giving the text of the Lord's Prayer a humorous turn in a popular folk song:

> "Our Father, who art in Heaven!"—
> White man owe me eleven and pay me seven
> "Thy Kingdom come! Thy Will be done!"—
> And if I hadn't took that, I wouldn't get none.[9]

There were black Christians who saw in the Bible's bloody accounts of holy war that God could and would secure their freedom through divinely sanctioned violence. Negro spirituals drew inspiration from the martial narratives and imagery of the Bible. "Joshua Fit the Battle of Jericho" celebrates the miraculous victory of the Israelite campaign against the impregnable city of Jericho reported in the sixth chapter of the book of Joshua. After seven days of silent marching around the city wall, seven Israelite priests blew their trumpets, the soldiers in their train raised a war cry, and the city walls disintegrated.

> Joshua fit the battle of Jericho
> Jericho, Jericho,
> Joshua fit the battle of Jericho
> And the walls came tumbling down.
>
> You may talk about your man of Gideon
> You may talk about your man of Saul
> There's none like good old Joshua
> At the battle of Jericho[10]

The second stanza mentions two biblical heroes. The first is Gideon, who with a diminutive force of three hundred Israelite irregulars armed only with trumpets and lamps hidden in earthen jars, executed a daring guerrilla raid on their Midianite foes. The second, Saul, is Israel's first king, who led the armies of the Lord into victorious war against the Philistines. The God of the enslaved Israelites comports himself as a god of war, and the captains of his hosts were messiahs, "Anointed ones," empowered by the Spirit to destroy Israel's enemies with the edge of the sword. American slaves heard these stories as a call to holy war on the Peculiar Institution, and the nineteenth century opened with some Christian slaves giving earnest heed to that call. As W. E. B. Du Bois would later eloquently put it in his essay "Faith of Our Fathers," the religion of the slave "became darker and more intense, and into his ethics crept a note of revenge, into his songs a day of reckoning close at hand. The 'Coming of the Lord' swept this side of death, and came to be a thing hoped for in this day."[11]

According to an account published after the Civil War by AME minister Moses Dickson, Dickson and eleven other men from several southern states met in Saint Louis in 1846 to form the Twelve Knights of Tabor, an underground organization dedicated to the overthrow of American slavery. A decade of conspiracy and strategy brought a secret network of militias called the Knights of Tabor to full flower before it was disbanded in 1857.

The knights were active in the Underground Railroad while recruiting forty-seven thousand men to their clandestine army of antislavery irregulars. The founding members chose a name for their organization from the fourth chapter of the book of Judges. Dickson explains that they called themselves the Knights of Tabor to recall the mountain from which the Israelite general Barak descended at the instruction of the prophet Deborah. At the foot of Mount Tabor the Israelite armies annihilated the infantry and chariots of their Canaanite oppressors. The name reminded its bearers of a biblical battle in which God granted victory to his oppressed people though they were vastly outnumbered. God, they believed, would likewise be with them and enable them to overcome otherwise insuperable odds. "Under the old name of Tabor," wrote Dickson later, "we resolved to make full preparation to strike a blow for liberty. We felt sure that the Lord God was on the side of right and justice, our faith and trust in him, and that he would help us in our needy time."[12]

The knights planned to converge from several points in Atlanta, and Dickson claims that by the summer of 1857 the conspiracy had more than 150,000 men secretly under arms. But in midsummer the anonymous "Chief" of the movement "called a halt" to the maneuvers of the knights because "it was plainly demonstrated to him that a higher power was preparing to take part in the contest between the North and the South."[13]

The "Chief" had prophesied the Civil War, which many Americans on both sides of the conflict interpreted as a crusade. African Americans understood the crusade as their own, with the Yankees as God's instrument of judgment. Thomas Wentworth Higginson learned the song "We'll Soon Be Free" from soldiers from Georgetown serving in his all-black Union regiment.

> We'll soon be free
> We'll soon be free
> We'll soon be free
> When the Lord will call us home
>
> My brother how long
> My brother how long
> My brother how long
> Before we done suffering here
>
> We'll fight for liberty
> We'll fight for liberty

We'll fight for liberty
When the Lord will call us home[14]

As a young drummer boy explained to Higginson, "They [the soldiers] think 'the Lord' mean for to say the Yankees." Several slaves in George-town were arrested and imprisoned when they were overheard singing the song publicly after learning of the outbreak of the War.[15] John Mason Brown, writing several years after the war of his encounters with slave songs, was struck by the prevalence of martial images in Negro spiritu-als. According to one spiritual, "Moses was a soldier, / In the army of the Lord," and in another,

> When Moses and his soldiers from Egypt land did flee,
> His enemies behind him, and in front of him the sea,
> God raised the water like a wall, and opened up the way,
> And the God that lived in Moses' time is just the same today.[16]

Black Union soldiers saw themselves as fighting in the Lord's army.

For blacks in the North who fought in the Union Army and those in the South who prayed for it, God was waging holy war in accordance with the holy scriptures. A group of slaves meeting in secret in Richmond, Virginia, found the War Between the States prophesied in an oracle of the book of Daniel. The slaves furtively read Daniel 11:13–15, "For the King of the North shall come and cast up a mound and take the most fenced cit-ies, and the arms of the South shall not withstand." Thomas L. Johnson, a member of the group, later recounted, "We often met together and read this chapter in our own way." Johnson and his comrades "eagerly grasped at any statements which our anxiety, hope, and prayer concerning our liberty led us to search for, and which might indicate the desirable end-ing of the great War."[17] The Bible, according to these slaves' clandestine reckoning, promised a Northern victory.

THE ETERNAL WORD

In Martin Delany's serialized antebellum novel of pan-African revolution, *Blake, or the Huts of America*, the protagonist Henry Blake is a runaway slave who travels through the American South and Cuba plotting insur-rection. Blake secretly organizes slaves in both countries to foil Southern expansionists who want to make Cuba a Caribbean extension of the slave regime in the United States. Blake surveys the religious affiliations of his co-conspirators and explains that his newfound religion of revolt is written in the hearts of the faithful.

> I, first a Catholic, and my wife bred as such, are both Baptists; Abyssa Soudan, once pagan, was in her native land converted to the Methodist or Wesleyan belief; Madame Sabastina and family are Episcopalians; Camina, from long residence out of the colony, a Presbyterian, and Placido is a believer in the Swedenborgian doctrines. We have all agreed to know no sects, no denomination, and but one religion for the sake of our redemption from bondage and degradation, a faith in a common Savior as an intercessor for our sins; but one God, who is and must be acknowledged common Father. No religion but that which brings us liberty will serve. The whites accept of nothing but that which promotes their interests and happiness, socially, politically, and religiously. They would discard religion, tear down a church, overthrow a government, or desert a country, which did not enhance their freedom. In God's great and righteous name, are we not willing to do the same? . . . Our ceremonies . . . are borrowed from no denomination, creed, nor church: no existing organization, secret, secular, nor religious; but originated by ourselves, adopted to our own condition, circumstances, and wants, founded upon the eternal word of God, our Creator, as impressed upon the tablet of each of our hearts."[18]

Henry Blake's words echo those of the prophet Jeremiah, who looked forward to a day when the written law of God—the Bible of the ancient Israelites—would be done away with altogether, no longer written in a book but permanently written on the human heart. God promises, "I will make a new covenant with the House of Israel and the House of Judah, not according to the covenant I made with their fathers. . . . I will put my law in their inward parts, and write it in their hearts" (Jer. 31:31–32). The Hebrew word for "law" in this oracle is *torah,* the name traditionally ascribed to the Bible of the ancient Israelites. Jeremiah's oracle promises that God will write a new Bible in the human heart.

That eternal word, that divine law, was justice. The crimson thread of justice winds through the history of slavery's children, and binds together several biblical images that have continued to be important for African Americans. The prophet Ezekiel's vision of a valley of bleached bones has become a recurring text in African-American arts and letters because it speaks to the permanent exile of Africans in the Western Hemisphere. The story of the Exodus has been the most influential of all biblical narratives among American slaves, who came to see divine worship as unfettered service to the God who had liberated Hebrew slaves en masse from Egypt. Even after Emancipation, African Americans continued to read the Exodus as promise of their future deliverance. In interpretations religious and secular, African Americans have understood Psalm 68:31, "Ethiopia shall soon stretch out her hands unto God," as an oracle affirming at the same time the glorious past and the glorious future of people of African descent. And the ubiquitous image of Jesus has been the biblical mirror in which African Americans have seen both their history of suffering and their hope of vindication, symbol of both the frustration and fulfillment of their destiny. These four images share several key features. They appear in different genres and in different periods throughout American history. They have arisen out of and have given rise to a sense of collective African-American identity: the images speak of and to African-American people and speak of and to African Americans *as* a people. And most important, it is in these biblical images that African Americans have held in tension both the injustice of history and the God of justice, catching a fleeting glimpse, as through a glass darkly, of the justice of God.

CHAPTER FOUR

Exile

O my fathers, what was it like to be stripped of all supports of life save the beating of the heart and the ebb and flow of fetid air in the lungs? In a strange moment when you suddenly caught your breath, did some intimation from the future give to your spirit a wink of promise? In the darkness, did you hear the silent feet of your children . . . in a land in which your bones would be warmed again in the depths of the cold earth in which you would sleep, unknown, unrealized and alone?

—*Howard Thurman, "On Viewing the Coast of Africa"*

IN 587 BCE, THE BABYLONIANS conquered Judah, the southern kingdom of ancient Israel. They destroyed the Temple in the capital city of Jerusalem, and took many Judean elites to Babylonia as prisoners. The shock of what came to be known as the Babylonian Exile registers across the width and breadth of Israel's sacred scriptures and is mourned in the poignant poetry of the psalmist:

> By the rivers of Babylon, there we sat down, yea, we wept,
>   when we remembered Zion.
> We hanged our harps upon the willows in the midst thereof.
> For there they that carried us away captive required of us a
>   song; and they that wasted us required of us mirth, saying,
>   Sing us one of the songs of Zion.
> How long shall we sing the Lord's song in a strange land?
> (Ps. 137:1–4)

In 539 BCE, King Cyrus of Persia overthrew the Babylonians, and his new imperial regime allowed the Judean exiles to return to Judah. The captivity of the Judeans, as the King James Version puts it, was "turned." Though some Judeans remained in Babylonia, others returned to their ancestral land and built the Second Temple in Jerusalem. Later, the communities of Judeans who remained scattered outside Israel became known as the Diaspora or Dispersion.

Like the ancient Israelites, African Americans experienced a violent exile, and these exiled Africans came to number among a vast, transatlantic African Diaspora. But unlike the captivity of the Judeans, theirs would turn out not to be turned. They would learn to sing their song in a strange land or not at all. As an anonymous African-American poet put it, echoing the words of the psalmist,

> By Babylon's streams we sat and wept,
> While Zion we thought upon;
> Amidst thereof we hung our harps,
> The willow trees upon.
> With all the pow'r of skill I have,
> I'll gently touch each string;
> If I can teach the charming sound,
> I'll tune my harp again.[1]

Frederick Douglass echoed this biblical cry of exile in his one of his most strident public denunciations of American slavery. In his address of July 4, 1852, "The Meaning of July Fourth for the Negro," Douglass denounces the hypocrisy of a national celebration of freedom in a land of slavery. "This Fourth July is yours, not mine," declares Douglass. "You may rejoice, I must mourn." Douglass quotes Psalm 137, likening the suffering of African-American slaves to the Babylonian exile:

> "By the rivers of Babylon, there we sat down. Yea! we wept when we remembered Zion. . . . O Jerusalem, let my right hand forget her cunning. If I do not remember thee, let my tongue cleave to the roof of my mouth."
>
> Fellow-citizens, above your national, tumultuous joy, I hear the mournful wail of millions! whose chains, heavy and grievous yesterday, are, to-day, rendered more intolerable by the jubilee shouts that reach them. If I do forget, if I do not faithfully remember those bleeding children of sorrow this day, "may my right hand forget her cunning, and may my tongue cleave to the roof of my mouth!" To forget them, to pass lightly over

their wrongs, and to chime in with the popular theme, would
be treason most scandalous and shocking, and would make me
a reproach before God and the world.[2]

Frederick Douglass was, in the words of Robert Hayden's elegiac poem,
"this former slave, this Negro / beaten to his knees, exiled, visioning a
world / where none is lonely, none hunted, alien."[3] Douglass identified
"the mournful wail of millions" of African-American slaves with the ancient blues refrain from Psalm 137, "the plaintive lament of a peeled and
woe-smitten people."[4] The cause for this lament, the engine of exile and the
resulting dispersion of millions of Africans in America, was slavery.

THE HOUSE OF BONDAGE

The mass deportation of people from Africa to the Americas was nothing
short of catastrophic for Africans on both sides of the Atlantic. For four
centuries, Africa bled a steady hemorrhage of stolen humanity. The population of West Africa, the native region of most of the African slaves, has
been estimated as about eleven million people at the beginning of the
sixteenth century, increasing to about twenty million at the beginning of
the nineteenth century. Throughout this period, as many as a hundred
thousand slaves were being exported annually. In Angola and the Congo,
enslavement exceeded natural population growth and depopulated entire
villages.[5]

Slavery was well known in Africa, and African rulers were the trading
partners of Arab and European slavers. Africans continued commerce in
human flesh with Arab slave traders after the European trade closed in
the nineteenth century. The trade crossed the sands of the Sahara, where
untold thousands perished from heat, thirst, and hunger. In 1849, a letter
to an Ottoman official mentioned sixteen hundred West African slaves
dying of thirst on their way to Libya. Of another slave caravan route, it
was said that someone unfamiliar with the desert might be able to find
his way just by following the trail of skeletons.

Although the Islamic countries of the Middle East and North Africa
imported more slaves from sub-Saharan Africa than did Europeans, the
Islamic world has no distinct, self-conscious groups of people of African
descent such as there are in the Western Hemisphere. Slaves captured
in the Arab trade had a higher mortality rate and a much lower fertility

rate than slaves brought to the Americas. One prominent feature of Islamic slavery that contributed to both factors was castration: eunuchs were prized as servants in harems and called for higher prices. Islam forbids castration, so the operation was hastily performed on hapless male slaves—often crudely, for as many as 90 percent of its victims perished under the knife—before they were brought to areas under Ottoman dominion. These men, by cruel design, would have no descendants.

Though eunuchs were in great demand, most slaves were girls and young women and their children, only the hardiest of whom survived the trek across the Sahara. Most of these women were retained for menial domestic service. Some bore their master a child and according to Islamic custom were subsequently freed, but not enough of them to leave a large, discrete population of African descent anywhere in the Islamic world.[6]

Muslim merchants and Tuareg tribal raiders of North Africa had plied the Saharan slave trade for centuries before the arrival of the Portuguese, the first Europeans to become regular business partners. In the mid-fifteenth century the Portuguese began to buy slaves from African traders instead of kidnapping slaves themselves. Apparently under royal direction, agents for the court of Prince Henry began buying slaves from African traders. The merchandise consisted of prisoners of war or raids waged for the purpose of slave capture, as well as convicted criminals or political enemies. Portuguese traders had learned the hard way that kidnapping slaves along the fishing villages of the West African coast was labor intensive, financially risky, and dangerous. African resistance to enslavement could be fierce, even lethal.[7]

By the sixteenth century the Portuguese and other Europeans were buying and selling slaves from all over the world. Slaves from far-off lands continued to be an ornament of European high society until the eighteenth century. Among them, Africans figured prominently. In 1556 the Genoese government circumscribed the slave trade to stem a glut of Africans for sale. Marseille was a market for slaves in the middle of the sixteenth century and a known port of call for Muslim peddlers of black flesh. African slaves became especially common in the Iberian Peninsula. The sale of slaves was advertised publicly in the streets of Seville, which by 1565 had a population of eighty-five thousand, of which six thousand were slaves. Most of these Spanish slaves were Africans. Yet the number of enslaved Africans in Portugal exceeded that of Spain: indeed, Portugal had more African slaves than any other European nation. By 1550 there were ten thousand slaves in Lisbon alone.[8]

It would be in the New World, however, that the labor of African slaves would lay the foundation for a new civilization. In the Western Hemisphere slavery became something it had never been in Europe: the principal source of labor for the economy. The two industries favored by the Europeans to produce enormous wealth—mining and plantation farming—both required massive labor. Hard labor: the work in the fields of the plantations was unremitting toil. And to the drudgery and disease that afflicted agricultural laborers the work of mining added constant danger. Arduous work on the land and beneath it would be the lot of Africans in the New World, work that no salary would adequately remunerate and few laborers would freely undertake. It would be the work of slaves.

It became clear to the Spanish and Portuguese from colonists to crowned heads that impressing Native Americans into service would not satisfy the exorbitant colonial appetite for slave labor. Many observed that the Africans could work long and hard under the tropical sun and were unusually resistant to fatigue and illness. This was no doubt a perverse effect of the Middle Passage, which had become an ongoing experiment in modern eugenics. The violence and disease of transatlantic transport had a winnowing effect on the gene pool of the slaves. As many as half the Africans brought to the New World died in transit: the fittest survived the ordeal, only some of them living to pass on their capacity for endurance to the next generation.

It was this hardy remnant that Europeans and Native Americans alike encountered in the colonies, and they agreed that the African survivors seemed ideally suited for the harsh service to which they had been condemned. Cristóbal de Benavente, public prosecutor of the Supreme Court in Mexico, wrote to the king of Spain in 1544: "Every day the gold mines are giving less profit, because of the lack of Indian slaves. In the end, if Your Majesty abolishes local slavery there will be no alternative to allowing blacks into the land, at least in the mines." Some natives agreed. In the 1580's a group of indigenous people in Mexico told the viceroy, Alvaro Manrique de Zuñigo, that the "difficult and arduous work" of the sugar plantations was "only for the blacks and not for the thin and weak Indians." Black labor was used in the production of sugar, rice, indigo gold, cotton, cocoa, and the extraction of Mexican silver: only the high altitudes of the Potosí silver mines in Peru precluded the use of Africans there. Between 1492 and 1820, five times as many Africans were brought to the Western Hemisphere as white Europeans who came voluntarily. From 1820 to 1870, as many Africans were imported to Brazil and Cuba as white emigrants arrived in all of Latin America.[9]

The slaves conveyed to the English colonies of British North America amounted to little more than 6 percent of the roughly fourteen million Africans who from the sixteenth century on were captured or purchased from among the many kingdoms and villages of different religions, languages, and cultures of sub-Saharan West Africa. It is one of the historical ironies of the New World that slavery and its racist legacy became more bitterly divisive in the United States than in Latin America, where the vast majority of slaves were sold. This irony is easier to understand when we consider that as early as the late seventeenth century, most slaves in the American colonies were born on American soil. These colonies were the only ones in the New World in which the African population consistently maintained its numbers by natural increase without continual, large-scale importation of slaves from Africa. Having a population of homegrown slaves proved cheaper than export: the United States is geographically the farthest of all New World slave societies from western Africa, and slaves arriving from Africa in the United States in the mid-nineteenth century cost thirty times their purchase price on the African coast.

Slavery developed in the English colonies of North America under two fundamentally different economies. The Northern colonies, from Pennsylvania northward, transplanted European mixed economies featuring smaller-scale agriculture, crafts, and trading. Slavery was but one source of labor and one mode of production among others as it had always been in Europe. For these colonies, the slave trade was their primary source of maritime wealth. Trading vessels were the indispensable links in the chain of commerce that firmly bound New England and the Middle Atlantic colonies to slavery.

The Southern colonies, from Maryland and Virginia southward, adopted the plantation system similar to that of Latin America with its large tracts of land and myriad levies of slave laborers. From its colonial beginnings, slavery in the Chesapeake was different from that of Massachusetts Bay. Unlike the New England colonists, the colony in Jamestown, Virginia, came to cultivate the labor- and land-intensive export staple of tobacco.

Tobacco export stimulated territorial expansion and immigration. Between 1618 and 1623 the colony grew from four hundred to forty-five hundred, notwithstanding an indigene attack in 1622 that killed three hundred. White indentured servants from Europe worked in the tobacco fields, and in 1619 the first African slaves arrived to work alongside them. In 1676 Bacon's Rebellion, the outbreak of the largest rebellion in any American colony before the Revolution and North America's first taste of class warfare, would change the demography of labor in the Chesapeake forever. In the rebellion, Africans and landless whites took up arms against the landowners. The colonial governor, Sir William Berkeley, was run out of town, and the rebels burned Jamestown to the ground. The rebels were briefly in control of the colony until their leader, Nathaniel Bacon, succumbed to swamp fever. By the next year Berkeley had returned and resumed control of the colonial government.

After the rebellion, planters reduced the importation of indentured servants and increased that of African slaves. Living conditions and thus life expectancy had improved for everyone in the colony, and so the investment in permanent slaves reaped a greater dividend. In 1705 the Christ Church, Virginia, assembly voted to grant fifty acres, ten bushels of Indian corn, thirty shillings, and a musket to indentured servants satisfying their term of service. "Vagrants"—that is, landless whites—were subject to enslavement or thirty-nine lashes. The property of African slaves, however, was confiscated and given to churchwardens to liquidate for the benefit of poor whites. In 1691 the Virginia colonial legislature proscribed manumission unless the former master paid for transport of the manumitted slave out of the colony. Interracial unions were proscribed, and white violators were to be banished. White women bearing the child of an African father were to be fined fifteen pounds, and the child was to be a slave for thirty years. The few free Africans in the colony were denied the right to own property and, consequently, the right to vote. Later, on the eve of the colonial War of Independence, the Virginia legislature recruited soldiers for the war with the promise of three hundred acres and a healthy male slave.[10]

Slavery bound Africans in America, along with their offspring, to their masters in a life of perpetual servitude. They could be sold at will to other masters: so, too, any domestic partner or children the slave might have. Neither law nor custom afforded protection to the slave's person or family: both law and custom reduced them to the plantation owner's most valuable liquid assets.

The Middle Passage of forced migration in North America, in which millions of Africans were kidnapped and transported across the Atlantic Ocean to the New World, was followed in the nineteenth century in the United States by a second, transcontinental Middle Passage.[11] At the end of the eighteenth century the transatlantic slave trade was being supplanted by the internal trade in slaves from the Northern states and the states of the Upper South to those of the Deep South and the new territories of the West. Immediately after the War of Independence, "Georgia traders" began trafficking in slaves from the North and the Chesapeake, uprooting these mostly American-born slaves and transporting them not only to Georgia but also to the Carolinas, Kentucky, and Tennessee. The War of 1812 briefly interrupted the internal slave trade, which then revived and rapidly expanded to provide labor for cotton production. The dominance of the United States in the global cotton market would be built on the backs of this hapless chattel, more than a million displaced persons. It would be the single largest internal migration in American history until their descendants began to leave the South in droves at the turn of the twentieth century.

SLAVES REMEMBERED

The impact of slavery on people of African descent in the United States cannot be overestimated. Optimistic anthropology of "African retentions" and revisionist historiography of the African-American "family" and other communal "institutions" under the slave regime cannot mitigate the brute fact of that annihilation. The devastation wrought by the First and Second Middle Passages and the legacy of inhumanity that followed in their train would leave deep wounds and long scars. Much of slave culture would be the keloids of collective consciousness.

In Toni Morrison's novel *Beloved*, the Middle Passage is shown to be an ordeal that dismembers African slaves. Morrison presents the stream-of-consciousness testimony of a prisoner of a slave ship as fragments of bodies and disembodied psychic impressions.

someone is thrashing but there is no room to do it in   if we
had more to drink we could make tears we cannot make sweat

or morning water so the men without skin bring us theirs
one time they bring us sweet rocks to suck   we are all trying
to leave our bodies behind   the man on my face has done it
it is hard to make yourself die forever   you sleep short and
then return   in the beginning we could vomit now we do not
   now we cannot   his teeth are pretty white points   someone
is trembling   I can feel it over here he is fighting hard to leave
his body which is a small bird trembling   there is no room
to tremble so he is not able to die   my own dead man is pulled
away from my face   I miss his pretty white points
   We are not crouching now   we are standing but my legs
are like my dead man's eyes   I cannot fall because there is no
room to   the men without skin are making loud noises   I am
not dead   the bread is sea-colored   I am too hungry to eat it
the sun closes my eyes   those able to die are in a pile   I cannot find my man   the one whose teeth I loved[12]

The memory of dismemberment is itself dismembered: without punc-
tuation or capitalization, phrases neither begin nor end but merely happen in the text as fragments of memory: hunger and "sea-colored" bread,
bodies, faces, eyes—and teeth, the bones of personal identity in forensic
medicine and in a smile. Bodies appear indiscriminately and unceremo-
niously "in a pile." Later in the novel, the grandmother Baby Suggs bitterly associates whites with those lost in the transatlantic Middle Passage.
"There's more of us they drowned," she says to her granddaughter Denver,
"than there is all the them ever lived from the start of time."[13]

African Americans first encountered the Bible in the throes of slavery, and ultimately they came to register the impact of slavery in biblical
terms. No West African cosmology could be impressed into such macabre
service. This is so for two reasons. First, much of West African culture was
annihilated in North America. The kidnapped Africans were stuffed into
the holds of ships and brought to the West Indies in a treacherous, transatlantic journey of terror. The overwhelming majority of these captives
left their native land never to return. The Africans had become disposable
commodities in a lucrative transatlantic traffic in human souls. Second,
there was no mythos, African or otherwise, adequate to the task helping
these African abductees find order in the moral chaos of American slavery.

The enormity of slavery required a new mythology as unprecedented and sui generis as the catastrophe it was to represent.

The lyric of a slave song that William Wells Brown reproduces in his autobiography captures the horrors of the First and Second Middle Passage, a plea for solidarity in suffering, and the hope of emancipation in the biblical image of jubilee.

> See these poor souls from Africa,
> Transported to America,
> We are stolen, and sold to Georgia—
> Will you go with me?
> We are stolen, and sold to Georgia,
> Come sound the jubilee!
>
> See wives and husbands sold apart,
> Their children's screams will break my heart,
> There's a better day a coming—
> Will you go along with me?
> There's a better day a coming,
> Come sound the jubilee!
>
> O, gracious Lord! When shall it be,
> That we poor souls shall all be free?
> Lord, break them slavery powers—
> Will you go along with me?
> Lord, break them slavery powers,
> Go sound the jubilee!
>
> Dear Lord, dear Lord, when slavery'll cease,
> Then we poor souls will have our peace,
> There's a better day a coming—
> Will you go along with me?
> There's a better day a coming,
> Come sound the jubilee![14]

In the Bible, legislation in the book of Leviticus stipulates that all slaves in Israel be set free at the end of the seventh cycle of sabbatical years in the ancient Israelite calendar, "the year of Jubilee." In American slave culture, the word *jubilee* came to be associated with a genre of joyous folksongs celebrating the hope of freedom—songs sung in perpetual exile.

"From the very beginning," observes historian of religion Charles H. Long, "the presence of slaves in the country has been involuntary; they were brought to America in chains, and this country has attempted to keep them in this condition in one way or another."[15] The historical challenge of African Americans has been the plight of all exiles: to be a people without a place. Theologian Cheryl J. Sanders writes of the exilic sensibility of African Americans throughout their tortured sojourn in modernity, "African Americans have responded to the experience of exile and alienation in America by expressing their longing for some place or space—geographical, cultural, spiritual—where they can feel at home." Thus Sanders argues for an African-American theology of exile. She bases her argument, however, not on the Old Testament image of the Babylonian Exile but on the New Testament letter called First Peter. Addressed to "the exiles of the Diaspora" (1 Pet. 1:1), the letter speaks to what Sanders calls "the exilic identity of the church."[16]

Some ancient Israelites had met the challenge of exile through written correspondence, the only way to manage a long-distance relationship in antiquity. The letter is the device through which those in exile continue to speak to those in the homeland. The prophet Jeremiah wrote letters to Judean exiles in Babylon and in Egypt. His reputation as a writer of tearful letters inspired the apocryphal Epistle of Jeremiah, written in the period between the Old and New Testaments. And in the New Testament, both the epistle of James and the epistle of First Peter open by addressing those "in the Diaspora," those communities of Judean descent still living outside the homeland.

But the genre of the letter allows for volition, for distance that might be consensual and temporary. African Americans suffered an exile that was coerced and permanent. As such it was not congenial to letters. The genre of preference for these permanent exiles would be the vision, the oracle. And the most compelling of oracles that they encountered in the Bible was that of another permanent exile, the prophet Ezekiel.

DRY BONES

The ongoing revelation that marked ancient Israel's peculiar history continued in exile. The Bible reports that Ezekiel received his oracles in Babylon, the land of captivity. In one of those oracles, God sends a spirit from the four points of the compass to restore the people of Israel. Once the people have been restored, God will then restore them to a land of their own.

And the hand of the Lord was upon me, and carried me out in the spirit of the Lord, and set me down in the midst of the valley, which was full of bones. And caused me to pass by them round about: and behold, there were very many in the open valley; and lo, they were very dry. And he said unto me, Son of man, can these bones live? And I answered, O Lord God, thou knowest. Again he said unto me, Prophesy upon these bones, and say unto them, O ye dry bones, hear the word of the Lord. Thus saith the Lord God unto these bones; Behold, I will cause breath to enter into you, and ye shall live. And I will lay sinews on you, and will bring up flesh upon you, and cover you with skin, and put breath in you, and ye shall live, and ye shall know that I am the Lord. So I prophesied as I was commanded: and as I prophesied, there was a noise, and behold a shaking, and the bones came together, bone to his bone. And when I beheld, lo, the sinews and the flesh came upon them, and skin covered them above; but there was no breath in them. Then said he unto me, Prophesy unto the wind, prophesy, son of man, and say to the wind, thus saith the Lord God; come from these four winds, O breath, and breathe upon these slain, that they may live. So I prophesied as he commanded me, and the breath came into them, and they lived, and stood upon their feet, an exceeding great army. The he said unto me, Son of man, these bones are the whole house of Israel: behold, they say, our bones are dried, and our hope is lost: we are cut off for our parts. Therefore prophesy and say unto them, Thus saith the Lord God; behold, O my people, I will open your graves, and cause you to come up out of your graves, and bring you into the land of Israel. And ye shall know that I am the Lord, when I have

opened your graves, O my people, and brought you up out of
your graves, and shall put my spirit in you, and ye shall live,
and I shall place you in your own land: then shall ye know that
I the Lord have spoken it, and performed it, saith the Lord.
(Ezek. 37:1–14)

Ezekiel's message of life after exile is nothing less than the declaration of
life after death, the pronouncement of a collective resurrection. In the biblical imagination of the slaves and their progeny, the text of the prophet's
vision of dry bones in Ezekiel is emblematic of African-American hope
that all the souls lost in the catastrophic exile of slavery might be restored
and revived, that their bones might yet live again.

The Negro spiritual "Dry Bones" recalls the vision of a dead, disjointed
people in Ezekiel 37:1–14: "Them bones, them bones, them dry bones /
Now hear the word of the Lord." It is precisely in the broken, lifeless desiccation of exile that the word of the Lord comes as a mighty, rushing wind
of restoration. The biblical vision of the valley of bleached bones became
a venerable image in African-American preaching. We may glimpse the
dawn of this text's special history of reception in the following testimony
of an ex-slave from Kentucky, who explains how he and his companions
would extemporaneously compose Negro spirituals.

Us ole heads used ter make them on the spurn of de moment,
after we wressle with the Spirit and come thoo. But the tunes
was brung from Africa by our granddaddies. Dey was jis 'miliar
song . . . they calls 'em spirituals, case de Holy Spirit done
revealed 'em to 'em. Some say Moss Jesus taught 'em, and I's
seed 'em start in meeting. We'd all be at the prayer house de
Lord's Day, and de white preacher he'd splain the word and
read whar Ezekiel done say—Dry bones gwine ter lib again.
And honey, de Lord would come a-shining thoo them pages
and revive dis ole nigger's heart, and I'd jump up dar and den
and holler and shout and sing and pat, and dey would all cotch
de words . . . and dey's all take it up and keep at it, and keep
a-adding to it and den it would be a spiritual.[17]

The ex-slave speaks of the songs as the product of concerted struggle,
based on "'miliar" (familiar) musical patterns inherited from their West

African forebears. The songs were nevertheless divinely inspired—revealed by the Holy Spirit or taught by "Moss Jesus" (Master Jesus). But it is the preacher's presentation of the text that provokes the spontaneous ecstasy of movement and musical expression in the singers.

Those things from the past that become part of the exile's present are perforce portable. The African ancestors of the slaves passed through the Middle Passage carrying little more than a tune, exiles at home, as Cornel West has noted, "only in a dynamic language and mobile music."[18] Music is the quintessentially portable element of exilic culture. And rhythmic West African music, always accompanied by some form of dance, is always somatic: music as the sound of rhythm, rhythm as the movement of music. The strongest of African residua are expressed through the body.

Slaves were the property of their masters—"chattels personal"—over which masters had complete control. The common law that British colonists brought with them had no provision for what Harriet Beecher Stowe would call the "absolute despotism of the most unmitigated form" that American slavery required. Slaves were rendered exempt from that body of common law that afforded rights of personal security and integrity to all persons.[19] The law balanced the rights of "absolute despotism" against those of "absolute property": the violent abuse of slaves would be construed as criminal only insofar as it threatened absolute claims of the master class to enjoy enslaved property. This balance of absolutes was struck, quite literally, on the back of the slave.

American slavery unleashed an all-out assault on the black body. One of the first laws of racial differentiation in the Virginia colony was that white indentured servants might not be stripped for punishment, as African slaves commonly were. American slavery not only gave masters complete access to the labor of slaves; it granted them complete access to the very bodies of slaves. The somatic dimension of African and subsequent African-American spirituality would answer American slavery's relentless assault on the black body. Under American slavery, slaves' very bodies were taken from them.[20]

In American slave religion, the slaves would take their bodies back. At the turn of the twentieth century in his famous essay "Faith of the Fathers," W. E. B. Du Bois identified as three persistent elements of traditional African-American Christian worship: the Preacher, the Music, and the Frenzy. "The Preacher" is the psychopomp of the faithful, inciting them to fervor through enthusiastic exposition of the Bible. "The Music," syncopated, kinetic strains by turns doleful and jubilant, is "the one true expression of sorrow, despair, and hope." "The Frenzy," or "shouting," is marked by outbreaks of ecstasy that Du Bois recognized as coeval with religion itself. This element of black religion was "the one more devoutly believed in than all the rest," according to Du Bois. "It varied in expression from the silent rapt countenance or the low murmur and moan to the mad abandon of physical fervor,—the stamping, shrieking, the shouting, the rushing to and fro and the wild waving of arms, that weeping and laughing, the vision and the trance. All this is nothing new in the world, but old as religion, as Delphi and Endor. And so firm a hold did it have on the Negro, that many generations firmly believed that without the visible manifestation of the God there could be no true communion with the Invisible."[21]

The premium placed on experience, where the spirit possession of West African religion meets the "experimental religion" of Evangelical Christianity, was the spiritual heritage of slave religion. Some Christian slaves, rejecting the hypocrisy of the faith of the master class, grounded their faith in their own ecstatic experience. Northern missionaries working among freedmen and women just after the Civil War found, sometimes much to their dismay and consternation, that their charges placed the emphasis of their faith on the Spirit and not the letter. One Northern missionary reported that the former slaves "wanted to see their children and friends get religion as they did. They fell under the mighty power of God . . . after mourning many days, and then came out shouting, for an angel, they said, told them their sins were forgiven."[22]

The slaves contrasted "getting religion" in this way with the Christianity of the master class that they had come to know and despise: "They said their masters and families were Bible Christians, and they did not want to be like them."[23] The slaves themselves recognized the difference in religious sentiments. That is to say, whites, even those sympathetic to the religion of the slaves, were not wont to "get religion" as they did, as the following testimony of a former slave suggests.

We went to church all the time. We had both white and colored preachers. Master Frank wasn't a Christian, but he would help

build brush-arbors for us to have church under, and we sure
would have some big meetings, I'll tell you.

One day Master Frank was going through the woods close
to where niggers was having church. All of a sudden he started
running and beating hisself and hollering, and the niggers
all went to shouting and saying, "Thank the Lord, Master Frank
has done come through!" Master Frank after a minute say,
"Yes, through the worst of 'em." He had run into a yellow
jackets' nest.[24]

The Evangelical faith of the Great Awakening underscored the affective
dimension of religion, its mantic potentialities. As historian Albert Raboteau explains, "The emotionalism of the revivals encouraged the outward
expression of religious feeling, and the sight of black and white converts
weeping, shouting, fainting, and moving in ecstatic trance became a familiar, if sensationalized, feature of the sacramental and camp meeting
seasons. In this heated atmosphere slaves found a form of Christian worship that resembled the religious celebrations of their African heritage."[25]
This overlap of Evangelical and African religious enthusiasm became the
core of African-American Christianity. The Bible became the numinous
medium through which Africans in North America held on to the precious vestiges of collective patrimony that survived the cultural slaughter
of the Middle Passage.

Contemporary reports of preaching in slave worship suggest that
the preacher's role most closely approximated that of the griot, "the living repository of history and tradition in the West African setting."[26] The
medium through which the griot communicates power is the story: to this
day one of the traditional descriptions of what African-American preachers do is "telling the story." The venerable West African griot, recounting
stories of the past, "had the capacity to make the past present, to 'resurrect'
the dead and present them alive."[27] In addition, in some West African
societies, "the epic bards' extensive knowledge of the history and culture
of the community, displayed in their narrative performances, [made] them
important sources of counsel and advice outside their professional duties
as storytellers."[28]

The cultural precedent of the role of the griot was complemented in
the role of the preacher in the Evangelicalism of the Anglophone New

World. African Americans were among the multitudes that found the Evangelical preaching a life-changing synthesis of biblical text and "experimental religion" that could transcend differences in class, caste, and culture. Preachers were the personal catalysts of religious experience in camp meeting religion. And they were also the dramatic interpreters of the Bible. Hearing the preacher "explain the word" is tantamount to divine encounter. The preached text provokes an epiphany: "The Lord" comes "a-shinin' through them pages."

The homeless African slaves fashioned a language of spiritual refuge out of elements of Evangelical Christianity with the syntax of their West African cultural heritage. James Weldon Johnson described the process this way:

> Far from his native land and customs, despised by those among whom he lived, experiencing the pangs of separation of loved ones on the auction block, knowing the hard master, feeling the lash, the Negro seized upon Christianity, the religion of compensation in the life to come for the ills suffered in the present, the religion which implied the hope that in the next world there would be a reversal of conditions, of rich man and poor man, of proud and meek, of master and slave. The result was a body of song voicing all the cardinal virtues of Christianity.[29]

At the end of the nineteenth century, Marion Haskell explained the process of improvisation that gave rise to Negro spirituals and the relation of the genesis of some of these songs to African-American preaching:

> Spirituals are often composed on the spur of the moment by a preacher or a member whose voice can insure the attention of the assemblage. At a meeting held in Columbia, South Carolina, the preacher chose as the subject of his sermon "Paul and Silas Imprisoned," and for an hour or more commanded the strictest attention of his hearers. At the end of this time interest began to flag visibly, and apparently the spirit of exhortation had fled from the minister. After a hard struggle to rouse the audience by another reading of the prison scene, he suddenly burst forth in a loud shout: "Y'all hear! Do yourself no harm!

Y'all hear! Do yourself no harm! Oh-h-h! Y'all hear!" At each repetition additional voices would join in, until the whole house had caught the words and rhythm.[30]

West African musical forms reemerged in North America in the slave folk songs that came to be called Negro spirituals. Melodies that had once celebrated the exploits of tribal warriors now praised Joshua, Gideon, David, and "King Jesus." "It was nothing else," Nathaniel Dett explained, "that this religious inheritance, their Oriental regard for the parable and prophecy, which made easy the incorporation of so much of Bible story: for in striving to give voice to his experiences the slave found in the Testaments, in the story of the children of Israel, for instance, much in the way of a text ready made."[31] African slaves clothed Holy Writ in vestiges of their African style and gesture that the violence of American slavery could not erase.

So remarkable was the ritual distinctiveness of indigenous African-American worship that observers have left us several vivid accounts of it. A decade before the Civil War, a slaveowner told Frederick Law Olmstead that the slaves of his plantation asked him to have the back rails removed from the benches of the plantation chapel to provide them "room enough to pray."[32] According to the testimony of Harriet Ware, an abolitionist teacher from Boston who accompanied Union troops when they occupied the South Carolina Sea Islands in 1862,

A true "shout" takes place on Sundays or on "praise" nights throughout the week either in the praise house or in some cabin in which a regular religious meeting has been held. Very likely more than half the population of the plantation is gathered together. . . . the benches are pushed back to the wall when the formal meeting is over, and old and young, men and women . . . all stand up in the middle of the floor, and when the "spiritual" is struck up, begin first walking and . . . shuffling around . . . in a ring. The foot is hardly taken from the floor, and the progression is due mainly to a jerking, hitching motion, which agitates the shouter, and soon brings out streams of perspiration. . . . Song and dance are extremely energetic, and often, when a shout lasts into the middle of the night, the monotonous thud, thud of the feet prevents sleep within half a mile of the praise-house.[33]

Before the ring shout, the whole congregation sang together somber hymns, called "spirituals." During the shout, however, the select chorus sang up-tempo "jubilee songs" or "running spirituals" that were the musical accompaniment to the ecstasy of the ring. H. G. Spaulding wrote in the *Continental Monthly* of what he witnessed at a slave worship service in the South during the Civil War. At the end of the service, "Three or four [people], standing still, clapping their hands and beating time with their feet, commence singing in unison . . . while the others walk around in a ring, in single file, joining also in the song. . . . Soon those in the ring leave off singing, the others keeping it up with increased vigor, and strike into the shout step."[34]

In the ring shout, a small chorus of people would provide vigorous accompaniment to worshippers who formed a circle: "Sometimes they dance silently, sometimes the song itself is also sung by the dancers. But more frequently a band, composed of some of the best singers, stand at the side of the room to 'base' the others, singing the body of the song and clapping their hands together or on their knees."[35] They would provide rhythm by clapping their hands, stamping their feet, and pounding the floor with the end of broomsticks. All would sing as those in the circle moved in unison counterclockwise, shuffling their feet in tempo without lifting them from the ground. The sound and tempo of the singing and dancing would gradually increase until members of the circle became ecstatic.

These same features have been observed in the funereal dances among the Ekoi people of southern Nigeria as well as the West African Ibo, Yoruba, Ibibio, and the Bakongo of central Africa, all ethnic groups prominently represented in the transatlantic slave trade. All these groups performed ritual circle dances counterclockwise to the rhythmic acceleration of a chorus to facilitate possession of the dancers by spirits of the ancestors. The dance was a complex ritual action to bring the living in direct contact with the dead and the human present in direct contact with the ancestral past. The ring shout appears to be a New World synthesis of a widespread West African ritual of ancestor invocation.[36]

AME bishop Daniel Alexander Payne was scandalized to find that the "heathenish ritual" of the ring shout was still practiced by "Praying and Singing Bands" of black Methodists he encountered as far north as Pennsylvania. Payne gives the following account of the ritual, which he witnessed at a "bush meeting" after the Civil War: "After the sermon they formed a ring, and with coats off sung, clapped their hands, and stamped their feet in a most ridiculous and heathenish way." Payne later argued with the leader of the ring about the religious efficacy of these "'Fist and Heal Worshippers,' as they have been called: "[The leader of the ring said]: 'Sinners won't get converted unless there is a ring.' Said I: 'You might sing till you fell down dead and you would fail to convert a single sinner, because nothing but the Spirit of God and the word of God can convert sinners.' He replied: 'The Spirit of God works upon people in different ways. At camp meeting there must be a ring here, a ring there, a ring over yonder, or sinners will not get converted.'" Payne complained that "the ignorant masses" of black Christians were inured of the ring shout, staunchly defended by its practitioners as "the essence of religion." And what he saw as "an incurable religious disease" not only affected "the stupid and headstrong" among the rank and file of the faithful. Payne despaired that "some of our most popular and powerful preachers labor systematically to perpetuate this fanaticism. Such preachers never rest till they create an excitement that consists in shouting, jumping, and dancing."[37]

What Payne derided as "fanaticism" persisted well into the twentieth century. Traveling through South Carolina in the 1920s, Cliff Furness observed the following during a worship service at a rural plantation:

> Several men moved their feet alternately, in strange syncopation. A rhythm was born, almost without reference to the words of the preacher. It seemed to take shape almost visibly, and grow. I was gripped with the feeling of a mass-intelligence, a self-conscious entity, gradually informing the crowd and taking possession of every mind there, including my own. . . . A distinct melodic outline became more and more prominent shaping itself around the central theme of the words, "Get right, soldier!" . . . Scraps of other words and tunes were flung together into the medley of sound by individual singers from time to time, but the general trend was carried on by a deep undercurrent, which appeared to be stronger than the mind of any individual present, for it bore the mass improvised harmony and rhythms into the most effective climax of incremental repetition that I have ever heard. I felt as if some conscious

plan or purpose were carrying us along, call it mob-mind, communal composition, or what you will.[38]

In 1927 an observer described the ring shout practiced in Georgia: "It was regularly permitted [on two fixed occasions—Christmas Eve and the last day of the old year] in all churches . . . but not as a part of the service. After that had closed, the wooden benches were pushed back and the center of the floor was cleared to give room for the circle of shouters."[39] In 1934 folklorist Alan Lomax found the ring shout alive and well not only in Georgia but also in Louisiana, Texas, and even in the Bahamas, whither British loyalist masters on the Georgia Sea Islands had absconded with their slaves in tow at the outbreak of the Revolutionary War. In 1942 Lydia Parrish reported that inhabitants of the Sea Islands off the coast of Georgia and South Carolina followed the same liturgical patterns observed before the Civil War: initial, solemn hymns that gave way to rapid rhythms and frenzied dancing.[40]

In the ecstatic worship of African-American slaves, ancient ritual was recapitulated in Christian rite. Solemn immersion in river water—the form of baptism favored by Baptist Evangelicals—bore an uncanny resemblance to the ritual immersion by which initiates became ecstatically imbued with river spirits in West Africa. In the early twentieth century Dorothy Scarborough observed the following scene at an African American baptism:

> With each immersion the excitement grew, the shouting became more wild and unrestrained, the struggles of the candidate more violent. . . . The crowd surged back and forth, and as one bystander would rush to greet a candidate coming out of the water, shrieking forth joy and thanksgiving, the crowd would be in ecstasy at once, each surrounded by a group of admirers trying to control him, or her—usually her. Each group would be a center of commotion in the general excitement.
>
> The shouter would fall on the ground, writhing about as if in anguish, tearing her hair, beating off those who sought to calm her.

On occasion the ecstasy of the ring shout might irrupt even in a secular setting. Frederick Douglass later wrote of his own participation in the ring shout, "I was myself in the circle, so that I neither saw nor heard as those without might see or hear." Douglass said of slaves with whom he had worked in the fields, "Sometimes you may hear a wild, hoarse laugh arise from a circle, and often a song. Soon, however, the overseer comes dashing through the field. 'Tumble up! Tumble up!, and to work, work,' is the cry." In the praise house, by the riverside, even in the field, the Holy Spirit overcame Christian slaves in the same way ancestral spirits had overcome their forebears in the cults of possession so important for traditional West African spirituality.[41]

The ring shout is the kinetic element of the Negro spiritual. The spiritual, even as a musical performance, is not complete without dance or swaying or rocking or tapping or clapping. This sensibility continues to mark African-American music both sacred and profane. The great gospel singer Mahalia Jackson was raised in the Baptist Church and recalls her early experience of music in the Sanctified church in her neighborhood in the mid-twentieth century: "Everybody in there sang and they clapped and stomped their feet and sang with their whole bodies." She once told a clergyman hostile to gospel music, "I was born to sing gospel music. Nobody had to teach me. I was serving God. I told him I had been reading the Bible every day most of my life and there was a Psalm that said: 'O clap your hands all ye people! Shout unto the Lord with the voice of a trumpet!' If it was undignified, it was what the Bible told me to do." This somatic sensibility has marked African-American music both sacred and profane. Of his first time hearing Charlie Parker and Dizzy Gillespie play together in 1944, the great jazz trumpeter Miles Davis recalled, "When I heard Diz and Bird in B's band, I said, 'What? What is this?' Man, that shit was so terrible it was scary. I mean, Dizzy Gillespie, Charlie 'Yardbird' Parker, Buddy Anderson, Gene Ammons, Lucky Thompson, and Art Blakey all together in one band and not to mention B: Billy Eckstine himself. It was a motherfucker. Man, that shit was all up in my body. Music all up in my body, and that's what I wanted to hear." Davis described it as the "greatest feeling I ever had in my life—with my clothes on."[42]

"It's a fallacy of Western civilization," observed contemporary jazz saxophonist Steve Coleman, "that the mind is doing all the thinking. In school, they only talk about understanding things with your mind. But you can also understand things with your body."[43] The ring shout is a way African-American Evangelical Christians understood the Bible with their bodies. This African-American way of knowing, this somatic apprehension, has not been in opposition to scripture: it is a matter not of the Bible versus ecstatic experience but of the Bible *as* ecstatic experience—music, the sound implied by the body's movement, and dance, the body's movement implied by sound, invoked in the spoken word "a-shinin' thoo them pages." In his visual interpretation of scripture as ecstatic experience in his linocut *De Good Book Says,* artist Wilmer Jennings captures a scene of mantic transcendence illustrating the peculiar Orphic insanity of African-American Christianity that was and continues to be realized in indispensable incantations of the Book. A frayed nimbus arcs around the head of the preacher, highlighting the small region between his open mouth and the open Bible that rests atop the pulpit. In the upper right, faint curved and straight lines suggest organ pipes. Ecstatic worshippers wave their hands in the pews from the far corner of the sanctuary, bow their heads, and hold themselves in rapt captivity to the Spirit. The Preacher, the Music, the Frenzy, cut concentric figures around the image at the center of the linocut—the open space between the preacher's parted lips and the pages of the open Book. We find a synthesis of ecstasy and exegesis that forecloses an opposition of the religion of the Spirit and religion of the Book in the provocative, well-nigh spontaneous alternative interpretation of the biblical accounts of divine deliverance that Evangelical Christian slaves told and retold in song.

BODY AND SOUL

Ezekiel's oracle is the text of the sermon featured in Oscar Micheaux's silent movie classic *Body and Soul* (1925), the film debut of Renaissance man Paul Robeson. Micheaux implicitly recognizes that the oracle of Ezekiel's valley of dry bones is a text the interpretation of which is expressed in the body. The Spirit takes bodily form, animating the bones and stretching the sinews of its hearers. The filmmaker brought this expression to the screen with one of the most distinguished black bodies of the day. Robeson had already become famous for his superb physique, a genetic gift that he had honed as an outstanding athlete in high school and college. Robeson posed nude for photographer Nickolas Muray and sculptor Antonio Salemme. Micheaux recognized that the sermon called for this bodily expression of the spirit, this spiritual expression of the body in *Body and Soul.*

In the film, Robeson plays the conniving, charismatic, and abusive Reverend Isaiah T. Jenkins, an ex-convict and self-ordained black preacher who preys on a small Southern town. Toward the end of the film, after Jenkins has robbed, raped, and bullied members of the town, he preaches a sermon entitled "Dry Bones in the Valley." The intertitle reads that this "is a sermon which is every black preacher's ambition." Demanding a larger collection from the congregation than the one he has already gathered and refreshing himself with liquor that he drinks from a tumbler behind the pulpit, Jenkins launches into his sermon. He galvanizes the congregation, which responds with enraptured exclamations, jumping out of the pews, and shouting. Jenkins himself is a dynamo of oratorical flourish, stabbing the air with forceful, grandiose gestures, pounding and then hoisting above his head his oversized pulpit Bible. Micheaux does not provide intertitles for the contents of the sermon in the silent film. Instead he relies on the somatic expression of the actors and the familiarity of his black audiences with the biblical text and the homiletic tradition that attends the text of Ezekiel's vision of the valley of dry bones in African-American Christianity.[44]

This vision of reanimated bones overtakes Herald Loomis, the protagonist of August Wilson's play *Joe Turner's Come and Gone* (1988). Wilson sets the play in a boarding house in Pittsburgh, Pennsylvania, in August 1911. In his description of the play that appears before the first act, Wilson describes its characters as migrants from the South, "the sons and daughters of newly freed African slaves." They "arrive carrying Bibles and guitars. . . . Foreigners in a strange land, they carry as part and parcel of their baggage a long line of separation and dispersement which informs their sensibilities and marks their conduct as they search for ways to reconnect, to reassemble."[45]

On Sunday afternoon, the owner of the boarding house leads his wife and the boarders in a "Juba." The "Juba," as Wilson explains in the director's notes, "is reminiscent of the Ring Shouts of the African slaves. It is a call and response dance." In his written stage directions, Wilson instructs the actors to "clap their hands, shuffle and stomp around the table"; the dance "should be as African as possible, with the performers working themselves up into a near frenzy. The words can be improvised, but should include some mention of the Holy Ghost." When Loomis enters the kitchen to find his fellow residents singing and "shouting," he becomes furious and disrupts the impromptu celebration. After a fit of ecstatic utterance, Loomis speaks of seeing skeletons rise up from the deep, take on flesh, and walk. Crawling on the floor with the prostrate Loomis, a fellow border named Bynum prompts him with questions and confirms, sometimes in advance, Loomis's answers. Bynum is a "root worker," an African-American folk healer who binds broken people and broken relationships: the name "Bynum" is Wilson's playful rendering of "bin' 'um," colloquial African-American pronunciation of the phrase "bind them." Later in the play Loomis, speaking to Bynum about Bynum's occult powers, says, "I know who you are. You one of them bones people." Yet Bynum coaches the prostrate Loomis through his vision in much the same way spiritually adept members of a Holiness Pentecostal congregation coach initiates at the altar who are possessed by the Holy Spirit. Bynum crawls on the floor to Loomis to help the stricken man find the words to speak of what he has seen.

BYNUM: Tell me about them bones, Herald Loomis. Tell me what you seen.

LOOMIS: I come to this place . . . to this water that was bigger than the whole world. And I looked out . . . and I seen these bones rise up out the water. Rise up and begin to walk on top of it.

BYNUM: Wasn't nothing but bones and they were walking on top of the water.

LOOMIS: Walking without sinking down. Walking on top of the water.

BYNUM: Just marching in line.

LOOMIS: A whole heap of them. They come up out the water and started marching.

BYNUM: Wasn't nothing but bones and they were walking on top of the water.

LOOMIS: One after the other. They just come up out the water and start walking.

BYNUM: They walking on the water without sinking down. They just walking and walking. And then . . . what happened, Herald Loomis?

LOOMIS: They just walking across the water.

BYNUM: What happened, Herald Loomis? What happened to the bones?

LOOMIS: They just walking across the water . . . and then they sunk down.

BYNUM: The bones sunk into the water. They all sunk down.

LOOMIS: All at one time! They just all fell in the water at one time.

BYNUM: Sunk down like anybody else.

LOOMIS: When they sink down they made a big splash and this here wave come up . . .

BYNUM: A big wave, Herald Loomis. A big wave washed over the land.

LOOMIS: It washed them out of the water and up on the land. Only . . . only . . .

BYNUM: Only they ain't bones no more.

LOOMIS: They got flesh on them! Just like you and me![46]

A sea of souls is the semiotic equivalent of Ezekiel's valley of dry bones. Just as the valley is the chasm that separates Babylon from the land of Israel, so the Atlantic yawns between America and Africa. It has become in turn the sign of the exile repeated in the transcontinental Middle Passage and yet again in the great migration driven by Jim Crow, the Ku Klux Klan, and the boll weevil in the last quarter of the nineteenth century and the first of the twentieth. As the wind summons the desiccated bones, the waves serve up the restless spirits, and Loomis catches trancelike glimpses of many thousands gone.

Wilson's directions to the cast to verbal improvisation during the Juba and Loomis's derisive reference to "tongues of fire" suggests the Pentecostal practice of the "speaking in tongues," ecstatic utterance in worship inspired by "the Holy Ghost." It is an echo of the unintelligible speech that Frederick Douglass mentions when he refers to his childhood experience of hearing fellow slaves sing Negro spirituals, "hymns," as he called them, as they worked in the field. Douglass reports that the songs were accompanied by loud exclamations and "improvised jargon" that were meaningless to him as well as to the master and the overseer but were filled with secret meaning for the older slaves. Folklorist Frank Dobie wrote that the lyrics of the Negro spiritual "A Song" "sound like a vivid but unintelligible description of a battle or a cyclone." The language of the spirit is the residuum of West African interjections that has now become unknown tongues.[47]

The ecstatic worship of the antebellum ring shout as choreographed encounter with spirit continues in the Sanctified or Pentecostal holiness tradition.

The organ drops out entirely and the voices . . . come together again and again. The organ returns with more power yet, and the congregation erupts into applause. Two women at the front of the church jump into the aisles and whirl in praise of the Lord. "Bless him, bless him, bless him, bless him!" the congregation shouts. "Praise him, praise him, praise him," they chant over and again. Fifteen or twenty people are in the aisles, some whirling, some leaping in place, some running up and down before the altar. A number of people have come from the aisles to assist those manifesting the spirit. Sometimes three or four people will surround a person in the spirit, gently supporting him or her, and rocking in rhythm to the driving hand claps and swelling, soaring organ.[48]

James Baldwin describes it in the conversion experience of John Grimes, the anguished protagonist of Baldwin's quasi-autobiographical novel, *Go Tell It on the Mountain* (1953). The experience of being overcome by the Holy Spirit, "slain in the Spirit," in the traditional parlance of the Sanctified churches, is the occasion for John Grimes's intense, telescoped encounter with the mortal suffering that has marked the history of slavery's children in the United States.

He began, for terror, to weep and moan. . . . It was the sound of rage and moaning which filled the grave, rage and weeping from time set free, but bound now in eternity; rage that had no language, weeping with no voice—which spoke now, to John's startled soul, of boundless melancholy, of the bitterest patience, and the longest night; of the deepest water, the strongest chains, the most cruel lash; of humility most wretched, the dungeon most absolute, of love's bed defiled, and birth dishonored, and most bloody, unspeakable, sudden death. Yes, the darkness hummed with murder: the body in the water, the body in the fire, the body on the tree. John looked down the line of these armies of darkness, army upon army.[49]

The young Grimes in effect returns to the horrors of the transatlantic Middle Passage: "the deepest water, the strongest chains, the most cruel lash." The dehumanization, rape, and sheer brutality of the transcontinental Middle Passage are "humility most wretched, the dungeon most absolute, of love's bed defiled, and birth dishonored, and most bloody, unspeakable, sudden death." The souls of the thousands drowned, burned, and lynched march before John Grimes as "these armies of darkness."

Baldwin's description of the multitude of murdered souls as "armies" obliquely suggests the legion of lost souls in Ezekiel's vision of dry bones. The vision is the third of four oracles in the book of Ezekiel introduced by the phrase, "the hand of the Lord was upon me," an idiom glossing a state of trance or ecstasy. Like the first such vision in Ezekiel 3:22–27, its venue is a valley near the exilic settlements of the Judean captives in Babylon. In Ezekiel 37, however, the prophet participates in the actuation of the vision: on orders from God, he prophesies to the bones, speaking *baharugîm ha'ēlleh*, "to these slain" (37:9).This phrase has led many commentators to read here the description of a battlefield of fallen soldiers. Understood as a killing field, the vision suggests the ancient biblical curse that Israelites disobedient to God's covenant would die unburied and their remains would become carrion (Deut. 28:25–26; Jer. 34:17–20). The nation of Israel had been unfaithful to its exclusive, long-term contract with God. Now those slaughtered by heathen armies would litter the battlefield without a decent burial, their bones blanching in the sun.

But Ezekiel makes no reference to a battle in this oracle, and there is no martial language in the vision. The prophet has given us no indication that the valley is a killing field. Nor does the prophet speak of the biblical curse of death without burial; his silence here is remarkable because it is out of character for Ezekiel to pass up an opportunity to indict Israel of sin and forego luxuriating over oracles of punishment. The fallen Israelites are not merely those Judean soldiers who fell before the Babylonians and the Israelite soldiers of the Northern Kingdom that fell to the Assyrians over a century before. Ezekiel explicitly says that the bones are "the entire house of Israel" (37:11).

The vision focuses exclusively on the enormity of exile. For exile is bigger than any mere human agency, so horrible as to transcend sin and warfare. Neither fallen soldiers nor unrepentant sinners, the armies of Ezekiel's vision are lost souls. The distinction is crucial. The valley of dry bones is the quintessential vision of human disaster that does not find fault or point fingers and refuses to limit the death toll to combatants.

Ezekiel's vision of dry bones offers none of the explanations for the Exile offered elsewhere in the Bible. The doctrine of the book of Deuteronomy claims that the exile would provoke national self-examination and that God would reward this contrition with peace and prosperity in the Israelites' homeland (Deut. 4:25–31, 30:2–5). The Holiness legislation in the book of Leviticus anticipates that the Israelites, accepting national humiliation as just recompense, will return to the homeland where God will remember his covenant with them (Lev. 26:41–42). Israel's repentance arouses God's mercy and moves him to fulfill the divine terms of the ancestral covenant. Jeremiah sees the exile as a punishment, the brutal penalties of which move God to pity; he grants a lavish forgiveness out of love and is happy to put the whole matter behind him (Jer. 32:40), fondly remembering the honeymoon of his relationship with Israel after the Exodus (Jer. 31:1–3). The God of Second Isaiah all but admits that the penalty of exile was excessive (Isa. 40:2), says he is sorry for exacting it (54:7–8), and promises never to do it again (54:9–10).

Ezekiel, the angry man of Israelite prophecy, will have none of this. In oracular tirades he inveighs against the utter depravity of Israel. According to Ezekiel's understanding of Israel's sacred history, God's courtship of Israel was troubled from the start. There was no honeymoon period. The nation had been corrupt from the beginning; the people were unfaithful to God even before the Exodus from Egypt (Ezek. 20). Even if those paragons of virtue Noah, Daniel, and Job were to be found in Jerusalem, their merits would not save the city from destruction (14:12–20). From top to bottom Israelite society was rife with idolatry, violence, extortion, violation of the weak and exploitation of the poor (22). God will unleash his wrath against the people for all their abominations, and his rage will be merciless (7:1–4). God ordained the fall of Jerusalem and the razing of its temple as punishment for national treachery (17:20).

But Ezekiel's vision of dry bones foresees a collective resurrection that does not treat of the problem of Israel's sin. The resuscitation of those long dead is an exercise of divine will. God acts, preemptively and unilaterally, to protect his reputation. He is motivated, ultimately, by anxiety over bad public relations. God will bring the nation back from the dead so that "ye shall know that I am the Lord when I have opened your graves . . . then shall ye know that I the Lord have spoken it, and performed it, saith the Lord" (Ezek. 37:12, 14). Neither Israel's past battles nor Israel's past sins are at issue. Israel's death and dismemberment overwhelm its past transgressions, and so Ezekiel is uncharacteristically silent about those transgressions here. In his oracle of the dry bones, Ezekiel suspends the causality of sin and consequence that is otherwise at the center of his own priestly ethics and prophetic vocation.

The vision of the valley of dry bones may have also been attractive to American slaves because of what it did not signify. It did not offer a view of the end of Exile that depended on notions of its cause. African Americans have fixed on a text that does not treat of the victim-blaming tendency of Deuteronomic thinking at its worst. The transatlantic and transcontinental Middle Passages could not be explained as recompense for past sins against the gods or lost wars against past enemies. The surplus of misery was just too great.

BY THE RIVERS OF BABYLON

The catastrophe of exile did not end Israel's story. The vision of valley overshadowed by death is followed in the book of Ezekiel by an oracle of the reunion of the dispersed tribes of the nation, restoration of the monarchy, and the reestablishment of the sanctuary. Immediately following the vision of the dry bones, Ezekiel receives another "Word of the Lord" that describes the nation's full restoration.

> The word of the Lord came again to me. . . . Thus saith the
> Lord GOD: Behold, I will take the children of Israel from
> among the heathen, whither they be gone, and will gather
> them on every side, and bring them into their own land. . . .
> Neither shall they defile themselves any more with their idols,
> nor with their detestable things, nor with any of their trans-
> gressions: but I will save them out of all their dwelling-places,
> wherein they have sinned, and will cleanse them: so shall they
> be my people, and I will be their God. And David my servant
> shall be king over them; and they all shave have one shepherd:
> they shall also walk in my judgments, and observe my statutes,
> and do them. And they shall dwell in the land I have given
> unto Jacob my servant, wherein your fathers have dwelt; and
> they shall dwell therein, even they, and their children, and their
> children's children: and my servant David shall be their prince
> for ever. Moreover I will make a covenant of peace with them;
> it shall be an everlasting covenant with them: and I will place

them, and multiply them, and will set my sanctuary in the
midst of them for evermore. My tabernacle shall be with
them: yea, I will be their God, and they shall be my people.
(Ezek. 37:15, 21, 23–27)

But this was not a vision that African exiles embraced in their North
American captivity. The folk tradition says nothing of the complemen-
tary vision of Ezekiel 37:15–28, the other half of the chapter in the book
of Ezekiel.

Ezekiel chapter 37 is not a seamless literary whole. The two distinct
visions, Ezekiel 37:1–14 and 37:15–27, constitute its composite text as it
has come to us in the Bible. But in the liturgical life of the book of Ezekiel,
Ezekiel 37:1–14 went its own way in Jewish synagogues as the accompanying reading from the prophets for the Passover and its Sabbath. In ancient
eastern copies of the Christian Bible, Syriac versions of the text have a
separate title for Ezekiel 37:1–14, and in some Syriac lectionaries this text
is the Easter reading. Tertullian knows the text of Ezekiel's vision of dry
bones as "a well-known passage in all the churches of Christ" (*omnium
ecclesiarum Christi lectione celebrata*), and in Latin tradition the passage was
read at Easter eve baptisms of catechumens.[50] What the ancient concate-
nation of the visions had put together, reading practices of subsequent
ancient communities had put asunder.

American Christian slaves followed suit. There is no postexilic moment for the slave singers, for they never return home. African Americans
could collectively recollect the challenge of constructing a community.
They could not relate collectively, however, to reconstructing one. The
claim that captivity had been turned did not ring true in historical experience. Africans in America could not return to their native land. The Africa
that lost them to slavery in the Atlantic world was lost along with their
freedom. The bards of the Negro spirituals sang of Ezekiel as one of those
biblical exiles who, like them, never returned home.

For the African exiles, the glory of the Lord was to be revealed not at
the end of the exile but at the end of the age. When American slaves sang
of Zion's walls in the Negro spiritual "Great Day," they sang of building,
not rebuilding, and of a dream under construction in the future:

Great Day, Great Day,
The righteous marching,

Great day,
God's going to build up Zion's walls"—a "Great Day" yet
    to come.[51]

Neither Negro spirituals nor African-American preaching traditions comment on the Bible's postexilic narratives. We may observe this silence in a featured sermon of the famous northern California radio broadcast of African-American preacher Carl J. Anderson. In his sermon, Anderson accurately situates the career of Ezekiel in the history of ancient Israel:

> While in Babylon, Ezekiel was with them in servitude
> He heard their cry as is recorded in the one hundred thirty-
>   seventh number of the Psalms
> Judah had lost her political existence as a nation
> And the temple was destroyed . . .
> And the walls of Jerusalem was torn down
> And the gates had been set on fire.[52]

The last two lines of this part of the sermon echo the Judean report of the destruction of Jerusalem in the book of Nehemiah: "And they said unto me, the remnant that are left of the captivity there in the province are in great affliction and reproach: the wall of Jerusalem also is broken down, and the gates thereof are burned with fire. And it came to pass, when I heard these words, that I sat down and wept, and mourned certain days" (1:3–4).

When Anderson moves to the climax of the sermon in his description of the desiccated bones Ezekiel encountered in the desolate valley, he likens that desiccation to the spiritual dryness he finds in the church: "And these bones were dry. Do you understand me? They were so dry no footsteps could be heard anywhere. Yeah, it's a sad thing. Yeah, to go to church and find Christians all dry." The preacher concludes with an existential reading of the Spirit's advent in the valley. There is no peace to Jerusalem, but there is peace for the solitary soul.

> I was in the valley of dry bones
> Yeah, I had no God on my side
> Yeah, I didn't have no spirit
> To make me shout
> But when I found the Lord

I found joy
Yeah, joy was found
I found joy
Peace to my dying soul[53]

Anderson identifies the presence of the Spirit in Ezekiel's oracle with the "shout," the frenzy of African-American spirituality: "Yeah, I didn't have no spirit / To make me shout." Anderson's sermon shows the implicit refusal of black preachers to turn to the tuning of Israel's captivity. The selectivity of Anderson's allusions is of a piece with the Negro spirituals' reticence to reach beyond the rivers of Babylon. Ezekiel's oracles of the new Temple and Judean repatriation are absent. The preaching tradition here has taken the cue of the black and unknown bards: neither poet nor preacher suffers the biblical prophets to speak of life after exile.

In the Babylonian Talmud, the rabbis say of the resuscitated skeletons of Ezekiel's vision, "they stood upon their feet, uttered a song, and died." Upon hearing of the valley of dry bones, African Americans likewise were swept up by the Spirit to stand upon their feet and utter "a wild, hoarse laugh . . . from a circle, and often a song," as Frederick Douglass had put it, in a land of permanent exile.[54] In the vision of the valley of dry bones, exiled Africans in America experienced the transforming power of God through the text of the oracle. Divinity shines through the pages of the Bible, the book that Reverend Jenkins totes on his shoulder as he prances from on side of the pulpit to the other at the climax of his sermon in *Body and Soul*. The oracle of God's reviving spirit does not merely recount an event of divine presence: the words of the text now signify that presence. Ezekiel's luminous text is the verbal image and likeness of God.

Centuries after the Babylonian exile, another Judean community read God's presence through Ezekiel's texts from self-imposed exile in the caves of Qumran on the northwestern shore of the Dead Sea. The poets of the Song of the Sabbath Sacrifice from the Qumran scrolls (4Q400–407) riff on the words and images of Ezekiel's inaugural vision in chapter 1, especially the language of the throne chariot (4Q404, 1, 2:1–16, and 4Q405, 20–21–22). The Qumran poets structure the liturgy of the songs, however, using elements of the Ezekiel's vision of the restored Temple in Ezekiel chapters 40–48, especially the heavenly ascent recounted in chapters 40–42. The community of protest in the Judean desert had withdrawn from the Temple, which it regarded as corrupt. Like Ezekiel before them they substituted sacred text for sacred space and found access to God through the scriptures they had taken with them in their retreat into the wilderness.[55]

Like the Qumran exiles, Christian slaves in the United States invoked the divine presence through the text of one of Ezekiel's oracles. They chose as their iconic text, however, not a vision of heavenly worship but a prophecy of earthly restoration. The Qumranites sought participation in an unsullied, angelic liturgy in an uncorrupted temple. Two of Ezekiel's four ecstatic visions introduced by the formula, "the hand of the Lord was upon me," are visions of the Temple. The second in chapters 8–11 is a vision of the fallen Jerusalem temple, and the fourth is the vision in chapters 40–48 of the new, heavenly temple that God will build at the end of the age. The Qumranites placed their hope in a pristine future temple, and so they focused their attention on the last of Ezekiel's four visions.

The exiled Africans and their descendants, however, yearned for a collective resurrection that included the resuscitation of their brutalized bodies. They neither looked back to Jerusalem nor looked forward to heaven; their text of choice was an oracle spoken in the midst of a community of exiles. The text "got all up into" their bodies, animating them to respond with music and movement to the transcendent God implied in the iconic text.

W. E. B. Du Bois remembered the anonymous authors of the Negro spirituals as "exiled Africans."[56] Du Bois understood the black and unknown bards as they understood themselves: they were singing their song in a strange land, never to return home. Ezekiel's wind-swept valley continues to remind slavery's children of their exile. They continue to be strangers in a strange land. And they continue to be haunted by the bones.

CHAPTER FIVE

Exodus

We poor creatures have need to believe in God, for if God Almighty will not be good to us some day, why were we born? When I heard of his delivering his people from bondage, I know it means poor Africans.

—*Polly, a slave, to her mistress*

IT LITERALLY MEANS "the way out." A loanword from the Greek, *exodus* signifies the road of escape. The biblical drama of Exodus recounts the story of the escape of the ancient Israelites from Egypt and their formation as a new people in Canaan. The Lord had commanded that the Egyptians "let my son [Israel] go" (Exod. 4:23), and the imperative phrase "Let my people go" is repeated seven times in the drama that climaxes in the Israelites' flight across the Red Sea.[1]

African Americans heard, read, and retold the story of the Exodus more than any other biblical narrative. In it they saw their own aspirations for liberation from bondage in the story of the ancient Hebrew slaves. The Exodus was the Bible's narrative argument that God was opposed to American slavery and would return a catastrophic judgment against the nation as he had against ancient Egypt. The Exodus signified God's will that African Americans too would no longer be sold as bondspeople, that they too would go free.

"For it is to me that the Israelites are servants ['*abadim*, literally, "slaves"]: they are my servants, whom I freed from the land of Egypt, I the Lord your God" (Lev. 25:55). The Israelites were set free to be the slaves of God. The foregoing is the concluding verse to the chapter in the book of Leviticus that outlines the conditions of the Jubilee, the last year of a forty-nine-year cycle in which all land returns to ancestral ownership and all Israelite slaves go free in the fiftieth year of the cycle.

> And if thy brother that dwelleth by thee be waxen poor, and
>   be sold unto thee; thou shalt not compel him to serve as
>   a bondservant:
> But as a hired servant, and as a sojourner, he shall be with thee,
>   and shall serve thee until the year of jubilee:
> And then shall he depart from thee, both he and his children
>   with him, and shall return to his own family, and unto
>   the possession of his fathers shall he return. (Lev. 25:39–41)

The legislation of Leviticus concludes with a proscription that American slaves hoped would one day be applied to themselves: "For they are my servants, which I brought forth out of the land of Egypt: they shall not be sold as bondsmen. Thou shalt not rule over him with rigour; but shalt fear thy God" (Lev. 25:42). African Americans came to associate the year of jubilee with the freedom for which they yearned with such longing. Negro spirituals that celebrated freedom came to be known as jubilee songs, and the word *jubilee* later came to designate the African-American quartets that sang this music in the late nineteenth century.

If these verses in Leviticus were the dream of the slaves, the verses that immediately follow them were their nightmarish reality:

> Both thy bondmen, and thy bondmaids, which thou shalt have,
> shall be of the heathen that are round about you; of them shall
> ye buy bondmen and bondmaids. Moreover of the children
> of the strangers that do sojourn among you, of them shall ye
> buy, and of their families that are with you, which they begat
> in your land: and they shall be your possession. And ye shall
> take them as an inheritance for your children after you, to
> inherit them for a possession; they shall be your bondmen
> forever. (Lev. 25:44–46)

These verses, and not the jubilee legislation of Leviticus, informed the view of slaveowners. Baptist preacher and proslavery apologist Iveson L. Brookes of South Carolina cited the passage above in 1851 when he wrote, "It was negro slavery, or the bondage of the Canaanitish descendants of Ham, whom God authorized to be held in hereditary bondage, under the laws of the Jewish polity."[2] For African Americans, strangers sojourning in the New Israel, this scripture was horrifically fulfilled.

A FURNACE OF IRON

African Americans were slaves when they collectively encountered the story of the Exodus: it was as slaves that they first learned of this story about slaves. The Bible told of a miraculous mass flight of slaves orchestrated by God himself. At the shore of the *yam suph,* the sea of reeds, the escaping Israelites are pursued by Egyptian chariots and cavalry led by Pharaoh to reclaim the Hebrew fugitives. Pinned between the desert and the sea, the Israelites panic at the sight of Pharaoh's army in the distance. God directs Moses to wave his staff over the sea, which divides and allows the Israelites safe passage. When Pharaoh's army attempts to pursue them, the waters come crashing down on the Egyptians, drowning Pharaoh's entire host. On freedom's shore, the Israelites sing one of the oldest canticles in all of scripture, the song of God's miraculous victory over Pharaoh's chariots.

> Sing ye to the Lord;
> for he hath triumphed gloriously;
> the horse and his rider hath he thrown into the sea.
> (Exod. 15:21)

It was precisely the miraculous glory of the Israelites' liberation that African-American slaves embraced so enthusiastically: the Negro spirituals would later echo this exultation of divine triumph. The spirituals sing of God's deliverance of the Israelites at the Red Sea and are our oldest testimony to the Exodus in African-American folk tradition.

The spirituals testify that with a mighty hand and an outstretched arm God intervened in the life of his captive children to free them from bondage. He had seen their affliction, heard their cries, knew their sorrows, and had delivered them. The weeping of the children of Israel and God's belated response to it are acts in the drama of Israel's deliverance celebrated in the Negro spiritual "Go Down, Moses."

> "Thus spoke the Lord,"
> Bold Moses said,
> Let my people go,
> If not I'll smite
> Your first born dead,
> Let my people go.

Go down, Moses,
Way down in Egypt land,
Tell old Pharaoh,
To let my people go.[3]

The question of the Negro spiritual "Didn't Ol' Pharaoh Get Lost?" becomes jubilantly rhetorical:

Didn't ol' Pharaoh get lost,
Get lost, get lost,
In the Red Sea, true believer,
O, Didn't ol' Pharaoh get lost,
Get lost, get lost,
In the Red Sea.[4]

The singers identified with the Hebrews not only in their bondage but also in their abjection: they too were slaves under an impossibly powerful regime. The story of Exodus provided the slaves with a biblical myth that allowed them to acknowledge the enormity of slavery and their own incapacity to do anything about it, while at the same time maintaining an expectation that God would make a way out of no way. This admixture of haplessness and hope was the faith of the slave.

The immediacy of African Americans' identification with the oppressed children of Israel was seemingly spontaneous and marked the vast gulf between the religion of the master and the religion of the slave. When preachers preached the Exodus, masters heard one thing, slaves another. A Northern missionary who read the Exodus narrative to slaves in South Carolina during the Civil War "was amazed at the impression it seemed to make. The remarks of the old men made were graphic and eloquent. It made them recount with praise to God their escape. The little church seemed like dreamland to me almost when they got stirred to talk."[5] In 1862 a white Methodist minister and pastor of a black congregation in Charleston, South Carolina, belatedly discovered that his charges were listening with enthusiasm to a sermon that he was unaware of preaching.

There were near fourteen hundred colored communicants. . . .
[Their] service was always thronged—galleries, lower floor,
chancel, pulpit, steps and all. . . . The preacher could not complain of any deadly space between himself and his congrega-

tion. . . . Though ignorant of it at the time, he remembers how the cause of enthusiasm under his deliverances [about] the "law of liberty" and "freedom from Egyptian bondage." What was figurative, they interpreted literally. He thought of but one ending of the war; they quite another. . . . It is mortifying now to think that his comprehension was not equal to the African intellect. All he thought about was relief from the servitude of sin, and freedom from the bondage of the devil. . . . But they interpreted it literally in the good time coming, which of course could not but make their ebony complexion attractive, very.[6]

This subversive reading of the Exodus is suggested to humorous effect in Paul Laurence Dunbar's poem "An Ante-Bellum Sermon" (1895). The slave preacher of the poem delivers a sermon in Southern dialect that is a homespun rehearsal of the Exodus. After God says to Moses, "Look hyeah, Moses, go tell Pher'oh / Fu' to let dem chillun go," the preacher continues,

> "An' ef he refuse to do it,
> I will make him rue de houah,
> Fu' I'll empty down on Egypt
> All de vials of my powah."
> Yes, he did—an' Pher'oh's ahmy
> Wasn't wuth a ha'f a dime;
> Fu' de Lawd will he'p his chillun,
> You kin trust him evah time
>
> . . . .
> Dey kin fo'ge yo' chains an' shackles
> F'om de mountains to de sea;
> But de Lawd will sen' some Moses
> Fu' to set his chillun free.

The slave preacher then offers this disclaimer:

> But fu' feah some one mistakes me,
> I will pause right hyeah to say,
> Dat I'm still preachin' ancient,
> I ain't talkin' 'bout to-day.

The preacher insists,

An' the love [God] showed to Isrul,
Wasn't all on Isrul spent;
Now don't run an' tell yo' mastahs
Dat I's preachin' discontent.[7]

Of course, Dunbar's preacher protests too much. That's just the point.

Dunbar was a city boy, but his parents had been plantation slaves in Kentucky. They regaled the young Dunbar with stories of Southern life before the Civil War. This material became grist for the mill of his literary craft and was associated with the romance of the halcyon prewar South that had become myth on both sides of the Mason-Dixon Line by the turn of the twentieth century. But Dunbar knew of the dark side of the myth of the happy "darky": the secret moral outrage fueled by the slaves' interpretation of God's justice in the Bible. The preacher continues:

I'se a-givin' you de Scriptuah,
I'se a-handlin' you de fac's.
Cose ole Pher'oh b'lieved in slav'ry,
But the Lawd he let him see,
Dat de people he put bref in,—
Evah mothah's son was free.

"But I think it would be bettah," cautions the preacher, "Ef I'd pause again to say, / Dat I'm talkin' 'bout our freedom / In a Bibleistic way."[8] The slaves themselves recognized the insurgency of their faith and prudently sought to hide their convictions through the subterfuge that is so much a part of life under all slave regimes. Slaves dissimulated about their religious experience on the rare occasions that they discussed these matters with whites. Some former slaves admitted as much. One ex-slave later confessed, "My master used to ask us children, 'Do your folks pray at night?' We said 'No,' 'cause our folks had told us what to say. But the Lord have mercy, there was plenty of that going on. They'd pray, 'Lord, deliver us from bondage.'"[9]

Dunbar's distinctive stylistic device was the use of African-American dialect in his poems. Single-handedly he turned dialect into a genre, and a genre into an oeuvre. Two years after "An Ante-Bellum Sermon," however, Dunbar wrote the poem "We Wear the Mask" in somber, standard English. Dunbar confesses,

We wear the mask that grins and lies,
It hides our cheeks and shades our eyes,—
This debt we pay to human guile;
With torn and bleeding hearts we smile,
And mouth with myriad subtleties.[10]

In "An Ante-Bellum Sermon," Dunbar lifts the mask ever so slightly at the poem's conclusion to allow the reader glimpses of an insurrectionary hope:

But when Moses wif his powah
Comes an' sets us chillun free
We will praise de gracious Mastah
Dat has gin us liberty;
An' we'll shout ouah halleluyahs,
On dat mighty reck'nin' day,
When we'se reco'nized ez citiz'—
Huh uh! Chillun, let us pray![11]

A deep chasm of experience and aspiration separated the faith of the master and the faith of the slave. That chasm would not close with the fall of the Confederacy. Though emancipation ostensibly rescinded the categories of master and slave, the stigma of their previous condition of servitude that attended the bittersweet end of slavery in the United States only broadened and deepened the social and psychic distance between slavery's children and their fellow Americans.

MY SERVANT MOSES

The book of Exodus begins by making an irony of the fulfillment of the promise that ends the book of Genesis. God tells Abraham that he will make the patriarch "exceedingly fruitful" (Gen. 17:6). Later in Egypt "the children of Israel were fruitful . . . and the land was filled with them" (Exod. 1:7). But it is precisely their greatness that marks them for misery. Pharaoh warns his people, "Behold, the people of the children of Israel are more and mightier than we" (Exod. 1:9). Threatened by the Israelites' high birthrate, the Egyptians reduce the Israelites to slavery. The Israelite population continues to grow, and a frustrated Pharaoh commands that all male Israelite children be killed at birth. It is in the shadow of this pogrom that Moses, the future leader of Israel's long march from slavery to freedom, is born.

Armed with magical powers and aided by his eloquent brother Aaron, Moses returns to Egypt after a long hiatus to confront Pharaoh and demand that he release the Hebrew slaves to serve the mysterious God of the desert. A contest of wills and wonders ensues, and after inflicting a series of ten plagues on the Egyptians, Moses receives Pharaoh's grudging permission for the Israelites to leave.

The Bible ascribes to Moses occult powers greater than those of his adversaries. But what is missing from Moses's wizardry is the very thing that makes magic so desirable—the promise of mastery. Moses is not the master of his own magic: "And the Lord said unto him, what is that in thine hand? And he said, A rod. And he said, Cast it on the ground. And he cast it on the ground, and it became a serpent: and Moses fled from before it. And the Lord said unto Moses, Put forth thy hand, and take it by the tail. And he put forth his hand, and caught it, and it became a rod in his hand" (Exod. 4:2–4). Moses is a wizard afraid of his wand, and rightly so: it obeys not his commands but God's. African-American folkloric retellings of the biblical story of Moses's contest with Pharaoh's court wizards emphasize that Moses merely lays his stick down and it does its work of itself.

> One day he was out minding his father-in-law's sheep, and the Lord spoke to Moses and said, "Pull off your shoes, for you is on holy ground. I want you to go back and deliver my children from Egypt." He said, "Moses, what is that you got in your hand?" Moses said, "It's a staff." He said, "Cast it on the ground." And it turned to a snake. And Moses fled from it. The Lord said, "Go back and pick it up." And Moses picked it up, and it turned back into a staff. The Lord said, "Go back and wrought all these miracles in Egypt and deliver my children from bondage."
>
> So Moses goes on back. He goes into to Pharaoh and told him what the Lord had told him to do. Pharaoh said, "Who is he?" "I can show you what He got power to do." And he cast his rod on the floor, and it turned into a serpent. Pharaoh said, "That ain't nothing. I got a magic can do that." So he brought

his magicians and soothsayers in, and they cast their rods on the floor. So theirs turned to snakes. And they crawled up to Moses' snake, and Moses' snake swallowed up their snakes. And that's where hoodoo lost its hand, because theirs was evil power and his was good. They lost their rods and he had his and theirs too.[12]

"Hoodoo," also known as "voodoo," "rootwork," and "conjure," is the residue of West African faith and practice flavored with Native American and European elements that survives in African-American folk healing and medicine. Hoodoo works cures and prodigies through occult ritual and herbal remedies. Practitioners, called "conjurors" or "rootworkers," manipulate words and objects to wield power over disease and misfortune. The "hand" is conjure terminology for amulets and other cultic objects fashioned by conjurors to ward off evil. Some Christian slaves associated "rootwork" with demonic activity: as one Negro spiritual puts it, "Satan is a liar and a conjurer, too, / If you don't mind, / He'll conjure you."[13] Resistance to magic inheres in biblical religion generally, which is hostile to any attempt to manipulate divine power.[14] In the figure of Moses African Americans could say yes to the miraculous while also saying no to the magical.

And yet, in the figure of Moses some African Americans said yes to both. They saw Moses as the conjuror par excellence. A contemporary hoodoo practitioner in New Orleans, calling himself Hoodoo Book Man, explained to an anthropologist, "Hoodooism started way back in the time that Moses days, back in old ancient times, nine thousand years ago. Now you see, Moses, he was a prophet just like Peter and Paul and James. And then he quit being a prophet and started the hoodooism."[15] Thomas Smith, a former slave from Yamacraw, South Carolina, was an octogenarian in the 1930s when he talked about his knowledge of hoodoo with an oral historian in the Savanna Unit of the Georgia Writer's Project under the Works Projects Administration. Smith said that Moses's magical powers still existed among African Americans. "That happen in Africa the Bible say. Ain't it show that Africa was a land of magic power since the beginning of history? Well then, the descendents of Africans have the same gift to do unnatural thing[s]."[16] Smith had experienced slavery in the South Carolina low country, where vestiges of West African culture among the slaves, many of whom had been brought directly from Africa, were strong: slaves on low country plantations even continued to observe African ethnic distinctions into the nineteenth century.[17] Elements of West African magic—hoodoo—figured prominently in the culture of these slaves.

A distinctive element, common to the West African worldview of the Fon, Ewe, Bantu, Dahomey, Whydah, and Yoruba peoples, was the cosmic power symbolized by the snake. The snake was the subject of veneration, fear, and folklore; its skin was used in the manufacture of charms and talismans, and its presence was considered an omen.[18] Some slaves who were hoodoo practitioners were reputed to be snake charmers. The Bible associates Moses with snakes precisely in the exercise of his miraculous powers. Moses's rod transmutes into a snake, and later the rod of his brother Aaron turns into a snake to overpower the transmogrified snakes of Pharaoh's court sorcerers (Exod. 7:10–12). The episode comports with the logic of hoodoo that the only match for strong magic is stronger magic.

African Americans were not the first to associate Moses with magic. In the first century BCE the Roman author Pliny writes in his *Natural History* that Moses was a great magician, as does the Greek author Apuleius in his *Apology,* and Moses figures prominently in esoteric European traditions of magic and secret wisdom. But the folklore of African Americans and other people of African descent elaborated further on this association of Moses with occult powers. On the basis of her ethnographic exploration of hoodoo in New Orleans, Zora Neale Hurston noted that all hoodoo practitioners "hold that the Bible is the great conjure book in the world," as well as that "Moses is honored as the greatest conjuror."[19] Hurston found the same to be so among people of African descent throughout the New World: "Wherever the Negro is found, there are traditional tales of Moses and his supernatural powers that are not in the Bible, nor can they be found in any written life of Moses. . . . All over the Southern United States, the British West Indies and Haiti there are reverent tales of Moses and his magic."[20]

Hurston's ethnographic studies of African-American culture in the South inform her novel *Moses, Man of the Mountain* (1939), a retelling of the Exodus story in a flavorful African-American Southern idiom. Though faithful to the biblical account, Hurston embellishes Moses's biblical biography with a masterful blend of ethnography, folklore, and flourishes of hoodoo. As a young man Moses has Pharaoh's court magicians teach him their tricks. After reading the book of Thoth, Egyptian god of wisdom and magic, Moses copies the text of the book on a piece of papyrus and washes the writing off with beer, which he then drinks so that he will not forget what he read and wrote. In Midian, Moses's father-in-law, Jethro, himself a practitioner of hoodoo, instructs Moses in magical arts: Moses's magical powers ultimately surpass even Jethro's, who declares Moses "the finest hoodoo man in the world."[21]

For African Americans, Moses was more than an expert magician or antimagician. He was, first and foremost, a leader of his people. Moses personifies leadership as divine vocation. Moses as an archetype of the faithful community leader is an image with strong antebellum roots. Slaves in the South Carolina low country sang of him as a divinely appointed leader of the people.

> God call Moses! (Ay Lord!)
> God call Moses! (Ay Lord!)
> God call Moses! (Ay Lord!)
> Time is a-rollin' on!
> Moses free the people! (Ay Lord!)
> Moses free the people! (Ay Lord!)
> Moses free the people! (Ay Lord!)
> Time is a-rollin' on![22]

In an essay entitled "Our Greatest Want" (1859), writer and activist Frances E. W. Harper commended to her readers the figure of Moses as an ideal political leader. Harper surveys the violent political leadership of Europe and laments its "carnage and blood." She condemns American politicians as mercenary "worshippers at the shrine of success," an idolatry practiced even by "some of us, upon whose faculties the rust of centuries has lain." Among these Harper indicts the leaders of her own community. "When we have a race of men whom this bloodstained government cannot tempt or flatter, who would sternly refuse every office in the nation's gift, from a president down to a tide-waiter, until she shook her hands from complicity in the guilt of cradle plundering and man stealing, then for us the foundations of an historic character will have been laid." African Americans need more than "gold or silver, talent or genius." The virtues of "unselfishness, earnestness, and integrity" must temper and tether these other possessions to "subserve the case of crushed humanity and carry out the greatest idea of the present age, the glorious idea of human brotherhood." Harper finds these virtues in Moses, who had turned from the privilege and prestige of "the slave power of Egypt" and chose rather "to suffer with the enslaved than rejoice with the free."[23] Later in her literary career Harper would revisit the figure of Moses as exemplar of virtuous leadership in the free-verse epic poem, *Moses: A Story of the Nile* (1869).

Speaking of his black soldiers, white Union Army commander Thomas Wentworth Higginson remarked in 1864, "There is no part of the Bible with which they are so familiar as the story of the deliverance of Israel. Moses is their *ideal* of all that is high, and noble, and perfect, in man. I think they have been accustomed to regard Christ not so much in the light of a *spiritual* Deliverer, as that of a second Moses who would eventually lead them out of their prison-house of bondage."[24] Preachers from antebellum times on have spoken of leadership in the language and image of the call narrative of Moses. A Virginia preacher's description of his calling at the beginning of the twentieth century is illustrative: "One day when I was working in the field all by myself, God told me he wanted me to [be] a leader for my people like Moses. I complained that I was not prepared. And God said, 'you go and I'll go with you and speak for you.' From that day I became some sort of leader of my people."[25]

Harriet Tubman, celebrated escaped slave and Union Army scout, was Moses to her admirers and the many fugitive slaves that she guided to freedom. Tubman crossed the Mason-Dixon Line repeatedly to conduct slaves along the Underground Railroad. For Tubman the image of Exodus and Promised Land had signified her own forays against the American regime of Pharaoh. She reworked the themes of Egypt and Canaan in her self-composed musical repertoire that spoke the secret language of escape. She coined a song to warn slaves in hiding "there's danger in the way" and that they should not come out in the open to meet her.

Moses go down in Egypt,
Tell old Pharaoh to let my people go;
Hadn't been for Adam's fall,
Shouldn't have to died at all.[26]

Moses continued to be an evocative ideal in African-American representations of authentic leadership in the twentieth century. James Weldon Johnson's sermonic poem "Let My People Go," paraphrases the call narrative of Exodus 3 mediated through a conscious elaboration of the Negro spiritual "Go Down, Moses": "Go down, Moses / Way down in Egypt land / Tell old Pharaoh / To let my people go."[27] Johnson supplements his poetic language with other divine summonses in the Bible. There is the still, small voice reminiscent of Elijah's conversation with God at Kidron: "And after the earthquake a fire; but the Lord was not in the fire: and after the fire a still small voice" (1 Kings 18:12). The reply, "here am I," is the response of Abraham, Samuel, and Isaiah as well: the poet echoes the Bible echoing itself. The invisible voice that speaks to Moses from the burning bush also suggests the story of the Apostle Paul's divine encounter on the Damascus road in Acts 9. The burning bush signifies God's voice, wherever and to whomever it speaks, as a call to leadership in a moment of crisis. It is the imagery of divine vocation.

In Beauford Delaney's painting *Burning Bush* (1932), the conical, fiery mass dominating the foreground implies simultaneously all the encounters on holy ground that mark the career of Moses and the milestones of the Exodus.[28] As the title of the work suggests, the pyramidal flame is the numinous bush from which God speaks to Moses in Exodus 3. But the blazing mound is also the lightning at Sinai where God dictates his law in Exodus 20 and, at the end of the book of Deuteronomy, the summit of Pisgah that Moses mounts in the final moments of his life. The entire career of the divinely appointed leader is signified in the single, flaming image. The painting contains no human figures: the luminous form in the foreground signifies simultaneously the burning bush, Sinai, and Pisgah. But there is no Moses. For Delaney the burning bush is a sign of divine presence that transcends human effort. The Exodus is initiated and consummated in the encounter with God. It is God and God alone who appoints the appointed and anoints the anointed. It is God and God alone who makes Moses the leader of the people. The painting affords the principals of the encounter—Moses, God, the children of Israel—neither foreground nor background. Delaney's image is divine vocation as pure event, a vivid color portrait of Providence.

In *Moses, Man of the Mountain*, Zora Neale Hurston treats the challenges of leading a fearful, recalcitrant people up from slavery. Among other themes, Hurston explores how bondage becomes the psychic norm of the slave born, bred, and expecting to die in slavery. When Moses announces to the Israelites that they are to leave the house of bondage,

Hurston writes, "the people cried . . . . They just sat with centuries in their eyes and cried."[29] Tears and fears show that liberation is a frightening alternative future for the children of Israel. In the play of the figures of Moses and the people that Moses led, Hurston signifies the terror as well as the promise of freedom for African Americans.

The figure of Moses attended African-American restive efforts to participate with greater equity in national life after World War II. Progressive Party politician Charlotta A. Bass appealed to the rhetoric of Exodus when in April 1952 she accepted the nomination as candidate for vice president of the United States on the Progressive ticket with presidential candidate Vincent Halliman. In her acceptance speech before the Progressive Party National Convention she defiantly promised her socialist comrades that "I will not retreat, not one inch, so long as God gives me the vision to see what is happening and strength to fight for the things I know are right." She concluded, "I accept this great honor. I give you as my slogan in this campaign—'Let my people go.'"[30] And when the Civil Rights Movement of the late 1950s and 1960s brought the cadences of black preaching into the public square, Martin Luther King, Jr., became the Moses of his people, marching toward the promise of a postapartheid society. King called Southern segregationists "pharaohs" who had used every means to hold African Americans in "the Egypt of segregation" and to bar them from the "Promised Land" of full citizenship.[31]

With poignancy King himself takes on the mantle of Moses in his last speech, delivered the night before his assassination in Memphis, Tennessee, on April 4, 1968. King structures his remarks with the same form that we find in Deuteronomy's report of the end of Moses's career on Mount Pisgah. Both testaments, that of King and that of Moses, open with the Exodus of the children of Israel from Egypt. Before ascending Mount Nebo, Moses concludes his address to the Israelites with a retrospective of the Exodus.

> And Moses called unto all Israel, and said unto them, Ye have
> seen all that the Lord did before your eyes in the land of
> Egypt unto Pharaoh, and unto all his servants, and unto
> all his land;
> The great temptations which thine eyes have seen, the signs,
> and those great miracles:

> Yet the Lord hath not given you a heart to perceive, and
>> eyes to see, and ears to hear, from this day.
> And I have led you forty years in the wilderness: your clothes
>> are not waxen old upon you, and thy shoe has not waxen
>> old upon your foot.
> Ye have not eaten bread, neither have ye drunk wine or strong
>> drink: that ye might know that I am the Lord your God.
>> (Deut. 29:2–8)

King goes on to say, however, that he would neither stop at the triumph of the Exodus nor choose to live in the moment of entry into the Promised Land of the Israelites.[32] The highlights that King reviews in his historical summary are not those of the biblical Exodus but those of the Civil Rights movement and the movements of emancipation that punctuated the early 1960s.

> Strangely enough, I would turn to the Almighty, and say, "If you allow me to live just a few years in the second half of the twentieth century, I will be happy." Now that's a strange statement to make, because the world is all messed up. The nation is sick. Trouble is in the land. Confusion all around. That's a strange statement. But I know, somehow, that only when it is dark enough, can you see the stars. And I see God working in this period of the twentieth century in a way that men, in some strange way, are responding—something is happening in the world. The masses of people are rising up. And wherever they are assembled today, whether they are in Johannesburg, South Africa; Nairobi, Kenya; Accra, Ghana; New York City; Atlanta, Georgia; Jackson, Mississippi; or Memphis, Tennessee—the cry is always the same—"We want to be free."[33]

At the end of the sermon, King turns to the testamentary language of Deuteronomy 34 to refer neither to the people nor to the movement but to himself. King himself has looked over; King himself bequeaths to the children that Moses led the legacy and challenge of the Promised Land he has seen but shall not live to enter. "We've got some difficult days ahead. But it does matter with me now. Because I've seen the mountaintop. And I don't mind. Like anybody, I would like to live a long life. Longevity has its place. But I'm not concerned about that now. I just want to do God's will. And He's allowed me to go up to the mountain. And I've looked over. And I've seen the Promised Land."[34]

Though King's many admirers hailed him as one like unto Moses, only here, in the shadow of death, did King identify himself with the figure of Moses. Like Moses, he looks over into the Promised Land that he knows he will not enter, and like Moses he charges his followers to take the land with a confidence. The mantle of Moses, that venerable ideal of African-American leadership, weighed on Martin Luther King, Jr., throughout his public life. He claimed that mantle only on the eve of his death.

The activists of the Civil Rights Movement seized upon the biblical tale of Moses and the people that Moses led to signify the terror and glory of freedom. In the generation that followed the movement, however, leaders were reticent to don the mantle of Moses and to speak of political action in the language of Exodus. On January 15, 1986, Jesse Jackson preached at Ebenezer Baptist Church in Atlanta, King's home church. The sermon inaugurated a week of commemorations sponsored by the Martin Luther King Center for Non-Violent Social Change, launching the first national celebration of King's birthday as a national holiday.

> Like Joseph, Dr. King could interpret dreams and nightmares, but he also had a vision. Now here is the challenge to our government. While Pharaoh had the good sense to give the job of staving off the famine to the man who interpreted the nightmares, our leaders denied Martin that opportunity. Pharaoh did not care that Joseph was a foreigner, that he was a Jew, that he was young, that he was in jail. . . . When Pharaoh started having these nightmares and learned that Joseph could interpret them, he went past all that—not just to steal Joseph's ideas—but to put him in a position of power an authority. Joseph was therefore able to save the economy, his own family, and Egypt. America couldn't get past race long enough to appreciate the prophetic truths of Dr. King. So, as opposed to bringing him in and hearing his voice, they locked him out. The result is that today we have Dr. King's memory, but we missed the opportunity to benefit from his wisdom.[35]

The biblical imagery is ultimately regressive. Jackson has made a rhetorical shift from the Promised Land back to Joseph the Dreamer and to a Pharaoh who, contrary to the biblical story, is heedless of the wise Dreamer.

At the Million-Man March on October 16, 1995, leader of the Nation of Islam Minister Louis Farrakhan summoned the image of the suffering children of Israel under Egyptian bondage. He did so, however, without mentioning Moses or the Exodus.

> And here we are, 400 years, fulfilling Abraham's prophecy.
>
> Some of our friends in the religious community have said, why should you make atonement? That was for the children of Israel. I say, yes it was. But atonement for the children of Israel prefigured our suffering here in America. Israel was in bondage to Pharaoh 400 years. We've been in America 440 years. They were under affliction. We're under affliction. They were under oppression. We're under oppression. God said that nation which they shall serve, I will judge.

Farrakhan speaks of judgment here in the future tense. He mentions Israel, Pharaoh, and 400 years of bondage. All of the elements of the exodus story are here—except the Exodus itself. According to Farrakhan's reckoning, African Americans have suffered their bondage for 440 years. Farrakhan mentions "Abraham's prophecy," referring to Genesis 15:13, where God warns Abraham that his descendants will suffer slavery in a foreign land for 400 years. But the count of 440 years corresponds to the traditional teaching of the Nation of Islam that the present era of evil commenced with the arrival of John Hawkins's British slave ship the *Jesus*, on the West African coast in 1555.[36] The Million-Man March, then, takes place in exactly the four hundred fortieth year of the present era. The Dutch slave ship *Jesus* actually arrived in Jamestown with what its manifest called "twenty negurs" in 1619, and the first slaves in North America were those brought to the Spanish colony of Saint Augustine in Florida in 1565.[37]

The date of 1555 in the Nation of Islam's mythology is, of course, mythic. But according to this dating, the African-American sojourn has exceeded even the adjusted span announced in the Bible on the eve of the Exodus: "Now the sojourning of the children of Israel, who dwelt in Egypt, was four hundred and thirty years" (Exod. 12:40). If divine deliverance of African Americans corresponds to that of the Hebrew children, that deliverance was now, according to biblical chronology, a decade overdue. And though there is no stated reason for the suffering of the ancient Hebrews in the Exodus story, Farrakhan, in another creative departure from the biblical figure, provides a contemporary answer to the question. The suffering of African Americans, though likened to that of the Israelites, is not due to Pharaoh's hard-heartedness: "Do you know why we are being afflicted?" Farrakhan explains, "God wants us to humble ourselves to the message that will make us atone and come back to Him and make ourselves whole again."[38] God, explains Farrakhan, has permitted affliction of African Americans for their own good.

Farrakhan, as had Jesse Jackson a decade earlier, evokes of the figure of a Joseph ignored by Pharaoh. In Farrakhan's allegorical twist, however, the figure of Joseph now signifies the collective wisdom of African-American leaders present at the march, including Jesse Jackson and, implicitly, Farrakhan himself.

> But, I think if you could clear the scales from your eyes, sir [Mr. President], and give ear to what we say, perhaps, oh perhaps, what these great speakers who spoke before me said, and my great and wonderful brother, the Reverend Jesse Jackson said, and perhaps, just perhaps from the children of slaves might come the solution to this Pharaoh and this Egypt as it was with Joseph when they had to get him out of prison and wash him up and clean him up because Pharaoh had some troubling dreams that he didn't have any answer to.
>
> And he called his soothsayers and he called the people that read the stars and he called all his advisors, but nobody could help him to solve the problem. But he had to go to the children of slaves, because he heard that there was one in prison who knew the interpretation of dreams. And he said bring him, bring him and let me hear what he has to say.
>
> God has put it for you in the scriptures, Mr. President.[39]

Though Farrakhan speaks more than thirty years after Martin Luther King, the leader of the Nation of Islam has taken a step backward in his deployment of the biblical image of Exodus. In Farrakhan's evocation of an oppressive Egypt, he goes only as far as the suggestion of the plagues of Exodus: "God said that nation which they shall serve, I will judge." But the menacing tone of the Negro spiritual "Go Down, Moses"—"If not I'll strike your first-born dead"—is absent. As more than a million people stood listening to Minister Farrakhan around the reflecting pool at the Lincoln Memorial that day, they heard no prophecy that promised to part the waters, let alone lead to the Promised Land. America is Egypt, and its leader is Pharaoh. But there is no mention of leaving the house of bondage.

THE WORDS OF THE COVENANT

In spite of obstacles, and in spite of the Israelites themselves, Moses leads the wandering multitude to Mount Sinai. There, through the mediation of Moses, God draws the fugitive horde into a covenant, a contractual agreement of exclusive fealty to him. The stipulations of the agreement are spelled out in the laws that God dictates to Moses on Sinai. Taken together, the compendium of these laws—henceforth the Law of Moses—becomes Israel's constitution. Israel's collective existence, initiated in the dramatic deliverance by the Lord of Hosts, is consolidated in the commandments of the God of law.

But the earliest summaries of the Exodus in the Bible do not mention Sinai: several ancient variations on Israel's recollection of the Exodus pass over the revelation of God's law in silence.

> A wandering Aramean was my ancestor; he went down into Egypt and lived there as an alien, few in number, and there he became a great nation, mighty and populous. When the Egyptians treated us harshly and afflicted us, by imposing hard labor on us, we cried to the Lord, the God of our ancestors; the Lord heard our voice and saw our affliction, our toil, and our oppression. The Lord brought us out of Egypt with a mighty hand and an outstretched arm, with a terrifying display of power, and with signs and wonders; and he brought us into this place and gave us this land, a land flowing with milk and honey. (Deut. 26:5–9)

We find similar summaries in Joshua 24:2–13 and in Psalms 78:12–55, and fulsome poetic rehearsals in Psalms 105, 106, and 136. None of these mention Sinai. We must await Nehemiah 9:7–31, an elaborate penitential prayer composed late in the history of ancient Israel, to find Sinai amid memories of the patriarchs, the Exodus, and the wilderness.

As in the earliest biblical summaries of the Exodus story, the connection between the deliverance at the Red Sea and the law at Sinai is seldom acknowledged in the African-American renderings of the Exodus. The figure of Moses is celebrated in a way that Sinai is not. In one of the additional verses of "Didn't Old Pharaoh Get Lost," we encounter a rare reference to Sinai in the Negro spirituals.

> And the Lord spoke to Moses,
> From Sinai's smoking top,
> Saying, "Moses, lead the people,
> Till I shall bid you stop."[40]

Sound and fury precedes the announcement of the Ten Commandments: "And it came to pass . . . that there were thunders and lightnings, and a thick cloud upon the mount, and the voice of the trumpet exceeding loud; so that all the people that was in the camp trembled" (Exod. 19:16). Likewise "the thunderings, the lightnings, and the noise of the trumpet, and the mountain smoking" punctuate the end of the Commandments (20:18). But in the Negro spiritual there is no mention of the law, not even the Ten Commandments. The revelation is not to Israel but to Moses. Not Ten Commandments but one: keep moving. Sinai is important in the minds of the unknown bards because Moses stood upon it. African-American reading of the revelation of the commandments tends to echo the ancient biblical traditions that remember Exodus without reference to Sinai.

The circumscribed African-American reading of Exodus was also at variance with that of the Puritan founders of what would become the United States. The Puritans imagined their migration from the Old World as an exodus to a New Canaan and an errand in the wilderness of the New World.[41] It is the biblical idea of covenant that informs John Winthrop's sermon "A Modell of Christian Charity," composed on his ship the *Arbella* en route to North America in 1630. Having left Egypt, the sanctified community must now take on the yoke of the covenant that God enjoins upon them on the other side of the Red Sea.

> Beloved there is now set before us life, and good, deathe
> and evill in that wee are Commanded this day to love the Lord

our God, and to love one another, to walke in his wayes and
to keepe his Commaundements and his Ordinance, and his
lawes, and the Articles of our Covenant with him that wee may
live and be multiplied, and that the Lord our God may blesse
us in the land whither we goe to posess it: But if our heartes
shall turne away soe that wee will not obey, but shall be se-
duced and worship . . . other Gods, our pleasures, and profitts,
and serve them; it is propounded unto this day, wee shall
surely perishe out of the good Land whither wee passe over
this vast Sea to possesse it.[42]

Winthrop delivers this speech en route to the Promised Land, with Egypt
far behind at a safe, cisatlantic distance. He refers to the Exodus from
England as a fait accompli. In the New World the settlers have the opportunity to realize covenantal life as a new nation, the New Jerusalem,
the City upon a Hill.

Puritan theology, which interpreted the experience of the English
settlers in North America in terms of biblical typology, had been reading
the Exodus as an American story for a century before the Revolution. The
Exodus story continued to influence the colonial imagination throughout
the revolutionary period. In the discussion of the official seal of the new
nation in 1776, Benjamin Franklin proposed the image of Moses, staff in
hand, parting the Red Sea as Pharaoh's army is drowned in its waters, with
the caption "Rebellion to tyrants is obedience to God." Thomas Jefferson
suggested a design with a scene of the Israelites in the wilderness led by
cloud and pillar of fire. In the mid-nineteenth century, Herman Melville
summarized the national self-understanding in 1850 in his early novel
White Jacket: or, The World in a Man-of-War. "We Americans are driven
to a rejection of the maxims of the Past, seeing that, ere long, the van of
nations must, of right, belong to ourselves. . . . Escaped from the house
of bondage, Israel of old did not follow after the ways of the Egyptians.
To her was given an express dispensation; to her were given new things
under the sun. And we as Americans are the peculiar, chosen people—the
Israel of our time; we bear the ark of the liberties of the world." As late
as 1865, James Russell Lowell could still extol America as "the Promised
Land / That flows with Freedom's honey and milk."[43]

Puritan preachers took to pulpit and public square to remind the New

Israel of duties that attended the blessings of the divine covenant. These calls to covenantal responsibility were warnings to return to a compact with God and with one's fellow citizens that had been effected at the founding of the nation. Jeremiah is the namesake for this form of public rhetoric, the jeremiad, because the prophet had called the kingdom of Judah to remember its covenant with God.

> The word that came to Jeremiah from the Lord, saying, Hear
> ye the words of this covenant and speak unto the men of Judah
> and to the inhabitants of Jerusalem; And say thou unto them,
> Thus saith the Lord God of Israel; Cursed be the man that
> obeyeth not the words of this covenant, which I commanded
> your fathers in the day that I brought them forth of, out of the
> land of Egypt, from the iron furnace, saying, Obey my voice,
> and do them, according to all which I command you: so shall
> ye be my people, and I will be your God: That I may perform
> the oath which I have sworn unto your fathers, to give them a
> land flowing with milk and honey, as it is this day." (Jer. 11:1–5)

The jeremiad assumes the notion of a shared national covenant, ratified in history and presently in force. Jeremiah called for a renewal of fidelity to a failed covenant that the Israelites would henceforth interiorize: "But this shall be the covenant that I will make with the house of Israel; After those days, saith the Lord, I will put my law in their inward parts, and write it in their hearts; and will be their God, and they shall be my people" (31:33).

African-American prophets demanded in biblical idiom that America live up to a law of liberty whites had never known in its observance and that blacks knew only in its breech. But the characterization of early African-American protests as jeremiads is not quite apt. The commandments to honor the rights of life, liberty, and the pursuit of happiness had been violated even as they were being promulgated by the Founding Fathers. For Americans to live out their founding ideals would be an unprecedented act of covenantal fidelity.

The spirit of African-American frustration with the national covenant—broken in its making—is that of Moses on the mountain, not Jeremiah in the Temple. In Exodus 32 the Bible recounts how, as soon as Moses returned from the mountain with the tablets inscribed with God's law, he found the Israelites in a spree of wanton apostasy. Moses had been on the numinous, terrifying mountain for some time, and the Israelites had become restless and anxious. In his absence, Aaron, Moses's brother, mouthpiece, and the father of what would to become the Israelite priesthood, was persuaded by the people to found a cult more accessible than the mysterious God of the mountain. They all melt down their gold to fashion a calf that would serve as the idolatrous focus of the Israelites' adoration. Moses descends from Sinai to encounter the people engaged in orgiastic worship of the calf, violating the very commandments he holds in his hands. The former slaves were even crediting their new idol with their deliverance from Pharaoh. In a fit of fury, Moses dashes the tablets to the ground, shattering them. Moses literally breaks the divine laws, angered that even as they were being coined on Sinai they were being broken in the Israelite camp.

The story suggests why Moses, not Jeremiah, is the proper point of figural reference for African-American protests against slavery. The protests arise very early in the history of American self-identification as the New Israel, too early to be a real analogue to the prophetic complaint of Jeremiah. Jeremiah laments Israelite apostasy at a later, more mature moment in the history of Israel's evolving consciousness of covenant. The African-American oracles decry a breech of national covenant at a time much closer to its ratification. African Americans would condemn the corrupt cult of the self-proclaimed New Israel. Their protests, coeval with the foundation of the nation itself, targeted the golden calf of white supremacy. As furiously as Moses, African-American prophets saw the divine law of freedom violated even as it was being enshrined in the founding documents and championed by the Founding Fathers.

Some even sought to break laws that had already been the broken. In the face of slavery's egregious violations, African Americans willfully read scripture contrary to the law's plain sense. The story of the Exodus became an apologia for disregarding the commandment against stealing.[44] In Martin Delany's antebellum novel *Blake*, the protagonist Henry Blake advises two enslaved co-conspirators to pilfer money from their masters. "God told the Egyptian slaves to 'borrow from their neighbors'—meaning their oppressors—'all their jewels,' meaning to take their money and wealth whenever they could get their hands on it, and depart from Egypt."[45] Ex-slave autobiographers Henry Bibb and William Wells Brown both speak of this sanctified stealing and its biblical justification.[46] Breaking the commandments under the slave regime was not merely a personal prerogative of the slave: because the master class had stolen so much from the slave—indeed, the slave's very life—depriving the master of ill-gotten gains became a moral imperative.

The traditions that now make up the biblical account of Exodus highlight the importance of law and covenant. Their canonical sequence shows, however, that the Israelites shared a common obligation to obey the Mosaic Law because they had collectively enjoyed the emancipation that God had secured for them at the Red Sea. The emancipation of the Exodus is imperfectly realized, however, in the collective historical experience of American slaves and their descendants. The laws of the land of their nativity—that is, the laws of the United States—enshrined the country's founding documents, developed out of a collective historical experience that was not only alien to the African-American aspirations to freedom but was hostile to them.

A HOLY NATION

Just as Exodus is the Bible's archetypal story of dramatic departure, so Genesis, the first book of the Bible and the book of beginnings, is littered with leave-takings. And all of them are prelude to the grand leave-taking of the Exodus that follows. God calls Abraham to leave his homeland near Ur by the Euphrates River in present-day Iraq and take his household on an uncertain trek westward. God promises to lead Abraham to a new, divinely granted homeland in which he and his descendents will proliferate and prosper. "Leave your country, your family and your father's house, for the land I will show you. I will make you a great nation" (Gen. 12:2). Abraham journeyed as far as Canaan, the region that his descendents would later enter as the Promised Land.

God's promise to Abraham becomes the legacy of his son Isaac. At God's direction, Isaac eventually migrates to Gerar in the coastland dominated by the Philistines and becomes a prosperous resident alien there. Isaac's journey is an occasion for God to repeat the promise that he made to Isaac's father. Isaac's son Jacob, while en route to visit the homeland and family that Abraham once left behind in Mesopotamia, has a dream of an expanded version of the promise first made to his grandfather. Later at Bethel, on the highland trade route to the southwest of the Jordan River valley, God again reminds Jacob of the promise that he will inherit a great land and father a mighty nation. When prolonged famine in Canaan drives Jacob and his extended family south to Egypt for survival, they move from a nomadic life to a settled agricultural society. God sends the elderly Jacob and his household to join his long-lost son Joseph in Egypt, where God finally fulfills the promise to make Jacob's descendents an innumerable host.

The recapitulations of the promise, each rehearsal more grandiose than the last, take the narrative of Israel's ancient patriarchs from generation to generation and from Mesopotamia to Egypt, setting the stage for the drama of divine deliverance of Exodus. The intergenerational promise addressed to each of the patriarchs accounts for God's special interest in a family of Levantine sojourners—that is, the election of Abraham and his descendants. The repeated promise binds them together in the biblical narrative and binds all of them in turn to the Exodus. God's promise to Abraham is repeated as the rationale for the Exodus: "And I will take you [Israel] to me for a people, and I will be to you a God: and ye shall know that I am the Lord your God, which bringeth you out from under the burdens of the Egyptians. And I will bring you in unto the land, concerning the which I did swear to give it to Abraham, to Isaac, and to Jacob" (Exod. 6:7–8). God again repeats his oath on the eve of Israel's entrance into Canaan, which he describes as "the land which I sware unto Abraham, unto Isaac, and unto Jacob" (Deut. 34:4) and "the land which I sware unto their fathers to give them" (Josh. 1:6).

Later in Israel's history, the prophet Hosea recalls that God summoned Israel out of the house of bondage in the earliest days of the nation's existence: "When Israel was a child, then I loved him, and called my son out of Egypt" (Hosea 11:1). The Lord God became Israel's God at the Exodus: "Yet I am the Lord thy God from the land of Egypt, and thou shalt know no god but me: for there is no savior beside me" (Hosea 13:4). An ancient Israelite psalmist sang that it was under the leadership of Moses that Israel became acquainted with the God of justice: "The Lord executeth righteousness and judgment for all that are oppressed. He made known his ways unto Moses, his acts unto the children of Israel" (Ps. 103:6–7). And even from exile in Babylon, the prophet Ezekiel reminded the Israelites that God's special relationship with the nation was initiated at the Exodus: "Thus saith the Lord God; In the day when I lifted up mine hand unto the seed of the house of Jacob, and made myself known unto them in the land of Egypt, when I lifted up my hand unto them, saying, I am the Lord your God . . . to bring them forth of the land of Egypt" (Ezek. 20:5–6).

But Israel's pretensions to election had proven to be both an important claim and an important problem. In the eighth century BCE, a Judean hillbilly named Amos challenged Israel's claim to be a chosen nation. The problem of election was "the nerve of a great part of his message," as Gerhard von Rad once put it.[47] Amos affirms that Israel has a unique relationship with God based on the might acts of God's deliverance from the land of Egypt.

> Hear this word that the Lord hath spoken against you,
>   O children of Israel, against the whole family which
>   I brought up from the land of Egypt, saying,
> You have I known of all the families of the earth: therefore
>   I will punish you for your iniquities. (Amos 3:1–2)

Later, however, Amos qualified the claim of election. "Are ye not as children of the Ethiopians unto me, O children of Israel? saith the Lord. Have not I brought up Israel out of the land of Egypt? and the Philistines from Caphtor, and the Syrians from Kir?" (Amos 9:7). The Ethiopians were at the southern edge of the civilized world that was known to the ancient Israelites in Amos's time. Yet Amos's rhetorical question suggests that God is as close to the Ethiopians as he is to the Israelites. Both the Philistines and the Syrians were Israel's neighbors and ancestral enemies: repeatedly in the past God had helped Israel put them to rout. But Amos here claims that God has given each of them a patrimony: God has "brought them up," just as he had "brought up" the Israelites from Egypt. What God has done for the Israelites, he has done for others. The election of Israel is not exclusive. The Exodus is not unique.

The New Testament opens with the polemic against election aimed at the point in biblical tradition where it is apparently most arbitrary: the divine favor granted to Abraham and his descendants in perpetuity. In the mouth of John the Baptist we hear what may have been a traditional slogan of election and its prophetic rejoinder.

> But when he [John the Baptist] saw many of the Pharisees
>   and the Saducees come to his baptism, he said unto them,

O generation of vipers, who hath warned you to flee from
the wrath to come?
Bring forth therefore fruits meet for repentance:
And think not to say within yourselves, We have Abraham
to our father: for I say unto you, that God is able of these
stones to raise up children of Abraham. (Matt. 3:7–9)

In the parallel version of this speech in the Gospel of Luke, John the
Baptist addresses his remarks to the people at large, "the multitude" (Luke
3:7). In the Gospel of John, Jesus rejects his Israelite critics' claims to be
children of Abraham because, "If ye were Abraham's children, ye would
do the works of Abraham" (John 8:39). The Apostle Paul is at pains in
several of his letters to identify who "the children of Abraham" properly
are (Rom. 9:7; Gal. 3:7). These passages attest that the identity politics of
Abrahamic descent was a controversy of earliest Christianity. All these
texts repudiate the principle of descent on the basis of bloodline or ethnic
identity. With Abraham, the universal scope of the primeval history in
Genesis chapters 1 through 11 narrows to the particular narratives of the
patriarch Abraham and his extended family. The New Testament theologi-
cally reverses the direction of the narratives in Genesis to tell a story that
embraces "all the nations of the earth."

This biblical transcendence of ethnicity ultimately appealed to those
Africans in America who became Christians amid a mixed multitude
of African peoples hailing from a geographical region of western Africa
roughly the size of the continental United States. The Middle Passage and
the biblical myth of the enslaved Hebrews became the elements informing
a collective African-American identity as newly minted as African Americans themselves. This collective identity, however, was not properly national: it was a consciousness of being a people without being a nation.

In traditional African-American treatments of the biblical patriarchs,
there is no theme of intergenerational election. Abraham, Isaac, Jacob,
and Joseph are vague figures whose familial connection to one another
is scarcely recognizable in the Negro spirituals. The Abraham of the Negro spirituals is not the Abraham of Genesis but the Abraham in Jesus's
parable of justice in the afterlife (Luke 16:19–31). The sacrifice of Isaac
is briefly mentioned at the beginning of the Negro spiritual "Didn't Ol'
Pharaoh Get Lost?": "Isaac a ransom / While he lay upon the altar bound,"

is an allusion without narrative context and without Abraham.[48] Thus the biblical story of the binding of Isaac in Genesis 22, which depends on genealogy, is reduced to a drama of human sacrifice.

The black and unknown bards remembered the patriarch Jacob for his associations with the New Testament and how his journey informed Christian self-understanding. The Negro spiritual "'Raslin' Jacob," recalls Jacob's nocturnal wrestling match at Jabbok stream: "And Jacob was left alone; and there wrestled a man with him until the breaking of the day" (Gen. 32:24). In the popular folk song "We Are Climbing Jacob's Ladder"—perhaps the first African-American song to enjoy "crossover" appeal—the Negro spirituals also sung of Jacob's dream of angels mounting a ladder between heaven and earth. "And he dreamed, and behold a ladder set up on the earth, and the top of it reached to heaven: and behold the angels of God ascending and descending on it" (Gen. 28:12). Commentators from antiquity on have suggested that this vision informs the cryptic prophecy of Jesus at the beginning of the Gospel of John: "Verily, verily, I say unto you, hearafter ye shall see heaven open, and the angels of God ascending and descending upon the Son of Man" (John 1:51). The report of Jacob's dream has been informed by the New Testament to forge an association of the heavenly ladder with the Christian life.

> We are climbing Jacob's ladder (3×)
> Refrain: Soldiers of the cross.
> Second verse: Every round goes higher, higher (3×)
> Third verse: We are climbing higher, higher (3×)
> Fourth verse: Sinner, do you love my Jesus (3×)
> Fifth verse: If you love him, why not serve him (3×)

The first through third verses are of the song as it appears in the 1977 edition of *The New National Baptist Hymnal*.[49] The latter verses appear in gospel singer Clara Ward's updated rendition of the song and make explicit the reading of Jacob's vision as an allegory of Christian discipleship.[50]

Also almost absent from the biblical imaginary of the Negro spirituals is Jacob's famous son, Joseph. One Negro spiritual remembers him as "Joseph by his false brethren sold, / God raised him above all," but passes over the details of his spectacular success in silence.[51] Literary critic Albert Murray once complained that "Negroes have been overlooking the special implications of Joseph's journey into Egypt, they have been overemphasizing the role of Moses as Messiah and grossly oversimplifying what the Exodus was really all about."[52]

> No one can deny to Moses, the great emancipator that he was, his position as epic hero of anti-slavery movements. But nei-ther should anyone overlook what Joseph, the riff-style impro-viser, did to slavery. He transcended it to such an extent that his "previous condition of servitude" became the sort of apocryphal cottonpatch-to-capital-city detail so typical of U.S. biography. Only a Horatio Alger could look at the elegantly tonsured and tailored Joseph at a function of state and believe that such a fine figure of a man was once not only a slave but a convict. As for Joseph himself, he never regarded himself as being any-thing other than a prince of the Earth.[53]

Indeed, the figure of Joseph first appears in American letters in an argument against the enslavement of Africans. The tract "The Selling of Joseph," published by Puritan merchant and judge Samuel Sewall in 1700, is the first Puritan anti-slavery tract printed in America. Alluding to the biblical story of Joseph, Sewall argued, "*Joseph* was rightfully no more a Slave to his Brethren, than they were to him: and they had no more Authority to *Sell* him, than to Slay him. And if *they* had nothing to do to Sell him; the *Ishmaelites* bargaining with them, and paying down Twenty pieces of Silver, could not make a Title. Neither could *Potiphar* have any better Interest in him than the *Ishmaelites* had." In 1701 John Saffin, a slave trader and judge who shared the bench with Sewall, published *A Brief and Candid Answer to a Late Printed Sheet, Entitled, The Selling of Joseph, a Rejoinder to Sewall.* "By all which it doth evidently appear both by Scripture and Reason," Saffin writes, "the practice of the People of God in all Ages, both before and after the giving of the Law, and in the times of the Gospel, that there were Bond men, Women, and Children commonly kept by holy and good men, and improved in Service." Saffin concludes his rejoinder with a poisonous piece of poetry, "The Negro's Character,"

> Cowardly and cruel are those Blacks Innate,
> Prone to Revenge, Imp of inveterate hate.
> He that exasperates them, soon espies
> Mischief and Murder in their very eyes.

Libidinous, Deceitful, False and Rude,
The Spume Issue of Ingratitude.
The Premises consider'd, all may tell,
How near good Joseph they are parallel.[54]

African Americans rarely identified themselves with the figure of Joseph for different reasons. Joseph's very success makes him less attractive than other figures to the bards: the "cottonpatch-to-capital-city detail so typical of U.S. biography" was not typical of the biography of the American slave. Joseph's boundless confidence and upward mobility, occasional reverses notwithstanding, was so unlike the collective experience of American slaves and their descendents that his story did not speak to their condition. On the other hand, self-confidence and savvy in enterprising slaves were virtues rewarded with a beating or worse under the American slave regime and were offensive to Jim Crow etiquette. Joseph's famous disclaimer, "But as for you, ye thought evil against me; but God meant it unto good" (Gen. 50:20), comes at the end of his story, not the beginning. The story of the ultimate vindication of African-American slaves and their descendants is yet to have a happy beginning, let alone a happy ending.

And in the collective experience of African Americans, there was no analogy to divine blessing coursing through an intergenerational bloodline. Writing after the Civil War, Episcopal clergyman Francis Grimké saw no evidence of divine election in African-American history. "In the case of the Jews, the record showed what the purposes of God were in regard to that people; but we have no such revelation touching ourselves. God spoke to Abraham, and God spoke to Jacob, and showed them what was to be; but where are the Abrahams and the Jacobs among us to whom he has spoken? There are those who are ready to speculate, but speculation amounts to nothing. What the divine purposes are touching this race no one knows."[55]

The calling and election of African Americans was anything but sure. African Americans identified with the children of Israel not on the basis of a claim to election but on the basis of their common experience of bondage. The identification is not ethnic: the children of Israel are not distant African ancestors, and indeed the villains of the story, the Egyptians, are children of Africa. African Americans did not relate to the Exodus ethnically but experientially, and only to the extent that the experience of oppression shared the same elements. African Americans implicitly eschewed election as a genealogical principle. They were like the Israelites, and the Israelites were like them, to the extent that both were an enslaved people pleading with God to provide a way out.

A PECULIAR PEOPLE

Historian of American religion Eddie Glaude has noted that "African American users of Exodus in the early nineteenth century were not primarily concerned with marking out the racial (blood) ties of fellows or the acquisition of land."[56] But it is these two elements, blood and land, that ground nationhood in modernity. Modern ethnicity makes certain assertions about collective identity based on claims to land and bonds of blood. But African Americans have been in no position to make claims on the basis of either.

Bloodlines were a problem for American slaves and their descendents. During slavery and for some time thereafter the rape of black women by white men was widespread: the children of these violent unions were not white but "Negroes" of lighter hue, relegated to the status and the community of their mothers. They could not be white. Racial mixture thus was always an element of African-American ancestry. Several of the most distinguished figures of black American history were of racially mixed parentage: Frederick Douglass, Booker T. Washington, Anna Julia Cooper, and W. E. B. Du Bois were all sired by white men. The racial politics of the United States determined that claims of and thus anxiety about the "purity" of blood would not punctuate the rhetoric of African-American identity.

For African Americans, filial ties historically have not been the cause for solidarity but its consequence. It is on the basis of this solidarity that Henry Highland Garnet calls his brothers in bondage to action. "Fellowmen! Patient sufferers! Behold your dearest rights crushed to the earth! See your sons murdered, and your wives, mothers, and sisters doomed to prostitution. In the name of the merciful God, and by all that life is worth, let it no longer be a debatable question, whether it is better to choose Liberty or death."[57] Garnet's remarks imply the reason why race could not be a matter of blood alone for African Americans. Many of the evils of slavery he decries are related to the violence of miscegenation. "Look around you, and behold the bosoms of your loving wives heaving with untold agonies! Hear the cries of your poor children! Remember the stripes your fathers bore. Think of the torture and disgrace of your noble mothers. Think of your wretched sisters, loving virtue and purity, as they are driven to concubinage and are exposed to the unbridled lusts of incarnate devils."[58] When Garnet speaks of the ties that bind black people in America, his language is neither national nor ethnic but familial. Garnet uses the language of family relations, especially filial relations, to talk about black solidarity.[59]

The collective historical experience of slavery and its aftermath had forged African Americans into a people in the iron furnace of American slavery. They were not and could not be a nation in the modern sense. Like the Israelites at the time of the Exodus, they were a "mixed multitude": Wolof, Ibo, Akan, Fon, Yoruba, and Mandinka mixed in the cauldron of the Middle Passage. Their sojourn in the New World added to this mixture Narraganset, Yamassee, Cherokee, Choctaw, and Creek and, through the miscegenation wrought by rape, Dutch, English, Irish, Spanish, Portuguese, and French.

The indelible stain of sexual violence was apparent to all. British writer and critic G. K. Chesterton was struck by the sheer physical consequences of miscegenation when he visited the United States. "Before I went to America," he writes, "I always thought the expression 'coloured people' was as fantastic as a fairy tale; it sounded as if some the people were peacock green and other a rich mauve or magenta. I supposed that it was either a sort of joke, or else a sort of semi-ironical euphemism or parody of politeness. But when I went there, I found that it was simply a dull description of fact. These people really are all colours; at least they are all shades of one colour. There must be many more coloured people than there are black people."[60] When in 1948 hysterical Southern Dixiecrats accused the federal government of seeking to "further *rape* the rights of the states," W. E. B. Du Bois answered with a counteraccusation. "The rape which you gentlemen have done against helpless black women in defiance of your own laws," wrote the outraged Du Bois, "is written on the foreheads of millions of mulattoes, and written in ineffable blood."[61] Novelist James Baldwin once told a white segregationist who brought up the issue of interracial marriage, "You're not worried about me marrying *your* daughter. You're worried about me marrying *your wife's* daughter. I've been marrying *your* daughter since the days of slavery."[62]

The people who emerged from this fitful blending of peoples were called many things, but the most common term with the least pejorative connotation was "Negro." The name pointed neither to land of origin nor to line of descent: it signified only color, color without reference to ancestry or territory. Identity was reduced to a matter of melanin: "Negro" and its more objectionable cognates simply mean "black." It was not and could not be a sign for nationality.

When African Americans did turn to the rhetoric of blood as a synecdoche for ancestry, the language was biblical, and the governing principle was the unity of humankind. This conviction of the humanity as an extended global family made the most influential words of the Apostle Paul in African-American life and letters those that he did not write. African Americans repeatedly quoted the sentence from the legendary Athenian oration that the writer of the book of Acts places on Paul's lips, "God . . . hath made of one blood all nations of men" (17:26). The phrase enters American letters in defense of African humanity in Samuel Sewall's "The Selling of Joseph." Alluding to the biblical story of Joseph, Sewall argued, "It is most certain that all Men, as they are the Sons of *Adam,* are Coheirs; and have equal Right unto Liberty, and all other outward Comforts of Life. God . . . *hath made of One Blood, all Nations of Men . . . Forasmuch then as we are the offspring of God* etc. Acts 17:26, 27." Thenceforth the Athenian declaration becomes a leitmotiv in African-American moral argument.[63]

In 1794 Olaudah Equiano cited the text as he scolded whites for their superciliousness: "Let the polished and haughty European recollect, that his ancestors were once, like the Africans, uncivilized, and even barbarous. Did nature make them inferior to their sons? And should they too have been made slaves? Every rational mind answers, No. . . . If, when they look round the world, they feel exultation, let it be tempered with benevolence and gratitude to God, 'who hath made of one blood all nations of men.'"[64] In a speech before the House of Representatives, Henry Highland Garnet cited the passage from Acts as his proof text for the full humanity of African Americans. In William Welles Brown's antislavery novel *Clotel,* Reverend Peck's daughter Georgiana cites Acts 17:26 against denials of black humanity. Pauline Hopkins's late-nineteenth century sentimental novel of race, romance, and mystery, *Of One Blood,* takes as its title the signal phrase from Acts 17:26.

In the twentieth century, African-American intellectuals continued to impress the phrase into service. Martin Luther King, Jr., imitating the form as well as the content of Paul's epistles in his "Letter to American Christians," would echo Paul's Athenian declaration of the familial bond uniting all humanity in Acts 17:26 as an argument against racial discrimination. After she and three other women were brutally beaten by local lawmen and male prisoners in a Winona, Mississippi, jail, voting rights activist Fannie Lou Hamer had opportunity to speak to the wife of her jailer. The woman claimed that she was striving to live a Christian life, apparently seeking to distance herself from her husband's actions. In the course of the conversation Hamer reminded the woman that the principle of the equality of all people regardless of color was enshrined in the Bible. Hamer's proof text, which she urged the woman to read for herself, was the verse from the Apostle Paul's declaration on the Areopagus.[65]

The blood-and-soil formula of modern nationalism was also ill suited to African Americans because they had no territory for which they could make credible proprietary claims. As Glaude has pointed out, "because the moral underpinnings of African American political action—its relation to black Christianity—the aim was not so much to gain land as to guarantee blessings through righteousness."[66] For African Americans, the Exodus was not a national story. Their Christian reading of the story was an implicit rejection of nationalism, because people of African descent in North America did not succeed in laying an ancestral or otherwise proprietary claim to territory. Certainly at its most concrete, the quest for the way out, and thus for freedom, invariably meant movement to a new territory. But in the African-American exodus, a territory does not a nation make.

African Americans, as a people of mixed blood and lacking land, have made their collective claim to peoplehood on the basis of neither a common ancestry nor a common territory but a common history. Even in the traditions of ancient Israel, and perhaps in its earliest traditions, the Exodus was an event that gave rise to a collective identity that did not require ties of ancestry and territory. Both the Hebrew slaves in Egypt and the African slaves in America entered history with pretensions neither to ancestry nor to territory. The promise of the biblical myth of Exodus was that, having neither, God would grant them both.

CANAAN LAND

Exodus informed the movement and territoriality that characterized African-American efforts to realize their freedom under slavery and subsequently. They were a peculiar people in search of a land of their own. The Promised Land was the biblical name for the patrimony that God had promised the Israelites. It became for African-American slaves the biblical typology for freedom. In 1862, a slave preacher leading a group of fugitive slaves behind Union lines cautioned them that "there must be no looking back to Egypt."[67] The unknown bard who coined the Negro spiritual "I Wish I Had Died in Egypt Land" unabashedly sings of a death wish attending the terror of freedom.

> O, I can't stay away,
> I can't stay away,
> I can't stay away,
> I wish I had died in Egypt land.
>
> Children grumbled all the way,
> "Wish I had died in Egypt land."
> Children they forgot to pray
> "Wish I had died in Egypt land."
>
> Now they wept and now they moaned
> "Wish I had died in Egypt land."
> Then they turned around and groaned
> "Wish I had died in Egypt land."
>
> Yes, the children they did right,
> "Wish I had died in Egypt land."
> When they went and had that fight
> "Wish I had died in Egypt land."[68]

Fear, hunger, thirst, sporadic warfare, episodic mutinies, and the Israelites' grumbling backward glances to Egypt mark the march to Sinai. In the adversity that attended their newfound freedom, they sometimes looked longingly to their former bondage and complained bitterly that liberty in such a hostile wilderness would be the death of them.

The sorrows of Egypt are remembered using the past tense of history. But when the singers speak of their own experience, they resist the past tense. In "Go Down, Moses" the judgment against Pharaoh is rehearsed in direct discourse. In the mouth of Moses, the plague is still an unrealized threat:

> "Thus spoke the Lord,"
> Bold Moses said,
> "Let my people go,
> I'll smite your first-born dead."

In the Negro spiritual "Walk Together Children," the verbs of the Promised Land are in the future tense: "We'll enter there, oh, children, / Don't you get weary, / There's a great camp meeting in the Promised Land." The Negro spirituals are a musical cartography that marks out the territory of freedom in the African-American imagination. In these songs, the Promised Land is not a home. It is a hope.[69]

In his last speech, Martin Luther King, Jr., identifies with Moses as he stands at the threshold of the land of promise. At the end of the book of Deuteronomy, the Israelites gather on the plains of Moab on the eastern side of the Jordan River, where the aged Moses rehearses the history of Israel's troubled journey to freedom and bequeaths to each of the twelve tribes of Israel a patrimony. Ascending to the peak called Pisgah on Mount Nebo overlooking the Jordan River valley and the land of Canaan beyond, Moses dies after viewing the land that the children of Israel would soon come to conquer and inhabit. Martin Luther King, like John Winthrop 338 years earlier, concludes his discourse with a paraphrase of Moses's farewell instruction to Israel. Unlike Winthrop, however, King is chillingly faithful to the testamentary rhetoric of Moses's speech. The rhetoric only works if the speaker is a testator—someone who bequeaths blessings that will take effect only after his imminent death. This was not so for Winthrop but tragically so for Martin Luther King. And though King is Moses the testator who "may not get there," he speaks of the collective fulfillment of the promise: "We as a people shall get to the Promised Land."[70]

The great Jewish scholar Abraham Joshua Heschel, who introduced King to the 1963 annual meeting of the United Synagogue of America as a modern prophet, once commented, "The exodus began but is far from having been completed. In fact, it was easier for the children of Israel to cross the Red Sea than for a Negro to cross certain university campuses."[71]

King spoke in the future tense of the Negro spirituals because, in the third quarter of the twentieth century, he still shared their yearning for a Promised Land in sight but beyond reach.

African Americans have tended to conflate the biblical image of the Promised Land with the end-time images of the New Testament, where fulfillment of the promise remains in the future. Even the deliverance at the Red Sea is spoken of as a future event in the song "God's A-Gwinter Trouble de Water."

> Wade in the water, children,
> Wade in the water, children,
> Wade in the water, children,
> God's a-gwinter trouble de water.
>
> See that host all dressed in white,
> God's a-gwinter trouble de water.
> The leader looks like the Israelite,
> God's a-gwinter trouble de water.
>
> See that host all dressed in red,
> God's a-gwinter trouble de water.
> Looks like the band that Moses led,
> God's a-gwinter trouble de water.[72]

The phrase "trouble de water" in the refrain appears not in the Old Testament but in the New. The phrase echoes John 5:4 as it is rendered in the King James Version of the Bible. There Jesus restores a hapless cripple who is unable to make his way to the waters of a pool reputed to have healing powers: "For an angel went down at a certain season to trouble the water." God will "trouble the water" in an undisclosed time to come. The figure of the Exodus provides the language to speak of escape to a freedom yet to be fully realized. The trumpet sounds in the Negro spiritual "New Jerusalem" sung by the Gullahs, the former slaves and their descendants of the coastal and island communities of South Carolina.

> The tallest tree in Paradise
> The Christian calls the Tree of Life
> And I hope that trumpet blows me home
> To my New Jerusalem!

The Gullah sang this "shout song" in the streets of Charleston on New Year's Day, 1866, at the Emancipation Jubilee commemorating the abolition of slavery. Contemporary observer Elizabeth Botume explained, "These people are living their 'New Jerusalem.'" Botume interpreted the song as a celebration of freedom. "Even the poorest, and those most scantily clothed, looked as if they already 'walked the golden street,' and felt 'that starry crown' upon their uncovered heads. It was indeed a day of great rejoicing, and one long remembered."[73]

The Land of Promise might be beyond the South, beyond the sea, anywhere beyond the reach of slavery. For those who found freedom, fulfillment defined promise. Former slave Nan Stewart recalled after her escape to freedom,

> Colored preachers use to come to plantation and they would read the Bible to us. I remember one special passage preachers read and I never understood it until I cross the river at Buffinton Island. It was: "But they shall sit every man under his own vine and under his fig tree; and none shall make them afraid; for the mouth of the Lord of Hosts has spoken it." [Mic. 4:4] Then I knows it is the fulfillment of that promise; I would soon be under my own vine and fig tree and have no more fear of being sold down the river to a mean master.[74]

For slaves in flight and those contemplating it, Canaan was, by typological definition, the land of freedom yet to be attained. Frederick Douglass pointed out that any "keen observer might have detected in our repeated singing of 'O Canaan, sweet Canaan, / I am bound for the land of Canaan,' something more that a hope of reaching heaven. We meant to reach the *North*, and the North was our Canaan."[75] Some of the Negro spirituals, those that sang of leaving "Egypt land," traversing the wilderness, and seeking the Promised Land, in effect belonged to a secret genre of songs of escape.

For slaves who did not run away as Douglass did, this escape sometimes took liturgical form in the ring shout. The shouters mimicked in their circular dance the march of the fleeing Hebrew slaves of Exodus as they sang "Going over Jordan" or "Canaan's Happy Shore."[76] The Negro spiritual "If You See John the Writer," sung by slaves in All Saints Parish, South Carolina, bears a specific, thinly veiled geographical reference.

If you see John the writer, tell him you saw me!
Tell him you saw me!
If you see John the writer, tell him you saw me
When you saw me I was on my way!

I'm traveling up the King's Highway!
I'm traveling up the King's Highway!
I'm traveling up the King's Highway!
When you saw me I was on my way!

I was on my way to a heavenly land when you saw me!
When you saw me!
I was on my way to a heavenly land
When you saw me I was on my way!

The singers are on their way "to a heavenly land." Heavenly, but not heaven: the old King's Highway, used by George Washington when he visited South Carolina in 1790, runs north and south through All Saints Parish. The slaves knew the thoroughfare as the highway to the North and to freedom.[77] Harriet Tubman, who was fond of Negro spirituals and loved to sing, composed several Negro spirituals herself. She sang one of her original compositions in earshot of her puzzled master the night before she became a fugitive slave.

I'm sorry I'm going to leave you
Farewell, oh farewell;
But I'll meet you in the morning,
Farewell, oh farewell.

I'll meet you in the morning,
I'm bound for the Promised Land,
On the other side of Jordan
Bound for the Promised Land.

I'll meet you in the morning,
Safe in the Promised Land,
On the other side of Jordan,
Bound for the Promised Land.[78]

The next morning, Tubman had disappeared.

When Radical Reconstruction failed in the South after 1877 and native terrorism of the newly organized Ku Klux Klan became the scourge of black life in the Cotton Belt, African Americans began to leave the South in droves in search of a Promised Land out West. The abolitionist and women's rights advocate Sojourner Truth lobbied the U.S. government to set aside lands for black settlement in "the West." "I have prayed so long that my people would go to Kansas," she preached, "and that God would make straight a way before them. Yes, indeed, I think it is a good move for them. I believe as much in that move as I do in the moving of the children of Egypt going out of Canaan—just as much."[79]

At first glance Sojourner Truth appears to have scrambled the biblical narrative of the Exodus. It is the children of Israel, not the children of Egypt, who left Egypt, not Canaan. Canaan is the indigenous name of the Promised Land. Unwittingly or tongue-in-cheek, she has twisted the biblical type to fit the shape of African-American experience. African Americans are children of America, for which the slave regime of Egypt is the premier biblical type. They are slaves in a country that understands itself as the Promised Land, a New Canaan. It is precisely this New Canaan that African Americans seek to flee. They sought escape, in effect, from the American Canaan.

Physician, novelist, explorer, and ethnologist Martin Delany concluded that emigration was indispensable for the greater destiny of African Americans. "Our race is to be redeemed," he wrote in 1852 in *The Condition, Elevation, Emigration, and Destiny of the Colored People of the United States.* "It is a great and glorious work, and we are the instrumentalities by which it is to be done. But we must go away from our oppressors; it is never to be done by staying among them."[80] In *Blake,* Delany's novel of pan-African revolution, the protagonist Henry Blake argues with Daddy Joe, an elderly plantation slave. "If a thousand years with us is but a day with God," Henry protests, "do you think that I am required to wait all the time?" Delany here obliquely refers to Psalm 90:4, quoted in the New Testament in 2 Peter 3:8 and frequently offered as an apology for Christian quietism: "For a thousand years in thy [God's] sight are but as yesterday when it is past, and as a watch in the night." Daddy Joe rebuts Henry's heresy with yet another scripture, Moses's command to the Hebrews to "stand still and see the salvation of the Lord" (Exod. 14:13).

"Don't, Henry, don't! The word say 'stand still and see the salvation.'"

"That's no talk for me, Daddy Joe; I've been 'standing still' long enough—I'll 'stand still' no longer."

"Then you have no call to obey God word? Take care, boy, take care!"

"Yes, I have, and I intend to obey it, but that part was intended for the Jews, a people long since dead. I'll obey that intended for me."

"How you going to obey it?"

"'Now is the accepted time, today is the day of salvation.' So you see, Daddy Joe, this is very different to standing still."

"Ah boy, I's feared you's losing your religion."

"I tell you once and for all, Daddy Joe, that I'm not 'losing' but I have altogether lost my faith in the religion of my oppressors. As they are our religious teachers, my estimate of the thing they give is no greater than it is for those who give it."[81]

At the conclusion of his conversation with Daddy Joe and his wife, Mammy Judy, Henry reveals his intentions to run away.

"Once and for all, I now tell you old people what I never told you before, nor never expected to tell you under such circumstances; that I never intend to serve any white man again. I'll die first!"

"The Lord have mercy on my poor soul! And how come you not gone before?"

"Carrying out the principles and advice of you old people 'standing still, to see the salvation.' But with me, 'now is the excepted time, today is the day of salvation.'"

"Well, well, well!" sighed Mammy Judy.[82]

Blake breaks with the counsel of his elders, which echoes the words of Moses to the terrified Israelites at the Red Sea, "stand still, and see the salvation of the Lord" (Exod. 14:13). But as Blake insists, exodus is the antithesis of "standing still." Delany has Henry Blake argue in fiction what Delany himself argued in fact: that African-American religion was sometimes a formidable impediment to the very liberation it signified in

its own biblical images. Martin Delany regarded African peoples' pur-
ported proclivity for religion as a mixed blessing. Though "a constitu-
ent principle of their nature and an excellent trait of their character," he
complained, "they carry it [religion] too far. Their hope is largely developed, and consequently, they usually stand still—hope in God, and really
expect Him to do that for them, which it is necessary that should do for
themselves."[83]

Like Henry Blake, Martin Delany practiced what he preached. He and
several other African Americans in South Carolina founded the Liberian
Exodus Joint Stock Company in 1878 to establish a steamship line to
transport African-American settlers to Liberia. It made only one voyage
before going bankrupt. It was the first of several African-American emigration schemes over the next half century that aspired to a transatlantic
exodus via steamship.

For other African Americans, the exodus would be transcontinental.
After the January 1879 anniversary of the Emancipation Proclamation,
black masses left southern Louisiana for Kansas, "the land whence came
John Brown."[84] Benjamin "Pap" Singleton was recognized as a Moses who
called black people to migrate to Kansas by the thousands. Singleton saw
himself as a man on a mission to lead African Americans out of the South.
As he testified before Congress, "Pity for my race, sir, that was coming
down instead of going up—that caused me to go to work for them. . . .
Right emphatically, I tell you today, I woke up the millions right through
me! The great God of glory has worked in me. I have had open interviews
with the living spirit of God for my people, and we are going to leave the
South. . . . My plan is for them to leave the country and learn the South
a lesson."[85] Those who followed Singleton's vision of milk and honey in
the Midwest came to be called "Exodusters."

Freed slaves also migrated en masse to the newly opened and sparsely
populated territory of Oklahoma. Activist Edwin P. McCable and other
émigrés lobbied to have Oklahoma admitted to the union as a state ruled
by African Americans akin to the success the Mormons had achieved in
Utah. After the turn of the century, however, Oklahoma received statehood
under the aegis of white political control that violently enforced a new
version of apartheid in the new state.[86] Jim Crow had followed African
Americans to Oklahoma to destroy their utopian hopes in yet another
would-be Promised Land.

In the last quarter of the nineteenth century and the first of the twentieth, many African Americans had concluded that it was past time to go somewhere else if they were to see salvation. Though newly enfranchised freed persons elected African Americans to public office at all levels throughout the South just after the Civil War, as early as 1868 the white majority of the Georgia state legislature refused to seat duly elected African-American representatives. In 1883 the Supreme Court declared the Civil Rights Act of 1875 unconstitutional. Lynching and other forms of racist terrorism began to sweep the South and even parts of the North and West. No region of the United States would be safe for black people, and once again African-American intellectuals looked to the land of their ancestors in search of refuge.

Presbyterian clergyman and polymath Edward Blyden argued for an African exodus. Born in Saint Thomas, Virgin Islands, in 1832, Blyden came to the United States in 1850 to study theology after having lived in the West Indies and Venezuela. Following an abortive eight-month search for a theological seminary that would admit him, he moved to Liberia in 1851. There he completed his education and was ordained a Presbyterian minister in 1858. In addition to enjoying a distinguished career as a clergyman and professor of Arabic, Blyden served as Liberian ambassador to Great Britain, president of Liberia College, and editor of the *Liberia Herald,* which became the journalistic forum for his learned denunciations of slavery. In an essay entitled "The Call of Providence to the Descendants of Africa in America" (1862), Blyden called on African Americans to lend their resolve and resources to building an African homeland in Liberia.

> Liberia, with outstretched arms, earnestly invites all to come. We call them forth out of all nations; we bid them take up their all and leave the countries of their exile, as of old the Israelites went forth from Egypt, taking with them their trades and their treasures, their intelligence, their mastery of arts, their knowledge of the sciences, their practical wisdom, and everything that will render them useful in building up a nationality. We summon them from these States, from Canada, from the East and West-Indies, from South America, from every where, to come and take part with us in our great work.

Blyden took rhetorical aim at those who resisted and derided African repatriation. The imagery of exile—"we bid them . . . leave the countries of their exile"—gives way to the imagery of exodus—"as the old Israelites went forth from Egypt," as Blyden likens detractors to the Israelite spies who returned an "evil report" of the Promised Land.

> When Moses sent out spies to search the land of Canaan, every man, on his return, seemed to be influenced in his report by his peculiar temperament, previous habits of thought, by the degree of his physical courage, or by something peculiar in his point of observation. All agreed, indeed, that it was an exceedingly rich land, "flowing with milk and honey," for they carried with them on their return, a proof of its amazing fertility. But a part, and a larger part, too, saw only giants and walled towns, . . . It was only a small minority of that company that saw things in a more favorable light. . . . In like manner, there is a division among the colored people of this country [the United States] with regard to Africa, that land which the providence of God is bidding them go up and possess.

"I come today," insisted Blyden, "to defend the report of the minority."[87]

In an address to an African-American emigration convention in 1893, AME bishop Henry MacNeal Turner offered an unvarnished presentation of choices before African Americans in the face of violence and disenfranchisement. "To passively remain here and occupy our present ignoble status with the possibility of being shot, hung, or burnt," he insisted, " . . . would be to declare ourselves unfit to be free men. . . . For God hates the submission of cowardice." Making a stand through armed self-defense, however, was out of the question: "to talk about physical resistance is literally madness. . . . The idea of eight or ten million of ex-slaves contending with sixty million people of the most powerful race under heaven!"[88] Exodus would be the only viable alternative.

Early in the twentieth century the movement of Chief Alfred Sam would lead a transatlantic exodus in search of a West African Promised Land. In the same year "Pap" Singleton was leading an exodus to Kansas, Alfred Sam was born on the Gold Coast in 1879. Educated in missionary schools in Africa, Sam traveled to the United States in 1913 and arrived in Oklahoma preaching that the deliverance of black people was to be found only in Africa. He issued his appeal with the fervor of a revivalist preacher. As his biblical namesake, however, this Moses too was not an impressive public speaker. But in the person of an articulate young clergyman who soon joined the movement, however, Chief Sam found a ready, willing, and very able Aaron. The clergyman became the chief ideologue of the movement, effectively providing it with a compelling biblical theology.

Born in Guyana in 1857 of Yoruba parents recently converted to Christianity, he was christened William J. Davis and grew up in Sierra Leone. As a student in Freetown he came under the influence Edward Blyden. Blyden's pan-African philosophy and broad erudition had a profound impact on the young William, who forsook his "Christian" name for one he felt was truer to his West African origins: Orishatukeh Fadama. Fadama studied at the University of London, then immigrated to the United States to take a theology degree at Yale Divinity School. After drinking deep draughts of liberal theology at Yale, Fadama concluded his theological studies in 1895 and was ordained a Congregational minister. Having failed to find denominational support for missionary work in Africa, Fadama joined the American Missionary Society. As a member of the society he was at last able to realize his vocation as a missionary. But not in Africa: the society sent him to those he described as his "kith and kin"—African Americans in the Southern United States.

Fadama went to the South in the confidence that the light of theological liberalism—the "new Theology," as it was called—would illumine the darkness of the Jim Crow South and constrain its purveyors of "Saxon haughtiness" to acknowledge that "'God is no respecter of persons.'" But Fadama would quickly learn that the South already had its own deeply entrenched and venerable theology—white supremacy. He would later write, "In the United States Anglo-Saxon teaching on race ideals is that all race varieties other than his are inherently inferior and dependent . . . the best in the Negro is treated as filthy rags. In the southern states particularly, the idea is enforced by means of the *argumentum baculinum*—brute force—and all kinds of class legislation which the imagination can devise." Fadama complained, "There are millions of Negroes in the United States who are laboring under this oppression, but, like dumb dogs, cannot bark, because if they bark the result is more oppression, with considerable suppression." In 1913, Fadama joined the African-American exodus from the South to Oklahoma.[89]

The hope of Fadama and other black migrants was deferred once again with the installment of white rule in Oklahoma after the state became part of the Union in 1907. Fadama, who had argued for selective African-American emigration to Africa even in his first year in the United States, then became a follower of Chief Sam.[90] He supplied the impassioned rhetoric and biblical imagery that made the compelling case for people of African descent in the United States to reverse both their direction and their fortune by retracing the transatlantic voyage of their forebears.

Chief Sam sold shares of his transatlantic trading company to finance the purchase of a ship to take African Americans back to West Africa. By early 1914 he had raised enough money to buy a cruise ship he christened the SS *Liberia*. It was to be the first vessel in what Chief Sam dubbed the Ethiopian Steamship Line. That September, even as Europe prepared to plunge into the global barbarism of World War I, the *Liberia* left the United States en route to the Gold Coast with Chief Sam, Fadama, and sixty other immigrants. Fadama published articles in the West African press making the case for Chief Sam's movement: using the ship's wireless communication, he became the West African advance man in absentia for Chief Sam.

On both sides of the Atlantic the movement faced serious opposition. In the United States W. E. B. Du Bois was dismissive, and in Britain Duse Mohamed Ali, Sudanese editor of the *African Times and Orient Review*, was skeptical. But West African reportage became sympathetic and then favorable in the wake of interference from the most formidable opponents to the movement: the British Colonial and Foreign Office. The British had requested that the U.S. government take measures to prevent the immigrants from leaving port. Failing that, the world's mightiest maritime power dispatched the British cruiser *Victoria* to intercept the *Liberia* off the West African coast. The British seized and impounded the steamer and towed it to Freetown, Sierra Leone. The Royal Navy explained the high-handed action as a "war precaution." The British confiscated the ship's wireless on the pretext that it had been manufactured in Germany.

The people of Freetown warmly welcomed the African-American immigrants as "Brethren," "members of the same ancient Negro stock," and "fellow believers in Jesus; fellow followers and disciples of the World's Redeemer." Chief Sam was honored as "the Moses of the African movement," "raised up to help to bring back African Israel to their own home from the foreign land, which had been to them a land of bondage."[91]

British detention and harassment notwithstanding, the African Americans finally arrived at the Gold Coast. They were disappointed by their African brethren's low standard of living, and the Americans' financial resources, now diminished by British indemnities, were less than enough to make a good go of what they considered to be rude and backward conditions. Most of the other immigrants scraped together what little they had left and returned to the United States. Even Chief Sam was dispirited. Unlike his biblical namesake, this Moses was alive in the Promised Land. But his movement was quite dead. For Fadama, however, even death in Africa was better than life in America. He settled permanently in Sierra Leone to write an unrepentant postmortem of the African movement, by now discredited in everyone's eyes but his. The theologian was firm in his resolve. But after the Gold Coast government seized the *Liberia* for unpaid taxes in the summer of 1915, he was also alone.

Back in the United States, tens of thousands of African Americans were fleeing the Jim Crow South for Northern urban enclaves. This mass migration quickly became known as "exodus fever," and soon the greatest demographic shift in American history was being seen and explained in the imagery of Exodus. In the minds of many African Americans, boll weevil infestations, floods in the Mississippi Delta, and the slumping cotton market that marked the second decade of the twentieth century were not merely the features of Southern agricultural disaster: they were the recapitulation of the plagues of Egypt visited on the oppressive regime of sharecropping servitude in Dixie. African-American preachers in the South "warned their congregations not to fight the pest because it was sent by God and therefore had some sort of divine status." In early 1917 the Reverend C. M. Tanner of Allen Temple AME Church in Atlanta was busy gathering evidence for a book he proposed to call "The Second Exodus." "The scripture is being fulfilled every day in our very sight," Tanner asserted, "and it is certainly the intention of divine providence to make our people in this moment profit by it."[92] "Boll weevil here, boll weevil there, boll weevil everywhere; Oh, Lordy, ain't I glad!" a black worker on a Southern road project was overheard to sing in the early 1920s. The white auditor reported that there was "a note of genuine gladness, almost of exultation in the voice singing it, like the note one hears between the lines in the Old Testament song of the Jews triumphing over the downfall of their enemies. It seemed a song of emancipation."[93]

A RESEMBLANCE AND A CONTRAST

As important as the imagery of Exodus has been to signify African-American hopes for freedom, some African Americans have found the account of the suffering of the Hebrews inadequate to the task of expressing the barbarity of American slavery and its aftermath. In a series of incendiary essays entitled *An Appeal to the Colored Citizens of the World,* David Walker accused the American slave regime of being more brutal than that inflicted on the Children of Israel in the Bible.[94] Born in Wilmington, North Carolina, in 1785, Walker was the son of a fugitive slave father and a free mother. Inheriting his mother's free status, he attended school and traveled throughout the Atlantic states. In 1827 he made his home in Boston, where he married a fugitive slave a year later. In Boston Walker became a leading abolitionist in the black community. His anti-slavery speeches appeared in *Freedom's Journal,* the first African-American newspaper published in the United States.

In what were to be the last two years of his life Walker would become more strident in his opposition to slavery. The three editions of his *Appeal,* first published in 1829, became increasingly more militant. Walker insisted that the contemporary American master class excelled the ancient Egyptians in brutality. Walker declared, "We, (colored people in these United States of America) are the most wretched, degraded, and abject set of beings that ever lived since the world began, and [. . .] the white Americans having reduced us to the wretched state of slavery, treat us in that condition more cruel (they being an enlightened and Christian people) than any heathen nation did any whom it had reduced to our condition." Walker asserted "that slavery as it existed among the Romans, (which was the primary cause of their destruction) was, comparatively speaking, no more than a cipher, when compared with ours under the Americans." Worse than the injury of servitude was the added insult of the refusal of whites to recognize the slave as a human being. "Show me a page of history, either sacred or profane, in which a verse can be found, which maintains, that the Egyptians heaped the insupportable insult upon the children of Israel, by telling them that they were not of the human family. Can the whites deny this charge? Have they not, after having reduced us to the deplorable condition of slaves under their feet, held us up as descending originally from the tribes of Monkeys or Orang-Outangs? O! My God! I appeal to every man of feeling—is not this insupportable?" Modern slavery had achieved depths of depravity unknown in former times. Even the God of the Exodus had never faced oppression like this before.[95]

In a speech he delivered in 1843 at the National Negro Convention in Buffalo, New York, Henry Highland Garnet rejected the Exodus figure as an appropriate one for African Americans. In "An Address to the Slaves of the United States," Garnet insisted that it was "impossible" for blacks to make "a grand exodus from the land of bondage" as the children of Israel had done. The country some African Americans sought to flee was the country of their nativity. "Forget not that you are native-born American citizens," he demanded, "and as such, you are justly entitled to all the rights that are granted to the freest." Nor was there another land that they could expect to receive them. "The Pharaohs are on both sides of the blood-red waters! You cannot move en masse, to the dominions of the British Queen—nor can you pass through Florida and overrun Texas, and at last find peace in Mexico. The propagators of American slavery are spending their blood and treasure, that they may plant the black flag in the heart of Mexico and riot in the halls of the Montezumas."[96]

As late as 1842, Garnet disavowed arms as a solution to the problem of American slavery: "I cannot harbor the thought for a moment," he opined, "that [the slave's] deliverance will be brought about by violence." But by 1843 his thinking had changed. The Supreme Court's decision in 1842 in *Prigg v. Pennsylvania* to uphold the Fugitive Slave Law of 1793 and the expulsion the same year of the abolitionist U.S. congressman Joshua Giddings of Ohio called for more than arguments. Garnet appealed instead to the revolutionary resistance of people of African descent: "Denmark Veazie," who was "a martyr to freedom"; the "patriotic Nathaniel Turner," whom "future generations will remember . . . among the noble and brave"; and the mutinies led by Joseph Cinque on the *Amistad* and Madison Washington on the *Creole*. Garnet resolved that violence was the only appropriate response to American slavery. Neither Denmark Vesey nor Nat Turner enlisted arguments of what Frederick Douglass called "moral suasion" as the weapons of their warfare. Nor did Henry Highland Garnet, passionately invoking their names, look forward to a peaceful dissolution of the slave regime. Slavery would fall by the sword. Two decades later the Civil War would vindicate Garnet's conviction.[97]

Writing after Emancipation, Francis Grimké argued that the "resemblance" between the ancient Israelites and African Americans might be pressed only so far. Scripture, in the light of the contemporary situation of African Americans, suggests "a contrast" as well as "a resemblance." Grimké asserted that some features of American slavery and its legacy were more irrational and inhumane than that of the ancient Egyptians. The children of Israel went down into Egypt voluntarily, whereas the African slaves were kidnapped and brought to American shores. Pharaoh resisted the departure of the Israelites. Yet, Grimké surmises, "While I do not apprehend that there will ever be any general movement to get rid of us . . . I do not believe that there would be any regrets or tears shed on the part of the whites if such a thing should occur." The legacy of American slavery kept African Americans captive both on the shore of the Red Sea and on the bank of the Jordan River. Freedom after Emancipation had devolved to a new form of bondage. Grimké lamented that even after the Emancipation Proclamation and the victory of the Grand Union Army, black people in the United States "still drag the chain." Canaan remained a land that the freed slaves could not enter.[98]

Others argued that African Americans had yet to find their own Moses or that he had yet to find them. They lacked, as African-American Baptist clergyman Nathaniel Paul put it in 1827, "the wise legislator to Israel."[99] Frances Harper put the matter poignantly. Though there are "millions of our race in the prison house of slavery, but we have yet a single Moses in freedom. And if we had, who among us would be led by him?" Toward the end of the nineteenth century, Henry MacNeal Turner despaired that there was no Moses in his day to lead African Americans back to Africa and out of the hopeless situation in the land of their birth. He wrote in the *AME Recorder* on January 25, 1883, "Now all I contend is this, that we must raise a symbol somewhere." "We are bitten," he continued, echoing the biblical story in which the children of Israel were attacked by snakes in the wilderness and magically relieved by a bronze serpent held aloft by Moses. "We are poisoned, we are sick and we are dying. We need a remedy. Oh for some Moses to lift up the brazen serpent, some goal for our ambition, some object to induce us to look up."[100]

Other African-American leaders tired of looking for the coming of one like unto Moses. W. E. B. Du Bois observed with some approval in 1917 that the exodus that was being called the Great Migration in effect had no Moses. "It is interesting to note that this migration is apparently a mass movement and not a movement of the leaders," he opined. "The leaders of the race are powerless to prevent [the Negro's] going. They had nothing to do with it, and, indeed, all of them, for obvious reasons, are opposed to the exodus. The movement started without any head from the masses, and such movements are always significant."[101]

A generation later, activist Nannie Helen Burroughs reminded her Depression era audiences that the land of promise is not so much given as taken. She demanded that African Americans must not wait for messianic leadership: standing now at the frontier of the Promised Land, their entry would be an exercise of collective will. Addressing an overflow crowd in 1933 at the Bethel AME Church in Washington, D.C., Burroughs entitled her remarks "What Must the Negro Do to Be Saved?" Arguing that black folks had politically outgrown the Exodus paradigm of divine deliverance, Burroughs's biblical point of departure is not Moses at the Red Sea but Joshua on the banks of the Jordan.

> Don't wait for deliverers. . . . I like that quotation, "Moses my servant is dead. Therefore, arise and go over Jordan." There are no deliverers. They are all dead. We must arise and go over Jordan. We can take the Promised Land.
>
> The Negro must serve notice on the world that he is ready to die for justice. To struggle and battle and overcome and absolutely defeat every force designed against us is the only way to achieve. Men must have life, the opportunity to learn, to labor, to love. Without these fundamental virtues we cannot achieve. We must not give up the struggle until this is obtained.

Burroughs chided the African-American political leaders of her day for their quiescence, commanding her audience to "Chloroform your 'Uncle Toms.' . . . I don't care whether they are in the church as the preacher, in the school as the teacher, in the ward as politicians." Burroughs contrasts diffident African Americans with "the Anglo-Saxon" who will "wade through blood for love of liberty, home, women, and life." She stops just short of insisting that to win these spoils African Americans must be willing to do the same. "We're a race ready for crusade," she insisted, "for we've recognized that we're a race on this continent that can work out its own salvation."[102]

Arna Bontemps, literary luminary of the Harlem Renaissance, dramatized the Denmark Vesey revolt in his historical novel *Black Thunder* (1936). Bontemps gives a fictional account of the biblical interpretation that put the slaves on the road to righteous revolution. During a secret meeting of the co-conspirators, the freed artisan Mingo reads to them aloud from the Bible.

> "There, there," he said abruptly, "Hold on a minute, Mingo. Read that once mo'."
>
> Mingo looked over his square spectacles. A cataracted left eye blinked. He smiled, turned the page back and repeated.
>
> "He that stealeth a man and selleth him, or if he be found in his hand, he shall surely be put to death. . . ."
>
> "That's the Scripture," Gabriel said. "That's the good Book what Mingo's reading out of."
>
> The Negroes murmured audibly, but they made no words. Mingo fluttered a few more pages.
>
> "Thou shalt neither vex a stranger nor oppress him; for ye were strangers in the land of Egypt. . . . Thou shalt not oppress a stranger. . . ." "Therefore thus saith the Lord: Ye have not harkened unto me, in proclaiming liberty, every one to his brother, and every one to his neighbor: behold, I proclaim a liberty for you, saith the Lord, to the sword—"
>
> "Listen!" Gabriel said.
>
> "—to the pestilence, and to the famine; and I will make you to be removed into all the kingdoms of the earth."

Mingo leafs through passage after passage from the Bible that indicts common practices of the slave regime: Mosaic legislation making kidnapping a capital offense in Exodus 21:16 and prohibitions against the exploitation of resident aliens in Exodus 22:21, 23:9, and Leviticus 19:33. All were the weightier matters of the law that the nominally Christian slave regime had left undone. Because of these injustices the master class had been condemned "to the sword, to the pestilence, and to the famine . . . into the hand of them that seek their life." This biblically mandated sentence was to be executed by the rebel slaves.[103]

But the biblical paradigm of Exodus turns out to be an ambiguous figure in Bontemps's novel. Gabriel's companion Juba rides through the night in the thunderstorm on the plantation master's favorite horse as a signal to the waiting slaves to commence the revolt. She braves the lightning, wind, and rain; the insurrectionists, however, regard the storm as a bad omen and refuse their summons to battle. True to the historical account, the combination of a torrential thunderstorm and the treachery of turncoat slaves foil the revolt. After the collapse of the conspiracy, Juba returns to the plantation, where she meets a group of slave women talking about the aborted revolt. One of the older women, "wrinkled and witch-like," points to the Bible as the reason for Gabriel's failure. "A man, do he 'spect to win, is obliged to fight the way he know. That's what's ailing Gabriel and them. He obliged to go at it with something he can manage. . . . Too much listening to Mingo read a white man's book . . . They ain't paid attention to the signs . . . Gabriel done forgot to take something to protect hisself. The stars wasn't right. See? All the rain. They ain't paid attention to the signs." The story of Exodus, the inspiration of Gabriel and his would-be revolutionary comrades, was at the same time the strength and the weakness of the revolt. Juba implores the old woman to make a hoodoo amulet to keep Gabriel safe as he flees the manhunt for the dispersed insurrectionists. The woman does so but in giving it to Juba casts doubt on its effectiveness: "He ought to come hisself," she complains, "that's the most surest way. He should of come a long time ago, did he have any sense."[104]

"YOU SHALL NOT CROSS INTO IT"

African Americans could not commemorate the escape from Egypt and into the Promised Land as a historical event. And they would look forward to one, in the words that the book of Deuteronomy puts in the mouth of Moses to speak of his own successor, who would be "one like unto Moses." Here Deuteronomy acknowledges that Moses must be superseded, and henceforth he becomes a figure of Israel's future as well as Israel's past. The Moses that leads the people to freedom is the Moses of the future who, as the preacher of Dunbar's faux-sermon puts it, "Comes an' sets us chillun free." The following are the last three of twenty-four verses attributed to the Negro spiritual "Go Down, Moses" as it appeared in the National Anti-Slavery Standard in December 1861.

We need not always weep and mourn,
O let my people go!
And wear these slavery chains forlorn,
O let my people go!

This world's a wilderness of woe,
O let my people go!
O let us on to Canaan go,
O let my people go!

What a beautiful morning that will be!
O let my people go!
When time breaks up in eternity,
O let my people go![105]

American slaves and their descendants would not look back to Exodus. They would look forward to it.

In later Israelite prophecy, the Exodus came to be viewed as but a means to a divine end that would transcend it. The prophet Isaiah hearkened back to God's election of Israel at the Exodus along with God's election of Zion as his holy mountain and David as his holy king. Yet Isaiah speaks of God's gracious choices in the past only to speak of the grace that the prophet anticipates in an age to come: in "that day," the holy city of Jerusalem will be delivered (17:12–14) and a descendent of King David installed on the throne (7:1–7). In a later generation, a brilliant poet prophesying in Isaiah's name looks back to the Exodus of the past only to look forward to the Exodus of the future.

Thus says the Lord,
who makes a way in the sea,
a path in the mighty waters,
who brings out chariot and horse,
army and warrior;
they lie down, they cannot rise,
they are extinguished, quenched like a wick:
Do not remember the former things,
or consider the things of old.
I am about to do a new thing;
now it springs forth, do you not perceive it?

I will make a way in the wilderness
and rivers in the desert. (Isa. 43:16–19)

This prophet of the Babylonian exile sees the Exodus as being reenacted in the present. The Exodus would be "a new thing," as Second Isaiah puts it: not a heritage but a hope.

In 1915 and after so many failed exoduses, Orishatukeh Fadama wrote of the leaders of Exodus as exemplary failures. Inspired leaders of Exodus were destined to fail, because the project of Exodus would always be bigger than any one great leader and any one great movement.

> Moses was dominated by a great idea, the emancipation of Israel. Had he been living in our modern twentieth century with its overpowering materialism, had he been a subject of Great Britain, he would be in prison, considered a stupid maniac. . . . He died without a realization of his cherished idea, a failure. But Providence used Joshua to carry out to a successful end what the leader failed to effect. The idea of Moses was carried out in piece meals. Most of the ideas of the World's thinkers are carried out the same way. In many cases they are mere projectors and injectors of ideas to be worked out by future generations.[106]

Fadama argues in effect that failure inheres in the project of Exodus. Success was beyond the reach of Moses just as the Promised Land was beyond the Plains of Moab. In this way, the story of Exodus is perversely fulfilled by remaining unfulfilled.

Orishatukeh Fadama, the African who had sojourned in America, had finally returned to his ancestral land: though not a land of promise, a land more promising—at least for him—than the United States. But African Americans, unable to find their Canaan in the land of their enslaved forebears, were less sanguine. David Walker, Henry Highland Garnet, Henry MacNeal Turner, Nannie Helen Burroughs, Francis Grimké, and even Martin Luther King, Jr., had argued variously that the biblical story of Exodus had not been fulfilled. Neither any African-American Moses nor the children of slavery that Moses led had ever found, let alone entered, the Promised Land.

At least, not yet.

CHAPTER SIX

Ethiopia

This, then, is the end of his striving: to be a co-worker in the kingdom of culture, to escape both death and isolation, to husband and
use his best powers and his latent genius. These powers of body
and mind have in the past been strangely wasted, dispersed, or forgotten. The shadow of a mighty Negro past flits through the tale
of Ethiopia the shadowy and of Egypt the Sphinx.

—W. E. B. Du Bois, "Of Our Spiritual Strivings"

PSALM 68:31, "Princes shall come out of Egypt; Ethiopia shall soon
stretch out her hands unto God," is the most widely quoted verses of the
Bible in African-American letters.[1] Psalm 68 is an oracle celebrating the
centrality of the Jerusalem temple in which the psalmist predicts, "Because of thy temple at Jerusalem shall kings bring presents unto thee"
(Ps. 68:29). The song may have been sung in antiquity during the Judean
pilgrimage to the Temple Mount. By the lights of its African-American
interpreters, however, the text did not point back to Zion. It was an oracle
pointed forward to Ethiopia.

Jeremiah, the prophet whose very biography in the Bible is the hinge
on which Israel turned from covenant to catastrophe, declares that one
day the turning of Israel's captivity would render obsolete the credo of
the Exodus. "Therefore, behold, the days come, saith the Lord, that they
shall no more say, The Lord liveth, which brought up the children of Israel out of the land of Egypt; But, the Lord liveth, which brought up and
which led the seed of the house of Israel out of the north country, and
from all countries whither I had driven them; and they shall dwell in their
own land" (Jer. 23:7–8). The prophecy of Psalm 68:31 looked forward to
the redemption of African people. All those who were scattered would
one day be gathered, that divine grace would be revealed in a manner

even exceeding the miraculous favor of the Exodus. The hope hung on a slender thread of scripture; it was neither a coherent vision like Ezekiel's valley of dry bones nor a fulsome narrative like the story of the Exodus. But this single verse of scripture became a text that nevertheless came to overshadow and supplant its biblical context.

Ethiopia, the biblical name of a venerable African nation, came to be shorthand for the biblical prophecy promising the exaltation of all African peoples. As a part of Africa that stands for the whole, Ethiopia took its place in African-American racial consciousness at the center of a biblical cartography of hope. African Americans took from the Bible the nomenclature of Ethiopia to speak of the magnificent future reversal of their collective fortune.

TAKING A TEXT

Europeans had been using the term *Ethiopian* to refer to African peoples since the ninth century BCE, when Homer applied it to the glorious, dark-skinned people at the southern edge of the world. European geographers came to refer to the peoples south of Egypt collectively as Ethiopians, and medieval Europeans looked to Africa for deliverance from the threat of Islam in the legend of Prester John, powerful king of an unconquerable Christian kingdom in Ethiopia that flanked the Islamic regimes of North Africa.[2]

In the English language, the word *Ethiopia* and its cognates epitomized everything dark or black. Shakespeare's Romeo says of Juliet, "It seems she hangs upon the cheek of night / As a rich jewel in an Ethiop's ear." In the New World, however, the term took on new meaning. There, images of Africa were freighted with the connotation of slavery. Three centuries after Shakespeare, Walt Whitman, writing of a "dusky woman, so ancient, hardly human," is referring to an aged African-American slave in his poem "Ethiopia Saluting the Colors." "Ethiops" continued to be synonymous with the adjectives "black" and "Negro" as a common way of referring to African slaves.[3] To provide theological direction for the conversion of slaves, in 1627 Jesuit Alonso de Sandoval published *De instauranda Aethiopum Salute: El mundo de la esclavitud negra en America* (On securing the salvation of the Ethiopian: the world of black slavery in America). Sandoval argued that because the slaves served their temporal needs, Spanish masters ought to see to the eternal salvation of their slaves. Proper religious instruction would insure the slaves a place in the world to come and show slaves that their proper vocation was obedience to their masters.

At the beginning of the eighteenth century, Puritan divine Cotton Mather made similar arguments for the religious instruction of African slaves in North America. In 1706 Mather charged New England slave-holders to instruct their slaves in the ways of Christianity, and to that end wrote the catechetical pamphlet *The Negro Christianized: An Essay to Excite and Assist the Good Work, the Instruction of Negro Servants in Christianity.* Appearing on the pamphlet cover were two quotations from scripture: one, Joshua 24:15, "As for me and my house, we will serve the Lord," the other, Psalm 68:31.[4]

Mather published his pamphlet after more than a decade of pastoral experience with "Ethiopians." Thirteen years earlier he published *Rules for the Society of Negroes* as a devotional constitution of sorts for a slave prayer meeting. In Mather's manuscript diary for October 1693, he describes how he came to write the *Rules.*

> Besides the other praying and pious meetings, which I have been continually serving, in our Neighborhood, a little after this Period, a company of poor Negroes, of their own Accord, addressed mee, for my Countenance to a Design which they had, of erecting such a Meeting for the Welfare of their miser-able Nation, that were Servants among us. I allowed their design and went one Evening and prayed and preached [on Ps. 68, 31], with them: and gave them the following orders, which I insert duly for the curiosity of the occasion.[5]

Itinerant Evangelical preachers were convinced that they were seeing the Ethiopian oracle fulfilled in the throngs of slaves who attended to their sermons in the British colonies of North America. Traveling through Han-over County, Virginia, the white Presbyterian evangelist Samuel Davies saw the enthusiastic response of African Americans at Evangelical revivals as the fulfillment of Psalm 68:31. Biblical prophecy was being fulfilled: "Ethiopia has . . . stretched forth her Hands unto God," Davies exulted. "There is a great number of Negroes in these Parts; and sometimes I see a 100 and more among my hearers."[6]

Although African slaves and their descendants early on learned to regard Africa with contempt and shame, they found in biblical preaching another, altogether different and altogether glorious image of their ancestral land. The Bible knew of mighty African peoples: it makes abundant references to Ethiopia, or "Cush," as the Authorized Version, following the transliterated Hebrew, renders it. Their blackness, their cultural and military superiority, and their potential for piety round out the biblical profile of ancient Africans. The Egyptians had not only enslaved the ancient Israelites but continued to be a source of worry as well as wonder for the precarious Israelite monarchy. The prophet Jeremiah mentions Ethiopia's mighty warriors (Jer. 46:7), and the Ethiopian king Tirhakah had attacked Israel's fearsome northern enemy, Assyria (2 Kings 19:9). Isaiah predicts that the Israelite exiles will be ransomed out of captivity with the enormous wealth of the African kingdoms of Egypt, Sheba, and Ethiopia (Isa. 43:3). And along with ancient Greek and Latin historians the Bible testified to the political, economic, and military might of ancient Ethiopia.

People of African descent in the United States referred to themselves and were referred to by others as Ethiopians and saw Ethiopia as the symbol for all people of African descent everywhere in the world. From the middle of the eighteenth century until the second quarter of the twentieth, African Americans and other people of African descent in the Anglophone New World summoned the Ethiopian oracle of Psalm 68:31 as the biblical slogan of African redemption.[7] African slave and precocious New England poet Phillis Wheatley looked forward to Africa's conversion to Christianity as the sole and sure hope of African peoples. In a letter to Boston pastor Samuel Hopkins she wrote, "Europe and America have long been fed with the heavenly provision, and I fear they loathe it, while Africa is perishing with a spiritual Famine. . . . Their minds are unprejudiced against the truth, therefore 'tis hoped that they would receive it with their whole heart. I hope that which the divine royal Psalmist says by inspiration is now on the point of being accomplished, namely Ethiopia shall soon stretch forth her hands unto God."[8] And among those Ethiopians she counted herself. In 1778 slave poet Jupiter Hammond dedicated a book of poetry to Phillis Wheatley, whom he described in the title as an "Ethiopian Poetess, in Boston, who came from Africa at eight years of age and became acquainted with the gospel of Jesus Christ."[9] Later in a sermon of 1783 Hammond refers to himself as "an unlearned Ethiopian."[10]

African Americans were especially inclined to refer to themselves as Ethiopians when soliciting a white audience. Phillis Wheatley penned a versified warning to the wayward students at the University of Cambridge in New England, later known as Harvard: "Let sin, that baneful evil to the soul / By you be shunn'd, nor once remit your guard / . . . An Ethiop tells you 'tis your greatest foe."[11] In 1788 Olaudah Equiano, kidnapped from his home in the kingdom of Benin and brought to the New World as a slave, submitted a petition to the British crown to abolish slavery and signed it using his adopted Dutch name, "Gustavus Vassa, the Oppressed Ethiopian." In a published address thanking Dr. Benjamin Rush and other white friends in Philadelphia, founder of the African Methodist Episcopal Church Richard Allen sought God "to add to your number until the princes shall come forth from Egypt and Ethiopia shall stretch forth her hands unto God."[12]

Prince Hall, founder of the African Masonic Lodge, traced the Ethiopian presence in the Bible in his public denunciations of slavery and of racial discrimination against free African Americans in Boston. In an address to his fellow Masons in 1797, Hall reminded them that Moses had learned the arts of governance from his father-in-law the Midianite Jethro, "an Ethiopian." King Solomon had graciously received the Ethiopian queen of Sheba into his court, and in the New Testament Philip the Evangelist had readily baptized the Ethiopian eunuch. Prince Hall's summary of the African presence in both Testaments was the common heritage of Christendom on both sides of the Atlantic.

Clearly, Prince Hall and other African Americans did not fashion the biblical image of Ethiopia out of the whole cloth of collective imagination; they tailored the images under the influence of European notions of Africa. Europeans had called Africans Ethiopians for centuries before the slave trade, and it was from Europeans that Africans in the New World learned that the prophecy of Psalm 68:31 applied to them. But African Americans interpreted the prophecy in ways that made them more than bit players and stage props in the divine drama of human history. The Ethiopian oracle was a prophecy that African people would be emancipated, and their emancipation would in turn herald the salvation of the world. In the minds of some African Americans, however, it also suggested that they would become emancipators. Prince Hall said of the revolution in Haiti, "Thus doth Ethiopia begin to stretch forth her hand from a sink of slavery, to freedom and equality."[13] In the slave revolt that gave birth to a new, free, black nation, Hall saw biblical prophecy being fulfilled.

In 1829 New York abolitionist Robert Alexander Young published *The Ethiopian Manifesto,* an apocalyptic essay in which he foretold the coming of a black messiah. "Ethiopians throughout the world in general, receive this as but a lesson presented to you from an instructive Book. . . . As came John the Baptist, of old, to spread abroad the forthcoming of his master, so alike are intended these our words, to denote to the black African or Ethiopian people, that God has prepared for them a leader."[14] Boston abolitionist David Walker's *Appeal* appeared in the same year, claiming that the God of the Bible, the God of justice, is "the God of the Ethiopians." He warned that the day was drawing near "when we [people of African descent] shall be enabled . . . to stretch forth our hands to the LORD OUR GOD." Walker declared, "The Blacks of Africa . . . have never been half so avaricious, deceitful, and unmerciful as the whites." As a consequence Walker was convinced "that if ever the world becomes Christianized (which must certainly take place before long) it will be through the means under God of the Blacks."[15]

"The besetting sins of the Anglo-Saxon race," complained Henry Highland Garnet, "are the love of gain and the love of power."[16] Even some Americans of European descent agreed. Swedenborgians, followers of the eighteenth-century Swedish philosopher and mystic Emmanuel Swedenborg, saw the decline of European churches as proof that Europeans were incapable of meeting the spiritual and moral requirements of the New Jerusalem. Africans, by contrast, were, according to the prevalent racial stereotype, naturally gentler, meeker, and more pious than the violent, acquisitive Europeans. Swedenborg believed in a historical sequence of "true churches." A new, more virtuous church somewhere else in the world would soon supersede the European church. Swedenborgians interpreted Psalm 68 as a prophecy that the Kingdom of God would be realized in the redemption of Africa.

By the beginning of the nineteenth century there were Swedenborgian churches in the United States, and the New Jerusalem Church movement held its first American convention in Philadelphia in 1817. A millenarian orientation coupled with emergent racial ethnology that posited inherent, permanent differences among Europeans, Africans, and indigenous peoples, informed a backhanded doctrine of African racial superiority. It was widely influential among many abolitionists, well beyond Sweden-borgian circles; it is Harriet Beecher Stowe's millennial view of African peoples in *Uncle Tom's Cabin*. The congeries of missionaries, coloniza-tionists, and abolitionists that ascribed to this hope of African exaltation in effect met anti-African racism with a millenarian, pro-African racism of their own.[17]

African-American self-identification reflected the old and new knowl-edge of Ethiopia as it crossed the Atlantic in print and anecdote. Samuel Johnson had translated the Ethiopian travelogue of a Portuguese Jesuit priest, *A Voyage to Abyssinia*, in 1735, early in his literary career, and John-son's comic satire *Rasselas, Prince of Abyssinia*, appeared in 1759. And British explorer James Bruce, one of the first Europeans to lay eyes on the source of the Blue Nile, published the popular account of his journey to Ethiopia's Lake Tana, *Travels to Discover the Sources of the Nile*, in 1790. Both are English masterworks in their respective genres, and they added luster to the romance of Ethiopia while also adding more precision to general knowledge about Ethiopia with the benefit of eyewitness accounts.

In 1809, shortly after the publication of both works, black Baptists in New York City, inspired by the example of the African Methodist Episcopal Church and disgusted with racial discrimination in their own, left their white coreligionists to found the Abyssinian Baptist Church. The church was destined to become one of the largest Protestant congregations in the world and pulpit of Adam Clayton Powell, Jr. Abyssinia was the name of the ancient Christian kingdom of the nation of Ethiopia. These African-American Baptists identified themselves specifically with Abyssinia—that is, with the ancient Christian legacy of Ethiopia.

African-American intellectuals touted the achievements of ancient African peoples that they called by their biblical names. Their great achieve-ments in the past gave the lie to the claim of African inferiority. Biblical Ethiopia, "Cush," and biblical Egypt, "Misraim," stand in the same ge-nealogical line in Genesis 10 and in the oracle of Psalm 68:31. People of African descent could claim with scriptural proof not one but two ancient African peoples who appear to be different branches of the same great, black family tree. In the nineteenth century, whites and blacks agreed on a plain-sense reading of the Table of Nations that suggested that Egypt and Ethiopia shared not only rulers, borders, and rivers but also the same bloodline. New developments in American science, however, would challenge that agreement. The American school of anthropology of Samuel G. Morton, Josiah C. Nott, and Harvard University's Louis Agassiz argued that black peoples did not found the Nile Valley civilizations. The Egyptians were dark-skinned Caucasians, and it was they who imparted their superior civilization to their Ethiopian and other African neighbors. Nonwhite peoples of the world had separate origins; the Bible, therefore, applied only to whites.[18] Speaking in 1847 before the Literary Society of Charleston, South Carolina, Agassiz said that he "believed in an *indefinite* number of original and distinctly created races of men," and that there are superior and inferior races due to multiple origins. The idea that people as different as Chinese, Africans, and Europeans had developed from a common pair in just a few thousand years, he concluded, was preposterous. Agassiz suggested in an issue of Unitarianism's *Christian Examiner* in 1850 that Adam and Eve were the progenitors of the white race exclusively.[19]

African Americans responded with a vigorous attack on the new, scientific racism. By the second quarter of the nineteenth century, histories valorizing African antiquity were becoming a genre. Among the more influential were the work of Robert Benjamin Lewis, *Light and Truth* (1836), in which he argues that many heroes of the Bible are in fact Africans; Hosea Easton, *A Treatise on the Intellectual Character and the Civil and Political Conditions of the Colored People in the United States* (1837); and James Pennington, *A Textbook on the History and Origins of the Colored People* (1841). African-American intellectuals were quick to translate the knowledge of these learned treatments from the printed page to the public square. In an address to Western Reserve College in 1853, Frederick Douglass argued that Negroes were builders of ancient Egypt and Ethiopia.[20] His arguments were primarily historical, anthropological, and ethnographic—a response to the scientific turn in contemporary anti-African racism. Douglass asserted that ancient, distant African ancestors had founded Egyptian and Ethiopian civilizations that "flourished . . . at a time when all Europe floundered in the depths of ignorance and barbarism."[21] Novelist, historian, and ex-slave William Wells Brown noted that, the opinions of the American school notwithstanding, the received wisdom of historians and ethnologists remained that the Ethiopians were black people and that their genius was responsible for the Egyptian pyramids and the great cultural achievements of Mediterranean Africa.

The basis of all these arguments was still the biblical witness to African peoples. On this point there was only hair's breadth of rhetorical distance between history and prophecy. In an address of 1848, Henry Highland Garnet reminded his audience that sacred and secular history bore witness to the glory of ancient Ethiopia. More important than the glorious past, however, was the glorious future: "Ethiopia is one of the few nations whose destiny is spoken of in prophecy. This is done in language so plain that we are not driven to dubious inferences. It is said that 'Princes shall come out of Egypt, and Ethiopia shall soon stretch out her hands unto God.' It is thought by some that this divine declaration was fulfilled when Philip baptized the converted eunuch of the household of Candes, the Queen of the Ethiopians. In the transaction, a part of the prophecy may have been fulfilled, and only a part."[22] In early 1850s Frances Harper set the plain language of prophecy to verse in her poem "Ethiopia."

> Yes! Ethiopia yet shall stretch
> Her bleeding hand abroad;
> Her cry of agony shall reach
> The burning throne of God.
>
> The tyrant's yoke from off her neck,
> Her fetters from her soul,
> The mighty hand of God shall break,
> And spurn the base control.
>
> Redeemed from dust and freed from chains,
> Her sons shall lift their eyes;
> From cloud-capped hills and verdant plains
> Shall shouts of triumph rise.
>
> Upon her dark, despairing brow,
> Shall play a smile of peace;
> For God shall bend unto her woe,
> And bid her sorrows cease.
>
> 'Neath sheltering vines and stately palms
> Shall laughing children play,

And aged sires with joyous psalms
Shall gladden every day.

Secure by night, and blest by day,
Shall pass her happy hours;
Nor human tigers hunt for prey
Within her peaceful bowers.

Then, Ethiopia! stretch, oh! stretch
Thy bleeding hands abroad;
Thy cry of agony shall reach
And find redress from God.[23]

BACK TO AFRICA

From colonial times, however, some African Americans concluded that
Ethiopia would not find redress in America: Africans in America would
return to Africa to see the fulfillment of God's beatific promises. The free-
born African-American preacher John Marrant was a passionate advocate
of African emigration following the American War of Independence. A
loyalist mariner during the Revolution, Marrant traversed the Atlantic and
arrived in Halifax in 1785 as a missionary of the Huntingdonian Connection, an Evangelical Calvinist sect that had separated from the Church of
England in 1783. When the American victory in the War of Independence
became imminent, most of the black loyalists, ex-slaves who had freed
themselves by joining the British, were returned to their former owners
or sold to West Indian plantations. About three thousand, however, sailed
for Nova Scotia in British ships. Landless, poor, and exploited by white
Nova Scotians, they hungrily heeded Marrant's message that emigration
to Africa and the restoration of a pure, covenantal black community there
were elements of God's providential design. Marrant argued that African
Americans' only hope was to return to West Africa to establish a free black
commonwealth there.[24]

Word of Marrant's Nova Scotia sermons led Prince Hall, founder of
the African-American order of Masons in the United States and vocal
proponent of African emigration, to invite Marrant to Boston to preach to
the African Masonic Lodge in 1789. In Boston among "Africans," Marrant
preached that the Garden of Eden might have been in "African Ethiopia."

He told the black Masons, "I could show also that one grand end or design of masonry is to build up the temple that Adam destroyed in Paradise." Africans nevertheless had survived humanity's fall and remained masters of "architecture, arts and sciences." Marrant believed that for African Americans to rise above their servile status in North America and attain "the level . . . with the greatest kings on the earth," they must "study the holy book of God," the Bible.[25] In it they would find the blueprint for their salvation. Marrant preached that the Masons of the African Lodge were to emulate Nehemiah, the Jewish functionary under Persian imperial rule who rebuilt the ruins of Jerusalem after the end of the Babylonian captivity. Marrant died in England in 1792, and his entire congregation, led by his chosen successor, Cato Perkins, and William Ash, a Prince Hall Mason, immigrated to Sierra Leone later that year.

African Americans who favored African emigration saw it as a device to fulfill the Ethiopian oracle. They claimed that the African-American presence would proffer to the benighted African natives the Christianity and civilization that they so sorely needed to stand with—and against—Europeans in the modern world. In 1816 wealthy African-American shipping magnate Paul Cuffee underwrote the repatriation of thirty-eight free African Americans in the West African colony of Sierra Leone, which the British had established in 1787 as a haven for freed African slaves. Cuffee traveled to West Africa in 1812 to explore sites for African-American settlement there. Before returning to the United States he visited Sierra Leone. He found the repatriated African settlers afraid that they would be overcome by the "heathenism" of their environment. Cuffee encouraged them that they could expect divine assistance in their sufferings and that ultimately, as a consequence of their work in Africa, Ethiopia "would stretch out her hand unto God."[26]

In the same year Paul Cuffee financed the emigration to Sierra Leone, a group of whites of varying sentiments founded the American Colonization Society; some members were abolitionists, others advocates of slavery. All agreed, however, that slavery afforded free blacks no acceptable modus vivendi in the United States. Emulating Sierra Leone, the ACS founded the colony of Liberia in 1822. Black Baptist missionary Lott Carey emigrated to Africa in 1820 and joined African-American settlers in Liberia. Of his work in the capital city, Monrovia, he wrote to friends in Virginia in 1826, "You may look through [these circumstances] to the time foretold in prophecy; i.e., Ethiopia shall stretch out here hands unto God."[27] Well after the colony declared its independence in 1847, the society continued to send African Americans there: by 1893 the ACS had repatriated more than sixteen thousand African Americans in Liberia.[28]

But African emigration looked very different from different sides of the color line. Thomas Jefferson once proposed to solve the problem of slavery by separating infants from their slave mothers and sending them to Santo Domingo (Haiti) as part of a phased plan to remove people of African descent from the United States. Later, after the outbreak of the Civil War, Abraham Lincoln considered the purchase of an island in the Caribbean for the forced emigration of African Americans. The import of African slaves and the export of African freed persons assured the viability of American slavery: the American system of color caste associated dark skin with bondage, and free blacks were living anomalies of the system. Emigration obviated the challenge of a multiracial American society and allowed whites to sidestep the claim of reparations to slaves who had forcibly invested their blood, sweat, and tears in building the nation. American slavery had deprived Africans of their freedom: now American slavery sought to deprive free African Americans of their citizenship by repatriating them—by force, if necessary—in Africa. African American opponents of the ACS—most prominent among them AME founder Richard Allen, founders Samuel Cornish and John Russworm of the antiemigrationist *Freedom's Journal*, and the *Journal*'s star editorialist, Frederick Douglass—suspected that the society's real objective was the forced emigration of free blacks to break the back of black abolitionism.

And there were other reasons for African American ambivalence about Liberia apart from the mixed motives of the ACS. Liberia was founded in what, for Alexander Crummell, grandson of a West African kidnapped and enslaved in North America, was the "seat of ancient despotism and bloody superstition." Born in 1819, Crummell grew up in New York, a close friend of Henry Highland Garnet and other member's of the city's African-American elite. He was ordained in the Episcopal Church, where he experienced so much racial discrimination that when he was offered a fellowship in England during a fundraising trip he readily accepted it and took a degree in theology there in 1853. The Episcopal Church in America then commissioned him to serve as a missionary to Liberia, where he served for twenty years before returning the United States. Crummell was a major influence on the pan-African thought of the young W. E. B. Du Bois, who late wrote of first meeting Crummell at a commencement at Wilberforce University, "Instinctively I bowed before this man, as one bows before the prophets of the world."[29]

In an essay entitled "The Progress of Civilization along the West Coast of Africa," Crummell wrote, "So far as Western Africa is concerned, there is no history. The long, long centuries of human existence, there, give us no intelligent disclosures. 'Darkness covered the land, and gross darkness the people.'" In a remarkable analysis of historical geography, Crummell explains why.

> Where peoples and nations have been so situated that they could be touched by influence and power, there men have gone upward and onward. . . . But so far as contact with the elements of civilization is concerned, so far as the possibility of being touched by the mental and moral influences of superior and elevating forces is implied, Africa might as well have been an island as a continent. The Desert of Sahara has served as effectually to cut off Africa from the ancient civilizations, as the ocean, for long centuries, separated the Sandwich Islands from the world's enlightenment. Here is the solvement of Africa's benightedness. Physical causes have divorced her from the world's cultivation and improvement. A great ocean of sand has shut her off from that law of both national and individual growth, namely, that culture and enlightenment have to be brought to all new peoples, and made indigenous among them.[30]

But in his time, Crummell saw Providence remedying the disabling legacy of Africa's isolation. The Negro had been "placed in juxtaposition with the Caucasian . . . that he might seize upon civilization . . . that he might develop those singular and vital forces, both of the living spirit and the hardy frame, in which I claim the Negro is unrivalled."

> The system of slavery, in the lands of the black man's thrall-dom, has been a system of greed, and overwork, and lust, and premature decay, and death, with but slight and incidental alle-viations. And yet there have been alleviations. God never allows

any evils on earth to be entirely aggregations of evil, without
their incidents of good. So here, in this matter, God has raised
up, even in their lands of servitude, a class of black men who
have already gone from America, from the British West Indies,
and from Sierra Leone; the pioneers of civilization and Christianity, to the land of their fathers. Thus God overrules the wrath
of man. Thus from blasting, deadly evil, is He ever educing
good. Thus does He pluck the sting of malignant intent out of
the disastrous histories of men; and transform those histories
into benignant providence.

With historic irony, God was using the Evangelical and philanthropic ener-
gies of the British and their North American cousins to undo the damage
they had done to West African peoples through the slave trade. "The whole
of Negroland seems, without doubt, to be given up to the English language," Crummell observed, "and hence to the influence of Anglo-Saxon
life and civilization. It is a most singular providence that the very people,
who have most largely participated in the slave-trade, should have been
brought, by the power of God's dealings . . . to bear the weighty burden of
lifting up this large section of humanity to manhood, and of illuminating
them with Christian light and knowledge."[31]

For all his confidence, Crummell was sensitive to the grave moral
problem that his analysis suggests, aware of "how wickedly, how blasphe-
mously, all this story has been used to justify the wrongs of the Negro, and
to fasten it all upon the will of God." To the question of theodicy Crummell
offers a biblical nonanswer.

But when Joseph told his brethren—"it was not you that sent
me hither, but God," he did not mean that they had not acted
brutally toward him; but only that, in all the dark deeds of men,
there is a higher, mightier, more masterful hand than theirs,
although unseen;—distracting their evil counsels, and direct-
ing them to goodly issues. God, although not the author of
sin, is, nevertheless, the omnipotent and gracious disposer
of it.

Through the transatlantic slave trade, God has used the crooked stick
of slavery to hit the straight lick of Negro uplift. Crummell concludes

his essay with "words of inspiration" that "come from God Himself": "'Ethiopia'—from the Atlantic Ocean to the Indian—from the Mediterranean to the Cape, 'shall soon stretch forth her hands unto God!'"[32]

The Ethiopianist pretension to divine mission accounts for Alexander Crummell's complex attitude toward Africa and Africans, at once committed, concerned, and condescending. Speaking in 1870 of the indigenous Africans as a "vast population of degraded subjects," Crummell had argued, "our [African Americans'] position and our circumstances make us the guardians, the protectors, and the teachers of our heathen tribes." At the same time, Crummell was also painfully aware that if the United States was a beacon of Christian civilization, African Americans made of themselves a fun-house mirror of its reflective glare. In their many years in Liberia, Crummell, himself a dark-skinned African American, had witnessed the catastrophe of color politics there. African-American and West Indian immigrants came to Liberia and formed two bitterly opposed parties—one black, the other mulatto. Early on in Liberian history the brown party imposed its rule on the black.

Edward Blyden, another dark-complexioned man of African descent, shared Crummell's distaste for the arrogance with which those of mixed heritage lorded over their darker-skinned brethren, especially the indigenous Liberians. Indeed, Blyden despised the mulatto regime of Liberia and came to insist that racial homogeneity was indispensable for the prosperity of any nation. Each race, he asserted, must follow its own peculiar development and destiny. Because of Liberia's racial politics, Blyden shared Crummell's deep distrust of immigrants of mixed ancestry and became an outspoken advocate of "pure races"; he saw the Liberian elite as pompous mulattos who emulated the worst of their white fathers. In his involvement with the American Colonization Society, Blyden sought to keep African Americans of mixed ancestry out of Liberia and claimed that only "pure Negroes" were suitable emigrants.

Yet Blyden's vision for Africa and Africans was far grander than anything encompassed in mere grades of color and caste. In one sweeping, oracular statement Blyden brought together a prophetic interpretation of the genealogies of Genesis, the fiery trials of exile, the advent of the Messiah, the global proclamation of the gospel, and the eschatological fulfillment of Ethiopia.

The all-conquering descendants of Japheth have gone to every
clime, and have planted themselves on almost every shore.
By means fair and unfair, they have spread themselves, have
grown wealthy and powerful. The have been truly "enlarged."
God has "dwelt in the tents of Shem," for so some understand
the passage. The Messiah—God manifest in the flesh—was of
the tribe of Judah. He was born and dwelt in the tents of Shem.
The promise to Ethiopia, or Ham, is like that to Shem, of a
spiritual kind. It refers not to foreign conquests, not to widespread domination, but to the possession of spiritual qualities,
to the elevation of the soul heavenward, to spiritual aspirations
and divine communications. "Ethiopia shall stretch forth her
hands to God." Blessed, glorious promise! . . . Let us go forth
stretching out hands to God, and if it be as hot as Nebuchadnezzar's furnace, there will be one in the midst like unto the
Son of God, counteracting its deleterious influences.[33]

Modern Christendom saw in the three sons of Noah the forebears of
modern races. Each is accorded a historical dispensation of dominion,
and each has a specific historical project the fulfillment of which was
ultimately a part of the divine plan for the redemption of all humanity. In
Blyden's interpretive schema the descendents of Shem and Japheth had
already taken their respective places on the stage of the ages. It remained
then for "Ethiopia, or Ham" to fulfill his vocation with divine assistance
in the present age.

Blyden lobbied among African Americans to rise to their racial vocation as emigrants to Liberia. After the outbreak of the Civil War, Blyden
sought to persuade African Americans to leave the United States for Liberia. In response to the widely held theory that tropical climate eroded
masculine vigor and moral rigor, he argued that African Americans already had in their cherished possession the all-powerful antidote to carnal
torpor—the Bible.

It was not Anglo-Saxon blood, nor a temperate climate, that
kept the first emigrants to this land from falling into the same
indolence and inefficiency which have overtaken the European
settlers in South America, but the Anglo-Saxon Bible—the
principles contained in that book, are the great conservative

and elevating power. Man is the same, and the human mind is the same, whether beneath African suns or Arctic frosts. I can conceive of no difference. It is the moral influences brought to bear upon the man that make the difference in his progress.[34]

So important was the Bible to Blyden's agenda of racial uplift that, in an open letter to Booker T. Washington published in the African-American newspaper the *New York Age,* Blyden called for "a new translation of the Bible adapted to the needs of the Negro." African Americans needed "a race of scholars able to deal with the whole question of original texts—to criticize with insight and accuracy the translation of others."[35]

In another essay on the meaning and means of African evangelization Blyden reads the figure of the Ethiopian eunuch in Acts 8:26–38 as a symbol of African self-determination in the light of the gospel. Already, from the twilight of New Testament times, Luke the Evangelist had understood the baptism of the Ethiopian eunuch of Acts 8:26–38 as the sign of the fulfillment of the programmatic proclamation of the gospel. The gospel of Jesus Christ was to be preached first in Jerusalem, then in Judea, Samaria, and finally to the farthest regions of the earth. Ethiopia, at the southern extreme of the habitable world, was the farthest reach of civilization for the ancient Greeks and Romans. Luke's report of the eunuch's conversion is the Holy Spirit's decisive signal that the new dispensation had reached the uttermost parts of the earth. African Americans would see the fulfillment of this prophecy in their own time in the evangelization of people of African descent both in the New World and the Old. The story of the Ethiopian, argued Blyden, shows "the instruments and the methods of Africa's evangelization. The method, the simple holding up of Jesus Christ; the instrument, the African himself."[36]

African Americans in the United States again turned to Africa as the place where they would work out the biblical synthesis of utopia and colonialism that would be their salvation. After 1858 Henry Highland Garnet's aspirations for emigration focused on Africa when he became president of the African Civilization Society, founded in 1859 to promote African-American emigration to Africa. "It is evident," stated the preamble to the society's constitution, "that the prophecy, 'Ethiopia shall soon stretch out her hands unto God' is on the point of fulfillment, and that the work, when commenced, shall be 'soon' accomplished, when compared with the apparently slow progress of the Gospel in other grand divisions of the globe."[37] Garnet embodied the complexity of the emigration question for African Americans. In the 1840s he had advocated that African Americans launch an armed attack on the slave regime in the United States and its expansion abroad in the Western Hemisphere. Yet he declared, "America is my home, my country, and I have no other." He was convinced that it was "too late to separate the black and white people of the New World" and that "this western world is destined to be filled with a mixed race."[38] Along with a number of other African-American intellectuals of his day, he favored limited emigration to other places in the Americas. The greater accessibility of Canada and the West Indies, word of poor living conditions in Liberia, and suspicions about the American Colonization Society made Africa unattractive to many African Americans.

Among the founding members of the African Civilization Society was Martin Delany. In 1850, the same year the Fugitive Slave Act defended the right of slaveowners to cross the Mason-Dixon Line to recapture escaped slaves, Delany was dismissed from Harvard Medical School when fellow students complained about having an African American in their class. Unable to find an American medical school that would accept him, Delany left for Scotland and took his degree in medicine at Edinburgh. Delany would become a physician, activist, essayist, novelist, ethnographer, and one of most distinguished intellectuals of his day. And a passionate Ethiopianist: he named his only daughter Ethiopia Halle Amelia. Delany wrote a serialized novel, *Blake,* in which the protagonist, Henry Blake, is an eloquent escaped slave and pan-Africanist patriot. Blake raises a clandestine, revolutionary vanguard of slaves and freed persons to foil Southern expansionists who want to make Cuba a Caribbean extension of the slave regime in the United States. In Cuba Blake comes upon a slave family in the city of Matanzas whose experience is emblematic of the pan-African scope of the novel. "This family proved to be a choice one . . . of a superior order, . . . native African, having learned English on the coast, French Creole at New Orleans, and Spanish at Cuba. . . . Their African name was Oba, the Cuban, Grande."[39]

In chapter 61 of the novel, Blake convenes a grand council of co-conspirators in Cuba. Among the attendees are "several fine looking mulatto officers . . . There were still others of the fairest complexion among the quadroons, who were classed as white, that faithfully adhered to the

interest of the African race, and were ready at any moment to join them."
Delany notes, "The term 'African race' includes the mixed as well as the
pure bloods." Among those in attendance is Blake's Cuban confidant,
Placido. The character's namesake is the famous Afro-Cuban poet executed for leading a revolution against Havana's Spanish imperial government in 1844. At the conclusion of the secret meeting, Placido reads "the
dismissing prayer prepared especially for the occasion."

> Oh Great Jehovah, God of Love!
> Thou monarch of the earth and sky,
> Canst thou from thy great throne above
> Look down with an unpitying eye!
> See Africa's sons and daughters toil,
> Day after day, year after year,
> Upon this blood bemoistened soil,
> And to their cries turn a deaf ear?
> Canst thou the white oppressor bless,
> With verdant hills and fruitful plains,
> Regardless of the slave's distress—
> Unmindful of the blackman's chains?
> How long, O Lord! Ere thou wilt speak
> In thy thundering voice,
> To bid the oppressor's fetters break,
> And Ethiopia's sons rejoice?
> . . . .
> Hasten, Oh Lord! The glorious time
> When everywhere beneath the skies,
> From every land and every clime
> Peons to liberty shall rise!
> When the bright sun of Liberty
> Shall shine o'er each despotic land;
> And all mankind from bondage free,
> Adore the wonders of thy hand.[40]

In this one prayer, Delany summarizes the Ethiopianist plot and politics
of his novel.

Earlier in his emigrationist thinking Delany had concurred with
Henry Highland Garnet that African Americans should seek a haven

elsewhere in the Americas. "God has . . . designed this great portion of the New World for us, the colored race," he asserted, "and as certain as we stubborn our hearts, and stiffen our necks against it, his protecting arm and sustaining care will be withdrawn from us." But later, along with Garnet and his other colleagues in the African Civilization Society, Delany trained his sights on Africa. In 1859 Delany led an expedition to the Niger Valley in search of promising cites for African-American colonization. In the "Official Report" of the expedition, Delany clearly stated his aspirations: "Our policy must be . . . Africa for the African race and black men to rule them."[41]

In 1877, after the demise of Radical Reconstruction, Delany, AME missionary Simon F. Flegler, and several other African Americans formed the Liberian Exodus Joint Stock Steamship Company. One year later the stockholders had raised enough money to purchase a steamship, the *Azor*—the "African Mayflower," Delany called it—to transport emigrant families to West Africa. The African-American colony failed shortly thereafter due to lack of funds, and eventually the investors were forced to sell the *Azor*.[42]

Between the end of Reconstruction and World War I, that moment of racial repression that historian Rayford Logan would call the Nadir Period, renewed interest in Africa and Africans was reflected in new works of African-American historiography that built on the antebellum intellectual tradition of combining biblical and secular sources in representations of African antiquity. Here too Martin Delany, ever the Renaissance man, made an important contribution, *The Origin of Races and Color* (1879). George Washington Williams quoted the Ethiopian oracle in opening of his two-volume history of African Americans, published in 1883. Scientific training and ethnographic experience informed the work of Delany and Williams: in most African-American historiography of the period, however, the biblical witness continued to be central. The titles of several signal works—J. E. Hayne, *The Negro in Sacred History; or, Ham and His Immediate Descendants* (1887), Harvey Johnson, *The Hamite* (1889), W. Forrest Cozart, *The Chosen People* (1924), and Joshua A. Brockett, *Zipporah: The Maid of Midian* (1926)—suggest as much.

African-American churches made even greater theological and material investments in Africa. The African Methodist Episcopal Church's widely circulating *AME Christian Recorder*, the nation's oldest continuously published African-American newspaper, carried Psalm 68:31 on the masthead. The *AME Review* declared in 1883, "Never will Africa's sons [in the United States] be honored until Africa herself sits among the civilized powers."[43] Even the secular African-American press claimed biblical warrant for immigration to Africa. Journalist John E. Bruce cited the Ethiopian prophecy in a Philadelphia speech supporting African emigration. And at the International Conference on Africa of 1895, sponsored by Gammon Theological Seminary in Atlanta, Georgia, T. Thomas Fortune, editor of the Harlem newspaper the *New York Age,* cited the Ethiopian prophecy in his invocation.[44] Between 1877 and 1900, African-American churches sponsored at least seventy-six missionaries in Africa, and African-American theologians thickened their descriptions of Ethiopianism in the light of their missionary projects.[45]

Episcopal priest James Theodore Holly is emblematic of the nineteenth-century African-American clergy whose personal pan-African experience informed an Ethiopianist vision. Born a Catholic in 1829 in Washington, D.C., Holly left Catholicism in 1851 to become a member of St. Matthew's Episcopal Church in Detroit, Michigan, where he had become editor of the abolitionist *Voice of the Fugitive.* Ordained a deacon in 1855, he became rector of Saint Luke's Episcopal Church in New Haven, Connecticut, and a year later was ordained an elder and traveled to Haiti as an Episcopal missionary.

Holly undertook the trip because he championed the cause of African-American immigration to Haiti; his firsthand experiences there further affirmed his aspirations. In 1861 Holly immigrated to Haiti with one hundred African Americans and there founded the Holy Trinity Episcopal Church. He was able four years later to persuade the Episcopal Church to support Holy Trinity financially and in 1874 to recognize the church as part of its "communion." At the time of Holly's death in 1911, the church had grown to two thousand members. Though several immigrants succumbed to disease and many became dispirited and ultimately returned to the United States, Holly remained in Haiti and soon became a Haitian citizen. He later worked as consul to Liberia and was ultimately consecrated as a missionary bishop, the first African-American bishop in the Episcopal Church.

In "The Divine Plan of Human Redemption in Its Ethnological Development," Holly propounds a racial philosophy of history based on "many self-evident postulates which will be readily accepted by all Christians, who acknowledge the Holy Scriptures of the Old and New Testaments as the divinely revealed rule of faith and practice." The "Ethnological development" of God's plan for the redemption of humanity is signified in the serial dispensations of each of Noah's three sons, "among whom were to be chosen the instruments for the accomplishment of God's designs toward the whole human race."

> Now in regard to the primal election of Shem to carry on God's purposes, it is a fact that Abraham, the father of the faithful and the friend of God, was a descendant of Shem. . . . Thus the purposes of God in Redemption were Semitic in their development during the whole of the Hebrew Dispensation, beginning with the elect vocation of Abraham, nineteen centuries before Christ, embracing the Divine Legation of Moses four centuries later on, and ending with the destruction of the Jewish Temple by Titus, the son of Vespasian in year 70 of the Christian era."

This dispensation of Shem was succeeded by that of Japheth, characterized by the spread of the Christian gospel. Japheth's dominion is coeval with the ascendancy of the "all those forms of denominations, Greek, Roman, Teutonic, or Anglican" that attend European hegemony in the world. This dispensation, too, has exhausted its fulfillment.

> Now, the Japhethic character of the Christian Dispensation is confined to its apostolic or evangelical phase. But the sons of Japheth no more than the sons of Shem can attain unto the perfect things without their Hamitic brethren. . . . Hence, after the nearly nineteen centuries of Gospel effort the Japhetic nations have not yet been able to realize among their most enlightened Christian nations the second clause of the Angel's song sung at the birth of Christ, viz: "Peace on earth, good will towards men."

It is the very nations of Christian Europe that are "the most warlike and predatory nations of this nineteenth century of the grace of Jesus Christ." Ultimately the European nations shall be annihilated in a climactic international battle and "the millennial phase of the Christian Dispensation" will be attended by the descendants of Ham.

Who, then, will be the elect among the nations for the carrying
out the designs of Almighty God during the last temporary
phase of Christianity, after the warlike Japhetic nations shall
be overthrown in the battle of Armageddon?

The inspired psalmist gives us the answer, in part at least,
to this question when he says, as translated in prayer-book
version of the Church of England: "When He hath scattered
the people that delight in war, then shall the princes come out
of Egypt; the Morians' land (Ethiopia) shall soon stretch out
her hands unto God" (Psalm 68:30, 31). Here we have the distinct mention of two of the sons of Ham, about whom Noah
guarded a significant silence while blessing Shem and Japheth
and in cursing Canaan. Scholars who can consult the Hebrew
text of this prediction know that the word rendered Egypt in
this Psalm is the name Mizraim, the second son of Ham, and
that the word translated Ethiopia, or land of the Moors, is the
name Cush, the eldest son of the same African patriarch. The
time, therefore, for the elect descendants of Ham to enter fully
into the active development of the final designs of God toward
the human race in the plan of Redemption will be at the
close of the present apostolic phase of the Gospel dispensation, when God shall scatter the Japhetic Christian nations
or peoples "that delight in war," in the coming battle of
Armageddon.[46]

Of the African peoples, Ethiopia is singled out for the special honor
of personal service to God. Holly deduces this from the absence of Ethiopians in another oracle that he interprets as a prediction of the Hamitic
dispensation, Isaiah 19:24–25: "In that day shall Israel be the third with
Egypt and with Assyria, even a blessing in the midst of the land, whom the
Lord of hosts shall bless, saying: Blessed be Egypt, my people, and Assyria,
the work of my hands, and Israel, mine inheritance." As Holly explains,
"Isaiah only names the three nations that will be engaged in active service
in traveling on the business of the Great King in going up and down the
highway of the nations. This would not seem to be the occupation of the
Ethiopians . . . for it is said of the Ethiopians that they shall stretch out
their hands directly unto God. That is, as I understand it, they shall serve

His Presence and around His Person, and shall not be sent on distant service." The honor of being God's personal attendants goes to the Hamitic peoples, reasons Holly, because "a son of Ham, Simon the Cyrenian, bore the cross of our Lord to the place of crucifixion. . . . When, therefore, our Savior shall be crowned and seated upon His throne of Glory, He will doubtless remember in a peculiar manner the race whose son carried His cross for Him, and choose from that race the crowned nobles who shall minister around His Person in His Royal Palace."[47]

Writing in the last quarter of the nineteenth century, African Methodist Episcopal American clergyman James Handy argued that the wickedness of modern Christendom is the chief impediment to evangelization of the world's non-Christian majority. In the fullness of times European and American Christians will be destroyed to make way for global Christianity.

> Will Africa receive the present Christian church, warped and twisted, mixed and adulterous as it is? Humanly speaking her millions turn from it, nevertheless there is a leaven in the midst that will yet permeate her millions. In the fullness of time, appointed by unerring wisdom, Mizraimites and Cushites from the center to circumference of Africa, shall unite in one Christian faith and fellowship, led on by Jesus Christ, the captain of one common salvation with her Egyptian princes in the van and her millions following.[48]

Thus Psalm 68:31 is "a passage grand in its conception, grand in its phraseology and grand in its promises." African crowned heads—"princes, her petty Kings"—shall be "ministers at the altar of God." They shall lead in worship a vast multitude "from her Atlas mountains, from her jungles, plateaus and her table lands, her Nile, Congo, Zambezi and Limpopo, her beautiful lakes, cataracts and falls, her coast and harbors, from the whole continent." "The moment," insists Handy, "is on the wing."[49]

ABYSSINIA

In 1896 the U.S. Supreme Court legally enshrined American apartheid in its decision of *Plessy v. Ferguson*. The decision was the rigor mortis of racial segregation that set in after the death of Radical Reconstruction and the rise of the unreconstructed South. Some African Americans looked

for a survival strategy in the United States and found it in the accommo-
dationist philosophy of Booker T. Washington. Others looked to Africa,
and there they found hope abroad at the very moment they had lost their
case for justice at home.

In March 1896 African Americans learned that the Ethiopians under
Emperor Menilek II had defeated an invading Italian army in the Abyssinian highlands of Adwa. It was the first time in modern history that
Africans had routed a European army in battle. The African victory put
the nation of Ethiopia on the screen of African-American political and cultural consciousness. Editor H. G. Smith of the *Cleveland Gazette* called the
Ethiopian victory an "Italian Waterloo" and wagged his finger at American
imperialists at home. "One lesson which the American people can learn
from the present crisis," he wrote, "is that the colonization and annexa-
tion fever is not only a source of danger but a menace to the stability of
home government."[50] An editorial in the *Savannah Tribune* charged, "This
overbearing spirit exercised by European nations over African nations
should be stopped."[51] The Ethiopians, for their part, saw their struggle as
a national one and were aloof to appeals to pan-African solidarity. When,
several years after the victory at Adwa, the Society for the Uplift of Negroes
approached Menilek II to become its honorary president, His Imperial
Majesty politely replied, "Yours is an excellent idea; the Negro should be
uplifted, but I am not a Negro."[52] African Americans, of course, saw the
king and his kingdom not as the modern African nation of Ethiopia but
as the reflection of a pan-African image in which they had come to see
themselves.

At the same time, events were transpiring farther south on the continent that would implicate Africans and African Americans together in
what promised to be another fulfillment of the Ethiopian oracle. In the
Transvaal of South Africa, the Ethiopian Church, an indigenous, independent church of black South Africans, voted to seek formal affiliation with
the African Methodist Episcopal Church in the United States. This union
was the fruit of seeds serendipitously sown six years earlier. Ethiopians
began stretching their hands to God by extending them to one another,
to the accompaniment of that most African music of North America, the
Negro spirituals.[53]

The United Church of Christ established Fisk University in Nashville, Tennessee, shortly after the end of the Civil War to provide higher

education for newly freed persons. An a cappella choir, the Fisk Jubilee Singers, was founded on the campus to sing Negro spirituals and other African-American folk songs. The songs—"Ethiopian airs," as some called them—were arranged and performed with the solemnity that emulated the gravity of sacred and classical music performances of highbrow European culture. The Fisk formula of staid public presentation appealed both to whites who were accustomed to the norms of concert performance and to blacks who were starved for affirmation of the cultural accomplishments of their people. The Fisk Jubilee Singers were a sensation and took their show on the road to raise funds for their financially struggling alma mater. Orpheus McAdoo organized the Virginia Jubilee Singers using the Fisk formula of presentation, with the hope of emulating their results. The choir went on tour in 1890, headed for South Africa.

The Virginia Jubilee Singers found an especially appreciative audience there among the Cape Coloreds and mission-educated Anglophone Africans. The Virginia Jubilee Singers did in soulful song what the Africans themselves yearned to do in the stifling air of South African racism: they put authentically black culture in the reputable Western dress of European art music. The Christian African elite of the Cape immediately sought to imitate the cultural coup of their African-American visitors. Shortly after the South African tour, South African Christians began to stage musical and dramatic shows featuring a decorous synthesis of European, traditional African, and now African-American musical forms. One of these creations was the African Jubilee Choir: its repertoire was half traditional African songs performed in native language and dress and half English songs in modern European dress.

A white South African businessman agreed to finance the choir's tour to England. The singers performed before Queen Victoria and Parliament but then ran out of money and struggled to return home. After reassembling, the choir launched a second tour; this time the United States was on the itinerary. After traveling as far as Cleveland, Ohio, the singers again went broke. This time they were stranded. Six of the singers were taken in by the African Methodist Episcopal Church, which gave them scholarships to the denomination's Wilberforce University. There they trained to be African missionaries for the AME Church.

In 1895, one of the stranded South Africans, Charlotte Manye, wrote to her sister in Johannesburg of her fate and of the largesse of the AME

Church. Charlotte's sister shared the letter with a close friend of the family, the Reverend Mangena Makone. Makone, ordained in the Methodist mission in the Transvaal, had fought racial discrimination in the Methodist Church of South Africa. He resigned from the Methodist clergy in 1892 and founded the denominationally independent Ethiopian Church the following year. Makone's aspirations were thoroughly pan-Africanist. He proposed that the young church send missionaries throughout Africa and establish relations with the Ethiopian Orthodox Church.

Charlotte Manye's sister intuited, quite rightly, that Makone would find of some interest a letter attesting to the existence of an independent African-American church then already a century old that could boast of its own university and a history of African missions. Makone immediately wrote to AME bishop Henry MacNeal Turner. Makone's was one of two letters the bishop received from South Africa in 1895. The other letter, however, sold Turner on AME intervention in South Africa. John Tule, a Tembu migrant worker in Cape Town, wrote to Turner's journal, *The Voice of Missions,* pleading that the AME Church send missionaries to South Africa: "Our people at home in the Transkei are in a bad state," Tule wrote, "needing two principal modes of life . . . Christianity and civilization." Neither the government nor the white missionaries colluding with it served the interests of black South Africans. "Send us ministers," he implored: "You are born of God. . . . Don't put your talents in safes . . . use them . . . to purchase the freedom of your brothers in South Africa, or in the whole of Africa."[54]

Both Tule and Makone anxiously awaited the South African advent of the AME Church. Makone, however, was not content to wait for the AME Church to come to the South Africans. The South Africans would come to the AME Church. In 1896, Makone sent the Reverend James Dwane to the United States as an envoy from the Ethiopian Church to negotiate with the AME hierarchy. The AME bishops met with Dwane, agreed to make the Ethiopian Church a part of the AME connection, and made arrangements for Turner to visit South Africa.

On his arrival in South Africa in 1898, Turner the pan-Africanist firebrand waxed the churchman and the politician. He consecrated Dwane as "vicar bishop" of the AME Church's new South African member of the Connection, and ordained fifty-nine African ministers. Turner downplayed his anti-racist radicalism in the presence of South African whites. He was granted an audience with President Paul Kruger of the Transvaal and favorably impressed the Afrikaner leader: the meeting was, according to Kruger, the first time he had ever shaken hands with a black man. No doubt Kruger saw in the AME presence a counterweight to British missionaries in South Africa, who were partisans of British imperialism and so worked against Afrikaner political interests. Before all-black audiences, however, Turner was characteristically, provocatively pan-African. "The time has now come," he declared at one such gathering, "to replace them [i.e., whites] with their antiquated methods and superannuated principles. Our new doctrine is more suited to the African awakening, and only the sons of new Africa may be trusted to propagate it, not aliens."[55]

The Ethiopian Church was incorporated into the AME connection the year of Turner's visit. The AME Church in South Africa would be plagued by years of schism and secession, provoked and exacerbated by African-American bishops who did not share Turner's pan-Africanist passion and did not disguise their disdain for indigenous African culture and self-determination. In 1901 the AME Church sent L. J. Coppin to South Africa to be its first resident African-American bishop. Unfortunately, the African Americans the AME Church dispatched to South Africa brought in their baggage condescension toward the Africans that the latter found as repulsive as that of the white missionaries. Perhaps even more so, for with this arrogance the African Americans brought few resources material or otherwise to make their superciliousness any less insufferable. A year later Dwane withdrew from the connection to lead an African order within the Anglican Church.

In 1908 the Ethiopian Church severed its ties with the AME Church and reestablished its autonomy. Ethiopia would stretch forth its hands unto God—not the African Methodist Episcopal Church. Nevertheless, the South African AME connection continued to grow to an estimated eighteen thousand full members by the middle of the second decade of the twentieth century. The Cape government began to see the African-American presence in South Africa as subversive and set about harassing the AME Church, the church's ambivalent cultural politics notwithstanding.[56]

"THROUGH THE SPECTACLES OF ETHIOPIA"
In a partial, fitful fulfillment of the Ethiopian oracle, the fates of West Africans and African Americans continued to intersect. In 1882 Henry

Highland Garnet, now an elder statesman of Ethiopianism, was chosen to be American ambassador to Liberia. Garnet died before assuming the post. He was buried with honors on the Liberian coast, in a plot overlooking the Atlantic Ocean. From the other side of the Atlantic, the hope of Ethiopia gave birth to a new generation of African-American artists and writers. In the last decade of the nineteenth century, poet Paul Lawrence Dunbar turned to verse to write of African-American aspirations in his "Ode to Ethiopia."

> Go on and up! Our souls and eyes
> Shall follow thy continuous rise;
> Our ears shall list thy story
> From bards who from thy root shall spring,
> And proudly tune their lyres to sing
> Of Ethiopia's glory.[57]

Pauline Hopkins's serialized sentimental novel *Of One Blood, or, The Hidden Self* (1902–1903) is a combination love story, mystery, and Ethiopianist legend. The novel takes its title from the biblical claim that "of one blood I [God] have made all races of man," but it is the African bloodline that the narrative traces from modernity to antiquity and back. The protagonist, Reuel Briggs, sets out on an expedition into Africa organized by a group of British scientists. According to one of the British scientists, Dr. Stone, the biblical progenitor Cush is "the grandson of Noah, an Ethiopian." The Bible, the "greatest authority" in these matters, shows that Egyptians, Ethiopians, Libyans, and Canaanites "were ethnically connected, being all descended from Ham." While roaming the ruins of Meroe, Briggs is kidnapped by the local inhabitants, who discover the distinctive birthmark on his chest that marks Briggs as heir to the Meroitic throne. The Meroites acclaim him king and arrange for him to be wed to their queen, Candace. With his royal consort, Reuel is destined to "give to the world a dynasty of dark-skinned rulers."[58]

The title of Sutton Griggs's novel *The Hindered Hand* (1905) is a reference to the "hand stretched forth to God" in the Ethiopian oracle: the oracle serves as the novel's epigraph. The two heroes of the novel, Ensal Ellwood, a black man, and his mulatto friend Earl Bluefield, consider various strategies of the survival for black people. They include among their range of options mass uprising and an international conspiracy to overthrow the

U.S. government. Here Griggs returns to the theme of black revolution that he explored in his first novel, *Imperium in Imperio* (1899), in which his black protagonists hatch a plot to wage race war to establish a black nation in Texas. But in *The Hindered Hand*, Griggs's characters also debate the prospects of solving the problems of the race by emigration to Africa.

Meta Warwick Fuller's *The Awakening of Ethiopia* (c. 1914) is a bronze apotheosis of the Ethiopian oracle. A woman in funereal swaddling turns with uplifted head. The lower part of her body is mummified; the bands on her upper body and torso, however, have begun to fall away. The woman bears an Egyptian royal headdress. These features, of course, suggest Egypt. Yet together with the title of the sculpture, the work signifies the full text of the Ethiopian oracle, which mentions both Egypt and Ethiopia in poetic parallel. The woman, in the words of Du Bois, is the personification of "a mighty Negro past." Writhing free "to escape both death and isolation," she is at once "Ethiopia the shadowy" and "Egypt the Sphinx."[59]

In 1915, the AME Church mourned the passing of Bishop Henry MacNeal Turner, who would be its last great African Methodist Episcopal champion of African emigration. And in that same year Turner's sometime political nemesis and most distinguished African-American leader of his day, Booker T. Washington, also went to his eternal rest. In that same year a worldly Jamaican immigrant, formerly a writer in London at Duse Mohammed Ali's *African Times and Orient Review* in the days when its editor was humbugging Chief Sam's African advent, arrived in New York City. As a seaman in the merchant marine the Jamaican had seen that people of African descent were everywhere "on the bottom," and he determined that Washington's formula for racial uplift was the solution to the problem that African people faced all around the Atlantic world. The Jamaican had come to the United States in the hope of meeting the great founder of the Tuskegee Institute. But Washington and his Jamaican admirer were never to meet.

The ambitious émigré settled in Harlem. But he did not set about to emulate the institutional success of Booker T. Washington. Instead, he founded a mass movement of African emigration. He capitalized the purchase of a steamer and chartered the ship to take people of African descent back to the continent, as had the Liberian Exodus Joint Stock Steamship Company in 1877, as had the National Baptist Convention in 1911, and as had Chief Sam in 1913. And like Chief Sam, he preached a gospel of African emancipation. His partisans too hailed him as a cis-atlantic Moses and a prophet of black self-determination. His name was Marcus Garvey.

Garvey explains his pan-African aspirations in an essay, "The Future as I See It."

> It is history, and history will repeat itself. Beat the Negro, im-prison the Negro, scoff at the Negro, deride the Negro, it may come back to you one of these fine days, because the supreme destiny of man is in the hands of God. God is no respecter of persons, whether that person be white, yellow or black. Today the one race is up, tomorrow it has fallen; today the Negro seems to be the footstool of the other races and nations of the world; tomorrow the Negro will occupy the highest rung of the great human ladder.[60]

This prophetic view of African peoples requires an eschatological reversal. And that reversal must be historically specific: the valleys would be exalted and the mountains would be made low among particular people in a par-ticular place. The people would be Africans. The place would be Africa. Garvey makes all this clear in his statement of the objectives of the United Negro Improvement Association (UNIA), which he founded in 1919:

> The establishment of a universal confraternity among the race; to promote the spirit of pride and love; to reclaim the fallen; to administer and assist the needy; to assist in civilizing the back-ward tribes of Africa; to assist in the development of indepen-dent nations and communities; to establish a central nation for the race; to establish commissaries or agencies in the principal countries and cities of the world for the representation of all Negroes; to promote a conscientious, spiritual worship among the native tribes of Africa; to establish universities, colleges, academies, and schools for the racial education and culture of the people; to work for better conditions for Negroes everywhere.[61]

The UNIA's doctrine offered African peoples a black God, a black Christ, and a black Madonna. Garvey explained that black people must learn to see God in their own image.

If the white man has the idea of the white God, let him worship his God as he desires . . . We, as Negroes, have found a
new ideal. Whilst our God has no color, yet it is human to see
everything through one's own spectacles, we have only now
started out (late though it be) to see our God through our own
spectacles . . . We Negroes believe in the God of Ethiopia, the
everlasting God . . . That is the God in whom we believe, but
we shall worship Him through the spectacles of Ethiopia.[62]

The idea of people of African descent seeing the images of their faith
"through our own spectacles," of course, was not new. Henry MacNeal
Turner had insisted on a black God for black people at the turn of the
twentieth century, and as early as 1844 Robert B. Lewis's volume *Light
and Truth* presented all biblical figures as black people. But Garvey turned
black theology into mass religion. He called his racially chauvinistic interpretation of Christianity "African Fundamentalism," a coinage that
obliquely suggested the Fundamentalist controversy in American Protestantism erupting around the same time as Garvey's movement. UNIA
members affirmed Garvey's doctrine in their recitation of *The Universal
Negro Catechism,* which the UNIA chaplain-general George Alexander
McGuire published in 1921.

Q. What prediction made in the 68th Psalm and the 31st verse is now
   fulfilled?
A. Princes shall come out of Egypt, Ethiopia shall soon stretch out her
   hands to God.
Q. What does this verse prove?
A. That Black Men will set up their own government in Africa with
   rulers of their own race.[63]

With fellow member Ben Burrell, UNIA choirmaster Arnold J. Ford wrote
the "Universal Ethiopian Anthem," which the UNIA officially adopted as
"anthem of the Negro race."

Ethiopia, thou land of our fathers,
Thou land where the gods love to be,
As storm cloud at night sudden gathers
Our armies come rushing to thee.
We must in the fight be victorious,

When swords are thrust outwards to gleam;
For us will the Vict'ry be glorious
When led by the red, black and green.
Chorus:
O Jehovah, Thou God of the ages,
Grant unto our sons that lead
The wisdom thou gav'st to Thy sages
When Israel was sore in need.
Thy voice thro' the dim past has spoken,
Ethiopia shall stretch forth her hand,
By Thee shall all fetters be broken
And Heav'n bless our dear Motherland.[64]

Garvey's mobilization of black people in the United States—the largest mass movement in American history—took as its proof text a biblical oracle that African Americans had been reading for two centuries as a prophecy of their deliverance.

Garvey's movement also occasioned a battle over, if not for, the Bible. Baptist clergyman James R. L. Diggs, pastor of Trinity Baptist Church in Baltimore, became acting chaplain-general of Marcus Garvey's United Negro Improvement Association in 1922. Born in Upper Marlboro, Maryland, in 1866, Diggs received bachelor's and master's degrees from Bucknell University, did postgraduate work at Cornell University, and taught Latin and French at Virginia Union University before going on to take a doctorate in sociology at Illinois Wesleyan University in 1906. One of only nine African Americans who had earned a doctoral degree in the United States at that time, Diggs may have been the first African American to do so.[65] Diggs preached the opening sermon at the Third International Convention of the UNIA in August 1922, taking as his text Isaiah 42:4, "He will not fail or be discouraged till he has established justice in the earth." When Garvey led the fight on the convention floor against granting permission to a "well known Bible Society" that sought to put a new Bible in the hand each of the seven thousand delegates, Diggs wholeheartedly supported him, and the measure was defeated. Diggs explained in a statement to a *New York World* reporter, "I am a Christian and a pastor, but I agree with the action of this organization in refusing to accept any Bibles from the Bible Society. We are not atheists by any means, and we are not rejecting the

Bible. What we are doing to-day is registering an emphatic protest against Christianity as it is interpreted in this country."[66] The UNIA suggested that the Bible society distribute the Bibles in the South, where they would be "circulated among those obsessed with race and religious prejudice."[67]

Garvey, a world traveler who never set foot in Africa but knew Europe and Latin America as well as his native Caribbean, held a pan-Africanist view of the historical relationship of African people in the New World with those of the Old. "We the Negroes in this Western Hemisphere are descendants of those Africans who were enslaved and transported to these shores, where they suffered, bled and died to make us what we are today—Civilized, Christian free men. Should we not, therefore, turn our eyes towards Africa, our ancestral home and free it from the thralldom of alien oppression and exploitation?" Garvey's view was not only historical but also strategic. He saw European colonization of Africa as the most recent and advanced phase of white supremacy. "Behind the murder of millions of Negroes annually in Africa," he wrote, "is the well organized system of exploitation by the alien intruders who desire to rob Africa of every bit of its wealth for the satisfaction of their race and the upkeep of their bankrupt European countries." Only an allied, pan-African front could frustrate European imperialism in Africa.[68]

In a speech delivered on January 1, 1922, commemorating both Lincoln's Emancipation Proclamation of 1863 and the British Empire's abolition of slavery in 1838, Garvey reminded his audience of the historical link between the people of African descent in the United States and those in the Caribbean. They shared a slave past and subsequent emancipation. Just as Lincoln had emancipated slaves in the United States, Queen Victoria had emancipated all the "hundreds of thousands of West Indian Negro slaves" of the British Empire. Garvey concluded by exhorting his audience, "And so tonight we celebrate this anniversary of our emancipation, we do it not with regret, on the contrary we do it with an abiding confidence, a hope and faith in ourselves and in our God. And the faith that we have is a faith that will ultimately take us back to that ancient place, that ancient position that we once occupied, when Ethiopia was in her glory."[69]

The U.S. government charged Garvey with mail fraud, and due in part to the dishonesty and incompetence of those to whom Garvey had given financial responsibility in the UNIA, he was found guilty in 1923 and sentenced to five years in prison. Several years after his conviction,

President Calvin Coolidge pardoned Garvey, only to have him permanently deported to Jamaica. The pan-Africanist leader vainly attempted to revive the UNIA from Jamaica and Britain, but exile from his Harlem power base in the United States proved fatal to his movement. Garvey died in obscurity in 1940.

Garvey's ideological influence nevertheless was enormous and reached well beyond the UNIA membership. In June 1920, Chicagoan Grover Cleveland Redding, a self-proclaimed prophet of the "Abyssinian Order," led a parade of his order in New York City that featured pamphlets commemorating a commercial treaty between the United States and Ethiopia signed in 1904. At the conclusion of the parade, Redding burned an American flag. Whites observing the desecration protested when Redding set a second flag ablaze, and a gun battle ensued. Several whites were shot and killed. Redding was arrested and subsequently hanged for murder. The Abyssinian Order was reputed to be an unofficial offshoot of the UNIA and may have known that an Ethiopian delegation had visited the United States the previous year seeking to renew the treaty.[70]

Though it had no official ties with the UNIA, the Universal Hagar's Spiritual Church carried the banner of Ethiopianism in the tradition of Spiritualist churches of George William Hurley. Hurley was born in Reynolds, Georgia, in 1884. A child preacher, he was ordained at eleven. As a young teen he became a member of "Father" Elias Dempsey Smith's Triumph the Church and the Kingdom of God in Christ. Smith founded the church in 1897, the same year in which, according to Hurley's official biography, "the spirit revealed to Father Hurley that he was the Second Coming of Christ." Smith established a church in Ethiopia and in 1920 moved to Addis Ababa never to return. Soon after Smith's departure, Hurley had a vision of "a brown skin damsel named Hagar," whom God commanded him to marry and "run on with the truth."[71]

And so he did. In the early 1920s Hurley began to systematize what would be his distinctive doctrine. Hurley left Georgia and joined the mass African-American exodus to the urban Midwest, and in 1923 established the Universal Hagar's Spiritual Church (UHSC) in Detroit. Hurley's teachings combined biblical interpretation with astrology, theosophy, and other esoterica, and in 1924 Hurley founded a "School of Mediumship and Psychology." The credo of the Universal Hagar's Spiritual Church, "What We Believe In," affirms a succession of "Ages, Times or Eras." Each age has an exalted leader; in this most recent age, God "has made his second appearance within Hurley," and "Hurley was born at the proper time to be the leader" who "will bring heaven to all nations that will believe." Toward the end of his life some of his followers called him "Christ Hurley." But more than his messianism and theosophy, it was Hurley's Ethiopianist theology that made him a man of his time. Hurley rejected the word "Negro" and insisted that "Ethiopian" replace it. The sixth of the "U.H.S.C. Ten Commandments" calls church members to "believe that the Ethiopians and all Nations will rule the world in righteousness."[72]

On November 2, 1930, Ras Tafari, whose Christian baptismal name was Haile Selassie, was crowned emperor of Ethiopia and received the rank of Negusa Nagast, "King of Kings." Thenceforth he would be known as Emperor Haile Selassie I, his royal epithets "King of Kings," "Elect of God," "Conquering Lion of the Tribe of Judah" all being titles that the book of Revelation applies to Jesus (Rev. 5:5, 19:16). Ethiopian tradition, however, applied these titles to the emperor: royal mythology claimed that the royal line in Ethiopia began with Menilek, first king of Ethiopia and child of the union of King Solomon of Israel and the queen of Sheba. The king of Ethiopia was thus a scion of the house of David.

Jamaican Leonard Howell concluded that the Ethiopian oracle was being fulfilled in the coronation of Haile Selassie and that the messiah promised in Acts 2:29, "he shall come through the lineage of Solomon, and sit on David's throne," had arrived in the person of the Ethiopian emperor. The passage in Acts and those in Revelation refer explicitly to Jesus, whom, Howell reasoned, had emerged from Africa as had Haile Selassie. Howell was inspired by the racially chauvinist exegesis of J. A. Rogers, an African-American clergyman in Perth Amboy, New Jersey, whose *Holy Piby, or, The Black Man's Bible*, published in the early 1920s, spoke of an African messiah who would fulfill biblical prophecy. Howell's adaptation of Rogers's interpretation in the light of contemporary Ethiopian history laid the theological foundation for the Jamaican movement that took Haile Selassie's given name as its own, Rastafarianism.[73]

In 1935, five years after the coronation of Ras Tafari, Italy invaded Ethiopia. African Americans were outraged. "There is not a Negro with other than ice water trickling through his arteries," wrote Harlem journalist George Schuyler, "who is not anxious to do something to help Ethiopia in her hour of extremity, who is not burning to strike through her a blow at white imperialism and aggression." Schuyler noted as self-evident the sympathies of African peoples in the conflict. "It would be a major catastrophe for the darker peoples of the world if Ethiopia should be defeated and subjugated by the Italians. This is the opinion of every intelligent colored person in the world today, and for once the view of the majority is correct."[74] During Ethiopia's anticolonial struggle Schuyler wrote a serialized novel, *Black Empire,* and other fiction about an international pan-African conspiracy to defeat the Italians and establish a black empire ruled from Africa.

From 1935 to 1938, Ethiopia's war against colonialism was a recurring theme in the poetry of Langston Hughes. "Call of Ethiopia" is the first of three poems he published between 1935 and 1936 that take Ethiopia as the title subject. "Call of Ethiopia" was followed in the same year by "Ballad of Ethiopia," and a year later Hughes published "Broadcast from Ethiopia," treating the Ethiopian defeat that constrained Haile Selassie to flee the country. In "Call of Ethiopia," Hughes praises Ethiopia as the vanguard of the African emancipation:

Ethiopia's free!
Be like me,
All of Africa,
Arise and be free![75]

And African Americans were not content merely to take up the pen against the Italians. African-American air force pilot John C. Robinson, the "Black Condor," commanded the Ethiopian air force during the war. Robinson assumed command from Herbert Fauntleroy Julian, a West Indian–born American and former Garveyite whom Emperor Haile Selassie had invited in 1930 to organize Ethiopia's small air force. The flamboyant Julian fell out of favor with the emperor, who gave his position to Robinson. Melvin B. Tolson, African-American poet and playwright who later became poet laureate of Liberia in 1947, mentions both Robinson "the Black Condor" and Julian, "the Black Eagle of Harlem" in his unfinished novel of Ethiopian resistance, *The Lion and the Jackal* (1935).

The Ethiopianist impact on the popular African-American imagination was not a recapitulation of Menilek's victory in 1896. This time, the story of Italian aggression and Ethiopian resistance would have a different ending: the Italians would occupy the country for five years before the

Ethiopians finally expelled them. Nevertheless, the anticolonial struggle in Ethiopia and the ideological residue of Garveyism continued to inspire Ethiopianist art and literature from the period of the Harlem Renaissance through World War II. In painting, Lois Mailou Jones's *Ascent of Ethiopia* (1932) belongs historically and ideologically to African-American pro-Ethiopian sentiment after the ascension of Makonnen. Above and around the profile of a pharaoh with dark skin and Negroid features, silhouetted figures move from contemplation of the pyramids in the light of a dark star at the upper left of the painting. They ascend a stairway to a hemisphere marked with symbols of modern art and architecture: skyscrapers, musical notes, and a painter busy before an easel. The entire realm of civilization rests on the head of the black Egyptian. Mural painter Aaron Douglas represents black Africans constructing the pyramids in *More Stately Mansions* (1944). The profiles of Douglas's Egyptian builders bear flagrantly Negroid features. The vivid figures, themselves monumental, intimate an apologia for African peoples in African-American arts and letters now over a century old: the greatness of African antiquity was the greatness of black people, people who looked very much like the people of African descent in America.

But in the postwar years, the tide of Ethiopianism receded among African-American intellectuals, in no small measure due to direct experience with Africa itself. Several African-American literary luminaries experienced moments of alienation and disillusionment in their encounters on the continent. Richard Wright, Gwendolyn Brooks, and Maya Angelou all wrote troubled travelogues of ambivalent relations with Africans on African soil.

Playwright and activist Lorraine Hansberry, however, is a remarkable exception. In reflecting on her childhood, Hansberry acknowledged her strident Ethiopianist heritage.

> Why ever since I was three years old, . . . I knew that somebody somewhere was doing something to hurt black and brown peoples. Little as I was I remember the newsreels of the Ethiopian war and the feeling of outrage in our Negro community. Fighters with spears and our people in passion over it, my mother attacking the Pope blessing the Italian troops going off to slay the Ethiopians. When the Pope died that was the

thought of him that came to my mind. I didn't know a thing
about Spain but I certainly did know about Ethiopia. . . . But
we just expected that things would change. We had been saying
for a long time: "Ethiopia will stretch forth her hands!" This
always meant that they were going to pay for this one day."

Hansberry's understanding of the Ethiopian oracle as a prophecy of justice informs two of her posthumously edited and published plays, *Young,
Gifted, and Black* (1969) and *Les Blancs* (1970). The main character of
Hansberry's novel *Young, Gifted, and Black* is Candace, the New Testament name for the queen of Ethiopia and the sovereign of the Ethiopian
eunuch baptized by Philip in the book of Acts. The section of the novel
preceding Candace's appearance is entitled "Queen of the Ethiopes." The
protagonist of Hansberry's play about European imperialism and West
African resistance, *Les Blancs*, is an African; Hansberry understood Africans as subjects of their own history. In placing Africans at the center
of African affairs, *Les Blancs* is an oblique rebuttal to Joseph Conrad's
Heart of Darkness. Les Blancs, like Conrad's infamous novel, takes place
in a venue resembling the Belgian Congo and treats the malevolence of
transplanted Europeans. Hansberry's ex-husband and literary executor,
Robert Nemiroff, noted that in the early draft of *Les Blancs*, the name of
the African protagonist was Candace.[76]

More than any other artist or intellectual in the generation after the
Harlem Renaissance, Lorraine Hansberry realized in her oeuvre the three-
point plan for pan-African cooperation that Harlem Renaissance philosopher Alain Locke had outlined in 1924 in his *Opportunity* essay "Apropos
of Africa." There Locke advocated that African Americans acquire factual
information about Africa, establish direct contact with Africa and Africans
through travel and exchange programs, and give sustained attention to
the academic study of things African, especially in the fields of art and
archaeology.[77] Hansberry had read Jomo Kenyatta, studied Africa in New
York in a seminar conducted by the great W. E. B. Du Bois himself, and
conversed with African expatriates as a graduate student at the University
of Wisconsin. Unlike other African-American intellectuals, she eschewed
the travelogue as a discursive means of coming to terms with her African experiences. Through drawing on her own Ethiopianist heritage and
acquiring a working knowledge of Africa that was mediated by Africans

and pan-Africanist African Americans, Hansberry saw Africa, in Garvey's words, "through the spectacles of Ethiopia."

In her art and her politics Hansberry joined a biblical ideal of justice with her actuation of Locke's pan-Africanist intellectual agenda. The fruit of this union was a keen Ethiopianist sensibility. God's justice, in concert with and in response to human action, governs the grand ebb and flow of events. Hansberry's expectations "that things would change," "that they were going to pay for all this one day," are not merely wishful notions derived from a cyclical philosophy of history. History, in the Ethiopianist view, is not cyclical. It is providential. This view was the legacy of the classic Ethiopianism of the nineteenth century. Neither fatalistic nor deterministic, as any cyclical view of history must be, Ethiopianism turns not on cosmic revolutions but on a dynamic tension of divine agency and human contingency that renders the universe a theater of morality. The historical timeline of Ethiopianism, a quintessentially biblical worldview, is quintessentially linear. Ethiopia's rise would be the consequence of divine justice and human will.

"SUCH HIGH HOPES"

Successful anticolonial struggles during the Cold War years added fifteen independent African states to the United Nations in 1960 alone. These successes matched hard-fought and hard-won political struggles of people of African descent on the other side of the Atlantic in the Civil Rights and Black Power Movements. During the anticolonial liberation of African nations in the 1960s, jazz virtuoso Dizzy Gillespie dedicated his composition "Kush," an alternative spelling of Cush, the biblical name for Ethiopia, to "Mother Africa." One of Gillespie's most popular works, "Kush" is performed in a 6/4 time that suggests ancestral African rhythms and opens with a sylvan tenor line from the flute of James Moody. The resonance with a long tradition of African-American identification with Africa should be self-evident: "If you can't get with that," Gillespie says of the dedication in a live recording from 1967, "shame on you, baby."

Romare Bearden's painting *Sheba* (1970) signified the Ethiopian oracle as it spans both Testaments. Whereas the profiled queen dominates the foreground, looming in the background is a male figure, presumably her vizier or chargé d'affaires. Bearden weaves together the Old Testament figure of Sheba, her association with Ethiopia, and the suggestion of the

New Testament figure of the Ethiopian eunuch of Queen Candace in Acts 8. He summons an image of Africa as royal, sovereign, and powerful —an image to match the politics of emerging African states and African-American demands to determine the destiny of their communities.

In 1975 the extraterrestrial lyrics of funk music composer George Clinton on his *Mothership Connection* album tacitly defended the claim of Africa's royal greatness, albeit in a facetious funk idiom. On the album, Clinton conceptualizes his band and his music as an invading UFO. Announcing his arrival on the planet in the song "Mothership Connection (Star Child)," a chorus sings repeatedly behind Clinton's voice the syncopated phrase, "Swing low, sweet chariot, /Stop, and let me ride." Throughout the song Clinton's spoken-word performance free-associates in evocative words from the slang of African-American popular music.

> Come fly
> with me
> it's free
> it's hip
> on the Mother Ship
> groovin'
> Swing.[78]

Clinton refers to himself and his band as "recording angels." They are the "band of angels" that accompanies the heavenly chariot in the Negro spiritual:

> I looked over Jordan
> And what did I see
> Coming for to carry me home
> A band of angels
> Coming after me
> Coming for to carry me home.

Clinton suggests both the theme of celestial deliverance that comes from the vernacular tradition of the Negro spirituals and the early myth among African-American slaves that native-born Africans had the ability to fly and occasionally used this power to escape from slavery and return to Africa. At the same time and in the same strophe, Clinton lays Afrocentric claim to the pyramids of Egypt as an outstanding accomplishment of African civilization. At one point in the original version of the song, Clinton raps the beginning of the first verse of the Negro spiritual "Swing Low, Sweet Chariot": "Swing low, sweet chariot / Comin' for to carry me home." In so doing he makes sure that his hearers do not miss the reference. Clinton raps, "We have returned to claim the pyramids," an oblique allusion to the anthropologist Erich von Daniken's then-popular theory of the extraterrestrial architecture of the pyramids. In the early 1970s, von Daniken argued that the Egyptian pyramids were built by an advanced race of aliens from another planet who had visited the earth at the dawn of history. The superior technology of the interplanetary visitors accounts for the extraordinary size and precision of these otherwise inexplicable ancient monuments. "Star Child" turns von Daniken's theory on its head, for the posited extraterrestrial origin of the pyramids effectively denies African peoples their glorious Egyptian past. The UFO thesis is a way of saying that genius is alien to Africa. Clinton quips and sings a rebuttal: the aliens are the geniuses of Africa, extraterrestrial black folks with extraterrestrial music.

Black people in the United States were again stridently claiming Africa as their ancestral home. Many African Americans made pilgrimages to West Africa in the 1970s, and some became citizens of African countries. The television miniseries *Roots*, based on Alex Haley's best-selling book of the same title telling of his family's African roots and transition from slavery to freedom in America, was a major media event as well as a cultural inspiration for African Americans.

But by the late 1970s the political and cultural fortunes of people of African descent on both sides of the Atlantic had crested. Afterward the realities of reaction in the United States and neocolonialism in West Africa saw cynicism supplant utopian hopes of black self-determination and pan-African concord. Alice Walker pilloried the Evangelical and quasi-imperialist pretensions of African-American Ethiopianism in her classic novel, *The Color Purple* (1982), in which the African-American missionary project in Africa is the mise en scène for the transatlantic failure of Africans. *The Color Purple*, in its representation of Ethiopianism's worse self, turns Ethiopianism against itself. In one long scene of the novel, the protagonist, Celie, gives her secondhand account of a story related by Samuel, a former missionary to Africa, who recalls a soiree in his aunt's parlor that was attended by none other than W. E. B. Du Bois.

I remember once, before Corrine and I were married, Samuel continued, Aunt Theodosia had one of her at-homes. She had them every Thursday. She'd invited a lot of "serious young people" as she called them, and one of them was a young Harvard scholar named Edward. DuBoyce was his last name, I think. Anyhow, Aunt Theodosia was going on about her African adventures, leading up to the time King Leopold of Belgium presented her with a medal. Well, Edward, or perhaps his name was Bill, was a very impatient sort. You saw it in his eyes, you could see it in the way he moved his body. He was never still. As Aunt Theodosia got closer to the part about her surprise and joy over receiving this medal—which validated her service as an exemplary missionary in the King's colony— DuBoyce's foot began to pat the floor rapidly and uncontrollably . . . Madame, he said, when Aunt Theodosia finished her story and flashed her famous medal around the room, do you realize King Leopold cut the hands off workers who, in the opinion of his plantation overseers, did not fulfill their rubber quota? Rather than cherish that medal, Madame, you should regard it as a symbol of your unwitting complicity with this despot who worked to death and brutalized and eventually exterminated thousands and thousands of African peoples.

Well, said Samuel, silence struck the gathering like a blight. Poor Aunt Theodosia! There is something in all of us that wants a medal for what we have done. That wants to be appreciated. And Africans certainly don't deal in medals. They hardly seem to care whether missionaries exist.

Samuel concludes his unflattering portrait of Du Bois with both an equally unflattering portrait of the Africans he served on the mission field and, ultimately, a pathetic outburst of tears.

Don't be bitter, I said.
How can I not? He said.
The Africans never asked us to come, you know. There's no use blaming them if we feel unwelcome.
It's worse than unwelcome, said Samuel. The Africans don't

even *see* us. They don't even recognize us as the brothers and
sisters they sold.

Oh, Samuel, I said. Don't.

But you know, he had started to cry. Oh, Nettie, he said. That
the heart of it, don't you see. We love them. We try every way
we can to show that love. But they reject us. They never even
listen to how we've suffered. And if they listen they say stupid
things. Why don't you speak our language? they ask. Why can't
you remember the old ways? Why aren't you happy in America,
if everyone there drives motor cars?[79]

A remarkable passage, one that brings together in a skein of failure, insight, and resentment the threads of late-nineteenth-century Ethiopianism
and late-twentieth-century cynicism.

Walker has targeted Du Bois as the poster child for a species of African-
American overconfidence that was neither tolerable for Africans nor sus-
tainable for African Americans in the late twentieth century. Du Bois
had been deeply influenced by the "pan-Negroism" of his spiritual men-
tor, Alexander Crummell. Of all people of African descent on the face
of the earth, claimed Crummell, the Negro who had weathered slavery
in America "has risen superior to the dreaded inflictions of a prolonged
servitude, and stands today, in all the lands of his Thralldom, taller, more
erect, more intelligent, and more aspiring than any of his ancestors for
more than two thousand years."[80] But unlike Crummell, the secular Harvard sociologist did not argue for African ascendancy as a providential
design. Du Bois's understanding of history on this point was informed
more by Hegelian philosophy than biblical theology. The vindication of
Africa would be accomplished not by the hand of God but by the *Volksgeist*
of African Americans, who would "take their just place in the van of Pan-
Negroism." In *The Color Purple,* Alice Walker shows Du Bois's dream of
an African-American vanguard to be a delusion that dies in the Congo.

Yet it was precisely in the Congo in the first decade of the twentieth century where African Americans were in the vanguard of opposition to the truly oppressive and dehumanizing force on the continent:
European imperialism. It was African-American outrage that turned the
public relations of the Belgian regime into an international scandal that
hastened Belgium's official departure from the Congo. The first testimony

that made public King Leopold's atrocities against the Congolese was the report of African-American historian and journalist George Washington Williams of his travels in the Congo in 1890. Williams called the Belgian monarch's abuses "crimes against humanity" and so introduced this phrase into the vocabulary of international law. But the world owed its awareness of the murderous colonialism of the Belgians in the Congo to the advocacy of a fearless African-American missionary, the Reverend William Henry Sheppard.[81]

Sheppard was a Presbyterian missionary, and cofounded the American Presbyterian Congo Mission in 1891 with white Southern coreligionist Samuel Lapsley. The two men worked together in the Congo for a brief period until Lapsley's death from tropical disease. Sheppard became an outspoken opponent of the Belgian colonial government and a staunch advocate of the Congolese, who were being murdered, mutilated, and terrorized in King Leopold's forced labor camps. Sheppard was one of a cadre of international activists who launched the Congo Reform Association (CRA), along with British consul and Irish nationalist Roger Casement and, in the United States, Booker T. Washington, W. E. B. Du Bois, and Mark Twain. Twain published a biting satire of the Congo, *King Leopold's Soliloquy,* in 1905.

King Leopold's private company in the Congo, the Compagnie du Kasai, sued Sheppard and his white colleague, newspaper editor William Morrison, for libel for an article Sheppard had published citing the disastrous effects of company rule on the Kuba people of the western Kasai. The anticolonial conflict in the Congo soon became an international incident: CRA, the American press, and international public opinion came to the missionaries' defense. With the eyes of the world on the courtroom in Kinshasa, the case came to trial in September 1909. Emile Vandervelde, socialist leader in the Belgian parliament and president of the Second International, traveled to the Congo to represent the defendants pro bono. Charges were soon dropped against Morrison, but the case against Sheppard went forward. Acquitted on a technicality, Sheppard became the international hero of the Congolese cause. The *Boston Herald* wrote of him, "Dr. Sheppard has not only stood before kings, but he has also stood against them. In pursuit of his mission of serving his race in its native land, this son of a slave . . . has dared to withstand all the power of Leopold."[82]

Sheppard was the point man in the first modern international campaign for human rights. Because of Sheppard's courageous advocacy, Booker T. Washington and W. E. B. DuBois, adversaries in almost all other matters, made common cause for the emancipation of the oppressed Africans of the Congo. This common cause was the Ethiopianism that struggled, albeit often unsuccessfully, to realize the counsel of Alain Locke: "We now see that the missionary condescension of the past generations in their attitude toward Africa was a pious mistake. In taking it, we have fallen into the snare of enemies and have given grievous offence to our brothers. We must realize that in some respects we need what Africa has to give us as much as, or even more than, Africa needs what we in turn have to give her."[83]

To be sure, William Sheppard's respect for indigenous African culture, including his command of several Congolese languages, was exceptional in an era when African-American missionaries looked down on their African charges as pagan inferiors. But it is an extraordinary exception that made history and makes sense of history. Little of this courage and pan-African solidarity, the stuff of fin-de-siècle Ethiopianism, shows up in the Congo of Walker's *The Color Purple*.

But some light does shine through the gloom, albeit only on the American side of the Atlantic. Celie's sister Nettie writes of her experience visiting Harlem during the missionary party's fund-raising tour of New York City:

> There are more than a hundred churches! And we went to
> every one of them. . . . [The colored people of Harlem] live in
> such beauty and dignity, Celie. And they give and give and
> then reach down and give some more, when the name "Africa"
> is mentioned.
>   They *love* Africa. They defend it at the drop of a hat.[84]

This passage rings truer than any of *The Color Purple*'s several scenes of missionary incomprehension and African apathy. W. E. B. Du Bois had characterized Africa as "at once the most romantic and the most tragic of continents."[85] Africa, in a romantic, tragic sense, was still the ancient home of African Americans, the antique touchstone of their collective identity.

And their collective destiny. In a letter to Celie, Nettie writes, "Everyone had such high hopes for what can be done in Africa." Then, speaking simultaneously of a glorious future and a glorious past, Celie explains the inspiration of such high hopes. "Over the pulpit there is a saying: *Ethiopia Shall Stretch Forth Her Hands to God*. Think what it means that Ethiopia is Africa! All the Ethiopians in the bible were colored. It had never occurred to me, though when you read the bible it is perfectly plain if you pay attention only to the words."[86]

CHAPTER SEVEN

Emmanuel

To some he is the grand prototype of all the distilled longing of
mankind for fulfillment, for wholeness, for perfection. To some
he is the Eternal Presence hovering over all the myriad needs of
humanity, yielding healing for the sick of body and soul, giving a lift
to those whom weariness has overtaken in the long march, and calling out hidden purposes of destiny which are the common heritage.
To some he is more than a Presence; he is the God fact, the Divine
Moment in human sin and human misery. To still others he is a
man who found the answer to life's riddle, and out of a profound
gratitude he becomes the Man most worthy of honor and praise.
For such his answer becomes humanity's answer and his life the
common claim.

—*Howard Thurman*, Jesus and the Disinherited

AT A BLACK BOY'S FUNERAL described in Toni Morrison's novel *Sula*
(1973), the very mention of the name of Jesus evokes among the women
mourners a sense of identity with him. Morrison verbally choreographs
the scene with movements of reverence and memories of pain.

> As Reverend Deal moved into his sermon, the hands of the
> women unfolded like pairs of raven's wings and flew high
> above their hats in the air. They did not hear all of what he said;
> they heard the one word, or phrase, or inflection that was for
> them the connection between the event and themselves. For
> some it was the term "Sweet Jesus." And they saw the Lamb's
> eye and the truly innocent victim: themselves. They acknowl-
> edged the innocent child hiding in the corner of their hearts,
> holding a sugar-and-butter sandwich. That one. The one who

lodged deep in their fat, thin, old, young skin, and was the one
the world had hurt. Or they thought of their son newly killed
and remembered his legs in short pants and wondered where
the bullet went in.[1]

Jesus is "the innocent child," "the son newly killed" whose mother, identifying with Jesus in her own innocence and his, agonizes at the sight of
his lifeless body.

African Americans have long had their own evocative piety of the
Sacred Name. A Southern planter wrote of what appeared to be a game
that a group of slaves would play in a darkened cabin. One after another
would call out, "Where is Jesus?"

> Some one would answer: "Here is Jesus." They would rush to
> the part of the cabin where the answer had been given, and, of
> course, not finding him there, would say, "He ain't here." Then
> another voice would cry out in the darkness from another part
> of the cabin: "Here is Jesus." Another rush would be made,
> when the statement, "He is not here," would be made. The
> calls and answers would be repeated for hours, sometimes all
> night. The women and men would become excited and frantic,
> would tear their hair, and scream and pray until the meeting
> was broken up in a frenzy.[2]

Scottish traveler David Macrae recalled a "poor black woman—a nurse
in a planter's family—who had become a Christian, and was never weary
hearing the children reading the Bible and telling her about Jesus":

> To her great delight, the little girl one day showed her the name
> of Jesus, and made her spell letter after letter, and look at the
> word until she knew it, and was able to point out when she saw
> it. After that it was a favorite employment with her to take the
> Bible and search for the name that was so precious to her. She
> had no idea in what parts of the Bible it was to be found; and
> so, opening it anywhere, she would travel with her finger along
> line after line, and page after page, through the wilderness of
> words that were all unintelligible signs to her, till she found the
> name of which she was in quest.

"And oh!" she said, in narrating her experience, "how that name started up like a light in the dark, and I say, 'There's the name of my Jesus!' It was de only one word I knew," she added, "but that one word made me hunger for more!"[3]

A Negro spiritual instructs those seeking true religion, "If you want to find Jesus, / Go in the wilderness." Traveling the pages of the through "the wilderness of words that were all unintelligible signs," as Macrae puts it, slaves followed the song's counsel and found Jesus there. A freedwoman in Beaufort, South Carolina, explained her knowledge of Jesus to a missionary this way: "Oh! I don't know nothing! I can't read a word. But oh! I read Jesus in my heart, just as you read him in the book. . . . I read and read him here in my heart just as you read him in the Bible. O, . . . my God! I got him! I hold him here all the time. He stay with me!"[4]

The sheer ubiquity of Jesus in African-American culture is recognized almost as an inside joke among African Americans. In the illustrated political satire *Birth of a Nation* (2004), the fictional black mayor of East Saint Louis, Fred Fredericks, is outraged by widespread voter fraud in the latest presidential election that has effectively disenfranchised his predominantly African-American constituency. Encouraged by a wealthy former schoolmate who offers to back his play financially, Fredericks announces the city's secession from the United States. The people of East Saint Louis vote to rename the city "Blackland," and Fredericks convenes a "Nation Time committee" to design a flag for the new nation. Later in the novel, members of Fredericks's cabinet are dismayed to discover that the committee has created a flag featuring a portrait of Jesus at the center. The mayor's best friend, Kendrick, explains, "Hey, it was mostly old people at the Nation Time meetings. . . . You know how old black people feel about Jesus."[5]

From the earliest folkloric reflections to the pathos of later belles lettres to the religious lore of hip-hop, the figure of Jesus has signified the suffering of black people, and the true significance of Jesus is signified in their sufferings. His humble and momentous birth, his parables and preaching, his shameful execution and glorious resurrection are everywhere in the African-American collective imagination. African Americans have seen Jesus, and they have seen themselves in him, as they have no other figure in the Bible.

TESTAMENT

African-American biblical imagery has been described as being obsessed by the Exodus and little else other than visions of the heavenly hereafter lifted from the book of Revelation—a book itself shot through with the language of the prophets and the Psalms of the Old Testament. One scholar has called this obsession an "Old Testament bias."[6] This widespread assessment apparently begins with Thomas Wentworth Higginson's study of slave songs in the third quarter of the nineteenth century. As commander of the first Union Army black regiment, the South Carolina Volunteers, he became an avid collector of Negro spirituals. In 1867 Higginson published an article in the *Atlantic Monthly* describing the songs that he had heard his black soldiers sing around their watch fires in the camps. "[The book of Revelation], with the books of Moses, constituted their Bible," Higginson writes, "all that lay between, even the narratives of the life of Jesus, they hardly cared to read or hear." In his subsequent book-length account of his Civil War experiences, *Army Life in a Black Regiment* (1870), he described the biblical reminiscences of his troops as "a vast, bewildered chaos of Jewish history and biography." Yet roughly half the lyrics Higginson's treats in the article either mention Jesus explicitly or depend on a detailed knowledge of the gospel narratives to be intelligible.

For the children of slavery, King Jesus and his kingdom were not revelation proprietary to the New Testament alone. Indeed, the distinction between the two Testaments was one without a difference. Though Moses and the Exodus are important and recurring figures in the songs of the slaves, the figure of Jesus is even more so. Among the Gullahs, African slaves of the South Carolina Sea Islands, the commanders of the Union occupation in 1864 found "religious slaves" for whom Jesus was a part of daily conversation. General William Tecumseh Sherman discovered that the children, however, did not know the Ten Commandments and had never heard of Moses. When he asked them to identify Jesus Christ, after a stunned silence some answered, "General Saxby," the occupying commander General Rufus Saxon. Others replied, "Master [Abraham] Lincoln."[7] Perhaps they offered these answers to flatter their new Union masters, but their logic is transparent enough: recognizing Jesus as their savior, the slaves recognized their Union saviors as Jesus.

According to the traditional Christianity doctrine of supersessionism, Old Testament scriptures are true insofar as they "prefigure" the later, superior Christian revelation—"The Old Testament is the New Testament concealed; the New Testament is the Old Testament revealed," in Augustine's handy phrase. Old Testament revelation is inferior because it is obsolete. But in the Negro spirituals, the New does not supersede the Old. The two Testaments, Old and New, are correlated to each other. Moses is not a "type" of Jesus. Both bear witness—eternally, equally valid witness—to what God has done and is doing in the world. They are placed side by side with others in the Bible, that "great cloud of witnesses," as the writer of the Epistle to the Hebrews puts it, who corroborate each others' testimony. Thus the remarkable juxtaposition of Moses, Mary and Martha, even Joshua and Jesus, in the earliest African-American folk songs.

Harriet Tubman evoked the image of the regal Jesus in the following composition that she used as an all-clear signal to slaves awaiting her direction along the Underground Railroad. When the slaves heard her sing this song, they knew it was safe to come out of hiding to meet her.

> Hail, oh hail ye happy spirits,
> Death no more shall make you fear,
> No grief nor sorrow, pain nor anguish
> Shall no more distress you there.
>
> Around him are ten thousand angels
> Always ready to obey command.
> They are always hov'ring round you,
> Till you reach the heavenly land.
>
> Jesus, Jesus will go with you;
> He will lead you to his throne;
> He who died has gone before you,
> Trod the wine press all alone.
>
> He whose thunder shake creation;
> He who bids the planets roll;
> He who rides above the tempest
> And his scepter sways the whole.
>
> Dark and thorny is the desert
> Through the pilgrim makes his ways.

Yet beyond this vale of sorrow,
Lie the fields of endless days.[8]

On arriving safely in Canada, Tubman and the group of fugitive slaves she had guided to freedom from the South sang together the refrain, "Glory to God in the highest, / Glory to God and Jesus too, / For all these souls now safe."[9] The themes of Exodus and Promised Land were prominent in the coded language of Tubman's extemporaneous compositions. But on those occasions when the Promised Land was in reach, she and the slaves she led to freedom sang of Jesus.

In the Negro spiritual "O Mary Don't You Weep," one Testament bears witness to the other.

O, Mary, don't you weep, don't you mourn,
O, Mary, don't you weep, don't you mourn,
Pharaoh's army got drownded,
O, Mary, don't you weep.

Mary here must be Mary the sister of Martha and Lazarus, who weeps at Jesus's feet after her brother's death (John 11:28–37). Her tears move Jesus to resurrect Lazarus from the grave where he had been lying dead for four days. This identification is confirmed by a variant of the song that mentions Mary and Martha together: "O, Mary, don't you weep, / O, Martha, don't you mourn."[10] Here the Exodus, God's definitive deliverance in the Old Testament, signifies the Resurrection, God's definitive deliverance in the New. The figure of Jesus, unmentioned but ever present, correlates across the Old and New Testaments these two mighty acts of God, Exodus as escape from the death of bondage and Resurrection as escape from the bondage of death.

The figure of the bereaved sisters Martha and Mary, mediated through the Negro spirituals, carries the semiotic impact of struggle and aspiration: here the reality of death and the hope of deliverance poignantly meet. This imagery informs the composition of Charles White's painting *O Mary Don't You Weep* (1956). White, who flourished between the late 1940s and early 1970s and resisted contemporary currents of minimalism, abstract expressionism, and conceptualism, renders the sorrowful sisters with the realism characteristic of his craft. The artist has eschewed abstraction to represent the struggles and aspirations of African-American life with gritty detail. The grim, forlorn woman at left heeds the counsel of the Negro spiritual and withholds her tears. Bereft, she is not alone. At right, the anguished but resolute woman who accompanies her is "Martha," Mary's sister in suffering. In the New Testament story of their suffering, they send word to Jesus that Lazarus their brother is dying. Jesus delays, Lazarus dies, and the women must bury their brother and mourn him four days before Jesus arrives to resurrect him. Both sisters confront Jesus with the same words: "Lord, if thou hadst been here, my brother had not died" (John 11:21 and 32). Jesus, by his very absence, defines the women's suffering in the biblical story, in the Negro spiritual, and in White's painting.[11]

The composers of spirituals sought and found Jesus in line upon line of the Bible, and they found him again and again—even where he does not appear. The Negro spiritual "Daniel Saw the Stone" suggests the presence of Jesus in the image in Nebuchadnezzar's dream of the stone "cut out the mountain without hands."

> Thou, O king, sawest, and behold a great image. This great image, whose brightness was excellent, stood before thee; and the form thereof was terrible.
>
> This image's head was of fine gold, his breast and his arms of silver, his belly and his thighs of brass,
>
> His legs of iron, his feet part of iron and part of clay,
>
> Thou sawest till that a stone was cut out without hands, which smote the image upon his feet that were of iron and clay, and brake them to pieces.
>
> Then was the iron, the clay, the brass, the silver, and the gold broken to pieces together, and became like chaff of the summer threshing floors; and the wind carried them away, that no place was found for them. And the stone that smote the image became a great mountain, and filled the whole earth. (Dan. 2:31–35)

The spiritual speaks of this Old Testament dreamscape in New Testament parlance. The first verse after the refrain of "Daniel Saw the Stone" declares,

> Never saw such a man before
> Cut out the mountain without hands
> Preaching gospels to the poor
> Cut out the mountain without hands.[12]

The reference to "such a man" here is not to Daniel, though Daniel is the only biblical figure mentioned by name in the song. "Such a man," glossed within the song as the stone "cut out the mountain without hands," is Jesus. It is Jesus, the Bible tells us, who preaches to the poor as a sign that the kingdom of God has come. The Gospel of Luke reports that Jesus in his inaugural sermon in Nazareth quotes the prophet Isaiah, declaring, "The Spirit of the Lord is upon me, because he hath anointed me to preach the gospel to the poor" (4:18). When John the Baptist sends emissaries to Jesus to find out if Jesus is indeed "he that should come," Jesus sends them back to tell John "what things ye have seen and heard; how that the blind see, the lame walk, the lepers are cleansed, the deaf hear, the dead are raised, to the poor the gospel is preached" (Luke 7:22). The stone is the coming kingdom that crushes all others. The king of that kingdom is Jesus.

Jesus is the premier figure of speech in Negro spirituals, the sacred folk music that has been called "a Third Testament" for African Americans.[13] As one Negro spiritual put it, "Everywhere I go, / Everywhere I go, my Lord, Everywhere I go, / Somebody's talking about Jesus."[14] In one figure, Jesus signified at once the betrayal, humiliation, brutal death, and miraculous resurrection of a broken people. A compelling image too capacious to be hemmed in by the canon that bears witness to him, he is a biblical figure bigger than either of the two Testaments, even bigger than both. The Negro spirituals might find Jesus in the Bible at the head of Joshua's armies, or on Mount Horeb, or in the fiery furnace with Shadrach, Meshach, and Abednego. In the spiritual "He's the Lily of the Valley" Jesus is at once the fair flower of Solomon's Canticle (Song of Solomon 2:1) and the driver of Elijah's heavenly chariot (2 Kings 2:11).

> He's the lily of the valley,
> Oh, my Lord.
> He's the lily of the valley,
> Oh, my Lord.
> King Jesus in His chariot rides,
> Oh, my Lord

With four white horses side by side,
Oh my Lord.[15]

In the Negro spiritual "Ride On, King Jesus," it is not the Joshua of the
Old Testament but the Jesus of the New who crosses the Jordan.

King Jesus rides a milk-white horse,
No man can hinder him.
The river Jordan he did cross,
No man can hinder him.

Jesus is depicted here astride a white horse in the bloody climax of the
book of Revelation (Rev. 19:11–19). At the same time he is Joshua, the
successor of Moses who leads the children of Israel across the Jordan into
the Promised Land (Josh. 3:1–4:19). He even surpasses Moses, for though
Moses does not enter the Promised Land (see Deut. 32:51–52), Jesus, the
Joshua of the New Testament, takes it by storm.

NOT PEACE BUT A SWORD

The armed Christ of the book of Revelation who rides into battle on
a milk-white horse had been a venerable biblical image in black Christianity from the days of slavery. And for the authors of the Negro spirituals, the Joshua of the Old Testament who sets Canaan aflame and the
Jesus of the New Testament who sets the cosmos aflame are one and
the same. It is as though the "black and unknown bards" somehow knew
that "Jesus" is but the Greek form of the Hebrew "Joshua." Thus in the
spiritual "He Is King of Kings," it is Jesus, not Joshua, who conquers
Canaan.

King of kings, Lord of lords,
Jesus Christ the first and the last,
No man works like Him.
He pitched his tent on Canaan's ground,
No man works like Him,
And broke the Roman kingdom down;
No man works like Him.[16]

Here Joshua does not foreshadow Jesus. Nor is Jesus fully realized the
figure of Joshua. Joshua *is* Jesus. The two, Jesus and Joshua, are identical

insofar as both insist on justice and judgment. Here we find no dichotomy of the bloodthirsty Jehovah of the Old Testament and the merciful deity of the New Testament revealed in Jesus gentle, meek, and mild. Jesus, as much for American slaves as he was for the author of the book of Revelation at the end of the New Testament, was a man of war.

Abolitionist David Walker evoked the name of Jesus as he charged slaves to be vigilant, watching for an opportunity to strike a blow for their freedom. In that day, "when that hour arrives and you move, be not afraid or dismayed; for be you assured that Jesus Christ the King of heaven and earth who is the God of justice and of armies, will surely go before you. And those enemies who have for hundreds of years stolen our rights, and kept us ignorant of Him and his divine worship, he will remove." Walker's Jesus is "the God of justice and of armies," who leads the slaves into battle against the master class.[17]

The Bible has offered slavery's children a martial paradigm of liberation by divinely sanctioned violence. The God of the enslaved Israelites comports himself as a god of war, much like the god Baal of the Israelites' neighbors in Canaan. The iconography of Baal—volcanic fire, thunderous storm cloud, and the quaking, shaking seismic violence of a celestial warrior—matches the persona of the God we encounter in Exodus. This is no accident: in the traditions of ancient Israel, the God who deeds Canaan to the Israelites sometimes appears very much like the god of Canaan. Although the Hebrew Bible rejected the image of Baal, it took over the imagery of Baal to speak of the God of Israel as a god of war.

In the Bible, Jesus is the son of this angry god. At the close of the New Testament Jesus becomes that god's most distinguished general. The book of Revelation renders Jesus waging war on the enemies of the Lord "with the sword of his mouth," riding a white stallion through a deluge of blood that would rise "even unto the horse bridles" (Rev. 14:20). Antebellum black revolutionaries waged war against the slave regime with Jesus in the vanguard, and so to join the battle, in W. E. B. Du Bois's words, on "this side of death" and "in this day."[18] In an infamous death-row confession made just before his execution in 1831 for leading a rebellion of hundreds of slaves in Southampton, Virginia, slave preacher Nat Turner reminded his interviewer that Jesus brought "not peace but a sword" (Matt. 10:34). Turner explained that the Holy Spirit had directed him through a revelatory understanding of the words of Jesus. Turner experienced a series of visions in which he saw images of black and white spirits at war with each other in rivers of blood. He observed prodigies in the sky that he inter- preted as the outstretched arms of the crucified Christ. While laboring in the fields he found the corn stained with blood, which he identified as the blood of Jesus. Turner's biblical mysticism guided him in the organiza- tion, timing, and execution of his plot.[19] The revolt began on August 21, and before it ended two months later with Turner's capture on October 31, fifty-five whites and two hundred blacks had been killed in the violence.

Solidarity with Jesus was the fount of the martial valor of one of Higginson's Union recruits, who explained to his commanding officer the source of his courage:

> Let me live with my musket in one hand the Bible in the
> other—that if I die at the muzzle of the musket, die in the
> water, die on the land, I may know I have the blessed Jesus
> in my hand, and have no fear. I have left my wife in the land
> of bondage; my little ones they say every night, where is my
> father? But when I die, when the blessed morning rises, when
> I shall stand in the glory, with one foot on the water and one
> foot on the land, then, O Lord, I shall see my wife and my little
> children once more.[20]

The soldier describes himself as standing in heaven, "in the glory, with one foot on the water and one foot on the land." He describes the pose of an angel who announces judgment in the book of Revelation: "And I saw another mighty angel . . . and he set his right foot upon the sea, and his left foot on the earth" (Rev. 10:1–2). The Bible assured this recruit that justice frustrated in time would be fulfilled in eternity.

Higginson suspected that to suit their condition on the battlefield his soldiers had retrofitted the martial imagery to the songs.[21] But there was much that Higginson did not understand of what he heard in the voices of the former slaves under his command. He did not, could not have under- stood that the same martial spirit had been the genesis of black folk songs for perhaps as much as a century before the outbreak of the Civil War. The violent restiveness of this spirit helps us to understand the more than 250 documented incidences of slave revolt in the United States from the beginning of the slave regime to its end.

Informed by the rich biblical imagery of the Last Days, African Americans have anticipated the return of the militant Jesus as the righteous arbiter of human destiny. His Second Coming would consummate ultimate deliverance in the consummation of all things at the end of time. "And I saw a great white throne, and him that sat on it, from whose face the earth and the heaven fled away; and there was found no place for them. And I saw the dead, small and great, stand before God; and the books were opened: and another book was opened, which is the book of life: and the dead were judged out of those things which were written in the books, according to their works" (Rev. 20:11–12). The Bible taught the slaves and their descendants that ultimately the entire world would fall under this sentence. Even death affords no escape: "And the sea gave up that dead which were in it; and death and hell delivered up the dead which were in them: and they were judged every man according to their works" (Rev. 20:13).

The last stanza of the Negro spiritual "Judgment" celebrates a forensic Jesus in the apocalyptic imagery of the New Testament:

> King Jesus sittin' in the kingdom, Lord,
> Oh, how I long to go there too;
> The angels singin' all round the throne,
> Oh, how I long to go.
> The trumpet sound the Jubilo,
> Oh, how I long to go there too,
> I hope that trump will blow me home,
> Oh, how I long to go.[22]

In "My Lord, What a Mourning," Jesus returns as the judge of the dead as well as the living:

> You'll see my Jesus come,
> To wake the nations underground,
> Look in my God's right hand,
> When the stars begin to fall.
> His chariot wheels roll round,
> To wake the nations underground.
> Look in my God's right hand,
> When the stars begin to fall.[23]

At his return Jesus will raise the dead—"wake the nations underground"—to face the recompense of their deeds.

The slaves' biblical reflections on the end of the age move from Revelation, the last book of the Bible, back through the teachings of Jesus to the Old Testament prophets, even as far as the first destruction of the world in Genesis. Though the flood is recounted in the first book of the Bible, African Americans associate that ancient cataclysm as a sign of the last days. For the slaves this sign speaks not of the ancient past but of the future judgment. The anonymous composers of the Negro spirituals compare the cosmic conflagration promised in the last book of the Bible with the global inundation recorded in the first: "God gave Noah the rainbow sign / No more water but fire next time." The cause of the first global catastrophe—the Deluge—is likewise that of "the fire next time." God's righteous outrage against human injustice is the impetus of cosmic catastrophe past and present: "And God saw that the wickedness of man was great in the earth. . . . And the Lord said, I will destroy man whom I have created from the face of the earth. . . . The earth also was corrupt before God, and the earth was filled with violence" (Gen. 6:5, 7, 11).

The Hebrew word for "violence" in the story of the flood, ḥamas, signifies any wrongdoing or false dealing: a false witness in the Hebrew Bible is 'ed ḥamas, one who does violence to the truth, literally, "a witness of violence." Once again, injustice is the biblical warrant for the fiercest violence. The God of the Bible, the God who destroys the world with water, is a God who meets violence with violence. Rap artist Ice Cube summons the example of the flood as the license for violent retribution human and divine in the song "When I Get to Heaven":

> The same white man that threw me in the slammer
> He bombed a church in Alabama
> So if I cocked the hammer God won't mind
> If I have to kill the human swine
> 'Cause God is a killer from the start
> Why you think Noah had to build his Ark?[24]

In traditions of the African-American vernacular, the rainbow is not so much promise as threat. The violence of the deluge is invoked against the violence of the present world order: the violence of human beings is overcome by the violence of God.

The story of Noah's ordeal is mentioned several times in the New Testament. Most influential in the Negro spirituals were the words of

Jesus in the Gospels: "But as the days Noe [Noah] were, so shall also the coming of the Son of Man be. For as in the days that were before the flood they were eating and drinking, marrying and giving in marriage, until the day that Noe entered the ark, and knew not until the flood came, and took them all away; so shall also the coming of the Son of Man be" (Matt. 24:37–39). The story is retold in African-American folklore: "And then Noah began to preach and tell them there was going to come a flood, and he starts to build an ark. It had never rained before and they thought he was just talking foolishness. And so they were marrying and giving in marriage until Noah built the ark and closed up the door. And when the flood came up they'd go and ask him to let them in. But he wouldn't. Then the flood destroyed them all."[25] The phrase "marrying and giving in marriage" is present neither in the Genesis account nor in the later Old Testament references to the flood. The phrase appears in the saying of Jesus about the end of the age: the folktale rehearses the Old Testament story using the words of Jesus. Jesus's saying about the flood as it is found in the Gospel of Luke provides the language of the ending of the folk version: "And as it was in the days of Noe, so it shall be in the days of the Son of Man. They did eat, they drank, they married wives, they were given in marriage, until the day that Noe entered into the ark, and the flood came, and destroyed them all" (Luke 17:26–27).

For those praying for the end of the present evil regime, God's promise not to wipe injustice of the face of the earth itself borders on injustice. The world that God condemned to the flood was a world already awash in violence. But by promising never to do so again, the God of the Bible in effect had tied his hands in the cosmic administration of justice. He has bound himself to a contract that will not permit him to flush evil out of the world. The New Testament writers found an escape clause, however, in Jesus's promise to return as a righteous judge. In the musical summary of the Bible that the church choir sings in James Baldwin's play *The Amen Corner* (1968), the contraltos bring together the themes of creation, Jesus, the first judgment of the deluge, and the Last Judgment of Revelation.

> I opened my Bible and began to read
> About all the things He's done for me;
> Read on down about Chapter One
> How He made the earth and He made the sun.

Read on down about Chapter Two
How He died for me and He died for you.
Read on down about Chapter Three
How he made the blind, the blind to see.
Read on down about Chapter Four
How He healed the sick and blessed the poor.
Read on down about Chapter Five
How it rained forty days and Noah survived.
Six, seven, about the same
Just keep praising my Jesus' name.
Read on down about Chapter Eight,
The golden streets and the pearly gates.
Read on down about Chapter Nine
We all get to heaven in due time.
Read on down about Chapter Ten
My God's got a key and He'll let me in.
When I finish reading the rest
I'll go to judgment to stand my test.
He'll say come a little higher, come a little higher,
He'll say come a little higher and take your seat.[26]

The summary condenses the Old Testament in "Chapter One." The next biblical event recounted is the Crucifixion, followed by the miracles of Jesus. Then the song returns to the Old Testament with the reference to Noah and the flood. The next biblical allusion is to end-time tableaux of the book of Revelation. "The golden streets and the pearly gates" is the beatific vision of the New Jerusalem (Rev. 21:21). The order of Baldwin's images is not canonical but eschatological: references to Jesus bracket the mention of the flood. Jesus is associated with both past and future events of divine judgment as he is in the Gospel sayings about "the days of Noe."

The sign of the rainbow after the flood signifies the tacit promise that the Negro spirituals read into Genesis from the Gospels and Book of Revelation: "no more water but fire next time." It is the divine threat, explicit in the New Testament and implicit in the Old, that God brought the world to a violent end once and stands ready to do it again by different but equally violent means.

And the ensign of that violent end is Jesus. In the Negro spirituals, the slave sang of "Jesus, walking down the heavenly road, / Out of his mouth came a two-edged sword."[27] They sang of themselves as "soldiers in the army of the Lord," and "singing with a sword in my hand."[28] The holy mountain of Zion is the command post for the armies of the Lord led by "their great General" Jesus in the anthem "They Look Like Men of War." S. C. Armstrong, a recruiter and commandant of the Ninth Regiment U.S. Colored Troops at Benedict, Maryland, heard this song sung by black soldiers around the campfires during the winter of 1863–1864. He found the song so compelling that it drew him out of his tent and into the cold to listen to this "magnificent chorus" that he dubbed "the Negro Battle Hymn." The soldiers were reading themselves and their struggle against the Confederacy into the imaginary of biblical holy war:

> Hark! Listen to the trumpeters
> They call for volunteers;
> On Zion's bright and holy mount,
> Behold the officers.
>
> Refrain:
> They look like men,
> They look like men,
> They look like men of war;
> All armed and dressed in uniform,
> They look like men of war.
>
> Their horses white, their armor bright,
> With courage bold they stand
> Enlisting soldiers for the King
> To march to Canaan's land.
>
> They follow their great General
> The great eternal Lamb
> His garments stained in His own blood,
> King Jesus is his name.[29]

This biblical imagery was not merely an apology for the unprecedented violence of the Civil War; it was a mandate for it. Former slave W. B. Allen explained, "God was using the Yankees to scourge the slaveholders, just as he had, centuries before, used heathens and outcasts to scourge his chosen people—the Children of Israel."[30] "What God says had got to come to pass, comes," testified ex-slave Jerry Eubanks, speaking of the Union victory. "This is written in the Bible. They says, 'The Yankees done it'—but colored people looks cross years at everything. God did it all."[31] The blood would flow, in the words of Revelation, "even unto the horse bridles." The slave regime was to be destroyed by force of arms, with the elect fighting on the side of the angels. All opponents of justice were to be pitilessly destroyed in the death-dealing judgment demanded by the scriptures and exacted by the saints. Marcus, a Gullah soldier who joined the Union Army after the Yankee occupation of the Sea Islands, recalled, "Master laugh one day. Ask me if I think Christ want black nigger in heaven. One thing sure. We'uns going to be where the crucify Lord am. And if that place be Hell, He going to make it heaven for we."[32] Black soldiers waging holy war in America looked forward to a place with Jesus on the other side of mortality.

Militant civil rights activist Robert F. Williams, whose advocacy of armed resistance to racist terror in the 1950s and 1960s anticipated the black militancy of the late 1960s and early 1970s, viewed the revolutionary spirit of Jesus's proclamation as compatible with armed revolt. Williams's working-class origins and military training kept him close to the American tradition of armed self-defense honored by whites, blacks, and Native Americans in the South. The militant tradition of African-American Christianity in the South, rooted in the Christian slave revolts and church-organized armed resistance during Radical Reconstruction, was also an important element of Williams's formation. As the embattled president of Monroe, North Carolina, chapter of the National Association for the Advancement of Colored People (NAACP), his charisma, outspoken insistence on bearing arms, and courageous willingness to use them in defense of African Americans made him a cause célèbre of leftist militants across the country and around the world. Williams ran afoul of the NAACP's cautious, conservative president Roy Wilkins and found himself to the political left of Martin Luther King, Jr. In 1959 the two popular civil rights leaders argued in published debate over the issue of violent resistance. King's eloquence and erudition carried the debate, but Williams's insistence on the right and the duty to defend oneself and loved ones against racist violence struck a resounding cord in the hearts of many African Americans throughout the United States.[33]

Williams's visit to Cuba in 1960 left him awestruck by the first fruits of national armed resistance to oppression. He later called the Cuban Revolution "the great miracle of the twentieth century."[34] Fidel Castro's speech celebrating the revolution's first anniversary in the Sierra Maestra in Oriente Province, the heavily Afro-Cuban region that gave birth to the revolution, was a quasi-religious experience for the African-American activist. Williams described the mountaintop celebration in his national newsletter, the *Crusader,* in biblical parlance: "For what can one say of a glory that mankind has never before approximated? . . . I simply say that I have seen the face of Cuba . . . in the beauty and happiness of her sons and daughters who made a pilgrimage to the Sierra Maestra to hear the modern version of the Sermon on the Mount."[35] Accompanying Williams's commentary, the *Crusader* featured a drawing of Castro with the caption "Fidel Castro: Spirit of Christ." For Robert Williams, Jesus was the image of the revolutionary and the revolutionary was the image of Jesus.

THE PROPHET

African-American Muslims as well as African-American Christians have held that Jesus will oversee the end of the world and the judgment of humanity. In much of African-American Islam, the end-time role of Jesus is similar to that of early medieval traditions of Islamic interpretation. According to the Qur'an, Jesus issues a summons to serve the one true God, threatens idolaters with hellfire, and promises paradise to those who die fighting in God's cause. The prophet Jesus is depicted in the Qur'an as a true Muslim who practiced ritual prayer and almsgiving. Jesus's disciples were "submitted ones," which is the meaning of the word "Muslim." They are counted "with those who bear witness," that is, those who recite the Muslim confession of faith. In Islam, Jesus is the premier witness of all those who bear witness to the true religion.

Several early Muslim commentators expected Jesus to return before the day of Resurrection and purge and unite all religious communities as the one true *umma,* or community of Islam. According to a report from the *Hadith,* or traditions of the life of the Prophet Muhammad, the prophet is said to have declared, "There is no Mahdi [Messiah] save Jesus son of Mary."[36] Early and medieval commentators argued that Allah would exalt Jesus as a harbinger of the Last Judgment, and they repeatedly interpreted a few obscure Qur'anic verses as anticipations of Jesus's return at the end of the age: according to this venerable line of Islamic interpretation, Jesus is the one whom the Qur'an says is "an eminent one in this world and the hereafter, one of those brought near [to Allah]." The Qur'anic verse, "He has knowledge ['ilm] of the hour" (43:61) became an oblique reference to Jesus's future return in the hour of judgment. In the Arabic text the word 'ilm, "knowledge," may also be read as 'alam, "sign" or "token": so interpreted, this verse is a reference to Jesus, whom God will send from heaven as a sign ('alam) of the end of the age.

Jesus is an important figure in the various Islamic traditions that began to develop in African-American communities in the twentieth century. Noble Drew Ali was the chief prophet of the Moorish Science Temple, which he founded in Newark, New Jersey, in 1913. Born Timothy Drew in North Carolina 1886, Ali studied in Egypt, where he claimed to have been recognized as a prophet. Ali taught that African Americans are "Asiatics" or Moors whose religion is Islam and whose Promised Land is Morocco. In 1927 he published *The Holy Koran,* a compendium of Christian, Islamic, and theosophical teachings that serve as the Moorish Science Temple's sacred scripture. In *The Holy Koran,* Jesus is a prophet of Allah. His name means "justice," and he was dispatched to earth by Allah to deliver the Israelites from their white European oppressors, the Romans. The first reincarnation of Jesus was the "Prophet Mohammed the Conqueror," who was to have beheaded Satan in 1453 CE.[37]

According to the traditional teaching of the Nation of Islam, Jesus is a great Muslim prophet second only to Muhammad. Elijah Muhammad, founder of the Nation of Islam and spiritual father of Malcolm X, taught that all the prophets of the Bible preached the same message of Islam. Contemporary hip-hop artists acquainted with the doctrine of the Five Percenters, the splinter group of the Nation of Islam influential among African-American urban youth, have also claimed the Islamic fidelity of Jesus. "[Jesus] was in fact a Muslim," insists rap artist Prince Hakeem. "Muslim means one who submits to do the will of God, and that's all Jesus did, the will of God."[38]

The Christ of African-American Christians could so easily be a prophet to African-American Muslims because he was a Christ bigger than Christianity, a Jesus who transcended the formulas of doctrine and dogma that Christian tradition has used to talk about him. And so the Jesus of African-American sacred music, folklore, and popular piety is the

Christ neither of the creeds nor of the communions that have historically confessed them.

Generally African Americans have found too terse the Pauline proclamation of a crucified and resurrected Messiah. The Jesus of the slaves resisted succinct, propositional formulations: for them, Jesus was, in the words of theologian James Cone, "an historical presence in motion."[39] Historically, African Americans have been more engaged with what Jesus did, said and suffered, than what had been said about him in the creeds. Apparently the slaves were ignorant of creeds of Nicaea and Chalcedon, and the churches of their descendents have historically worn Nicene and Chalcedonian confessions very loosely. Sociologist of religion Joseph Washington has claimed that the religion of black people in America, obsessed with the narratives and discourses of Jesus, is not Christianity but "Jesusology," a tacit, heterodox rejection of the orthodox Christology of the creeds. Washington saw this Jesus-centered faith as a sign of the theological poverty of African-American Christians, to whom orthodox, genuine Christianity was unknown and uninteresting. "Instead of experiencing a sense of participation in the Cross, the Crucifixion, and the Resurrection, the Negro relates singularly to the life and ministry of Jesus." Washington accuses African-American Christians of reducing Jesus "to the role of exemplar."[40]

African-American art and sacred music have done what the venerable Christian creeds, which make such quick work of the tortured and triumphant life of Jesus, have not: they have insisted on telling the story of the life and death of Jesus. The words and deeds of Jesus mark an entire genre of contemporary African-American religious music called gospel. In the gospel song made famous by Mahalia Jackson, "Lord, Don't Move This Mountain," not only the words but even the valuations of scripture have been turned around. The lyrics suggest the saying of Jesus that just a little faith is enough to move a mountain (Matt. 17:20). But the song is not a plea for more faith: indeed, Jesus's words affirm that only a little faith will do. The song is a plea for strength: "Lord, don't move this mountain, — /But give me the strength to climb it." In one of Isaiah's oracles, which promises holy mount Zion as the inheritance of Israel, the prophet commands, "take up the stumbling block out of the way of my people" (Isa. 57:14). The gospel song, however, insists that God not remove the stumbling block. It is an ordeal to be obviated but not eliminated: "Please

don't move that stumbling block / But lead me, Lord, around it."[41] The
Bible affirms that faith moves mountains, and that stumbling blocks must
be moved. But the gospel song affirms that precisely because mountains
and stumbling blocks here are a part of Christian life, they must not be
moved. In effect, the plea of the singer is at cross-purposes with the very
biblical texts to which she alludes. The words of Jesus speak directly to
their condition, even if they do so against their own plain sense.

African Americans intuited that the stories Jesus was so famous for
telling—the Lost Sheep, the Prodigal Son, the Good Samaritan—were
stories ultimately about African Americans themselves. In the parable
of the Lost Sheep, African Americans found Jesus tenderly finding
them.

> What man of you, having an hundred sheep, if he lose one
> of them, doth not leave the ninety and nine in the wilderness,
> and go after that which is lost, until he find it? And when
> he hath found it, he layeth it on his shoulders, rejoicing. And
> when he cometh home, he calleth together his friends and
> neighbours, saying unto them, Rejoice with me, for I have
> found my sheep which was lost. I say unto you, that like wise
> joy shall be in heaven over one sinner that repenteth, more
> than over ninety and nine just persons, which need no
> repentance. (Luke 15:4–7)

It is ultimately Jesus himself who sings in the Negro spiritual "Done
Found My Lost Sheep."

> My Lord had a hundred sheep.
> One of them went astray.
> He left the ninety-nine,
> And went to the wilderness to seek and find.
> If you find him, bring him back,
> Across the shoulders, across your back.
> Tell the neighbors all around,
> That lost sheep has now been found.
> I found my lost sheep,
> I found my lost sheep.
> In that Resurrection Day,

The sinner finds no place to rest
Go to the mountain,
The mountain moves.
Go to the hill,
The hill runs, too.
The sinner travels on trembling ground,
Poor lost sheep was never found.
Sinner, why don't you stop and pray,
Then you would hear the Shepherd say,
I found my lost sheep,
I found my lost sheep.

Elijah Muhammad argues that the lost sheep of the parable are African Americans. "[Allah] has made us to understand," writes Muhammad, "these Bible parables are referring to us, the so-called Negroes, and our slavemasters":

> We, the so-called American Negroes, are mentioned in the
> New Testament under several names and parables. I will name
> two: the parable of the Lost Sheep and the parable of the Prodi-
> gal Son. We could not be described better. . . . Regardless of
> the sins that we have committed in following and obeying our
> slave-masters, Allah (God) forgives everything today, if we, the
> so-called Negroes, will turn to Him and to our own kind. If the
> wicked can rejoice over finding his lost animal, or a piece of
> silver, or a son who had a desire to leave home and practice
> the evil habits of strangers, how much more will Allah and the
> nation of Islam rejoice over finding us, . . . [we] who have been
> lost . . . for 400 years.[42]

In Luke 15, the Evangelist has brought together parables about a lost sheep (15:4–7), a lost coin (15:8–10), and a lost son (15:11–32) to illustrate the theme of lost and found in the teaching of Jesus. According to the racial doctrine of Elijah Muhammad, the lost sheep of the parable allegorically portray the "so-called Negroes" as the "the lost-found Nation of Islam."

In James Weldon Johnson's poetical retelling of Jesus's parable of the Prodigal Son (Luke 15:11–32), Babylon is the cipher for life in the big city. The story becomes a parable of the many young, black men who fled the poverty and racism of the rural South only to meet the poverty and racism of the urban North with its fast life and fast women.

> Then the young man came to himself,
> He came to himself and said:
> In my father's house are many mansions,
> Every servant in his house has bread to eat,
> Every servant in his house has a place to sleep;
> I will arise and go to my father.
> And his father saw him afar off,
> And he ran up the road to meet him.
> He put clean clothes upon his back,
> And a golden chain around his neck,
> And made a feast and killed a fatted calf,
> And invited the neighbors in.
> Oh, sinner,
> When you are with the crowd in Babylon,
> Drinking the wine of Babylon,
> Running with the women of Babylon,
> You forget about God, and you laugh at Death.
> Today you have the strength of a bull in your neck
> And the strength of a bear in your arms,
> But some day, some day,
> You will struggle with bony Death,
> And Death is sure to win.
> Young man, come away from Babylon,
> That city at the border of hell,
> Leave the dancing and the gambling of Babylon,
> The wine and whiskey of Babylon;
> Fall down on your knees,
> And say in your heart:
> I will arise and go to my Father.[43]

African Americans have become drunk with the wine of hedonistic captivity of their new urban homes after the great northern migrations of the early twentieth century. They have come to Babylon, "city on the border of hell."

Just as African Americans saw their own moral declension in the parable of the Prodigal Son, so they also saw their own moral agency in the parable of the Good Samaritan. Since the third-century Egyptian exegete Origen, the parable of the Good Samaritan has been subject to an allegorical reading that interprets the Samaritan as a stand-in for Jesus and the waylaid traveler as a sign for the abject sinner that the Savior comes to save. African-American interpretation, however, resists this allegory for one in which the Samaritan is not Jesus but the African-American reader. In so doing, the reading insists on the agency of African Americans themselves. The parable of the Good Samaritan becomes the script of a morality play in which African Americans assume the title role.

At the end of the eighteenth century, Prince Hall, founder of the first fraternal order for men of African descent, exhorted his Masonic brethren to practice "love and benevolence to all the whole family of mankind, as God's make and creation." The penultimate example of this universal love is the Good Samaritan, whose compassion is second only to that of Jesus himself.

> I shall mention the good deeds of the Samaritan, though at
> that time they were looked upon as unworthy to eat, drink, or
> trade with their fellow men, at least by the Jews; see the pity
> and compassion he had on a poor distressed and half-dead
> stranger, . . . See that you endeavor to do likewise.—But when
> we consider the amazing condescending love and pity our
> blessed Lord had on such poor worms as we are, as not only to
> call us his friends, but his brothers, we are lost and can go no
> further in holy writ for examples to excite us to the love of our
> fellowmen.[44]

In his sermon "Who Is My Neighbor," Martin Luther King, Jr., tacitly concurs with Prince Hall that the Samaritan exemplifies what mercy demands of all people without exception and without exclusion. Through the figure of the Samaritan, Jesus defines the neighbor as someone—anyone—in need. "Who is my neighbor? 'I do not know his name,' says Jesus in essence. 'He is anyone toward whom you are neighborly. He is anyone who lies in need at life's roadside. He is neither Jew nor Gentile; he is neither Russian nor American; he is neither Negro nor white. He is "a certain man"—any needy man—on one of the numerous Jericho roads of life.'"[45] Like Prince Hall, King points out that at a profounder level the parable is not only a story about love, but about the storyteller, for "we have, in addition to the inspiring example of the good Samaritan, the magnanimous life of our Christ to guide us."[46] King considers only briefly the actions of the Priest and Levite in the parable, and Prince Hall makes mention of them only in passing as counterexamples. Their moral cowardice pales in the brilliance of the Samaritan's moral courage. In the linoleum cut of African-American artist James L. Wells that illustrates the parable, the dangerous road, the supine traveler, the attentive Samaritan and his waiting burrow dominate the foreground. A city, presumably Jerusalem, looms small and distant behind them in the background. The Priest and the Levite have faded from view; Wells has deemed them unworthy of iconic mention.[47] With the hatred of the city of Jerusalem behind him, the Samaritan cares for his neighbor with gratuitous love. The parable of the Good Samaritan teaches black people that the compassion that Jesus commanded transcends all peculiarities and idiosyncrasies of the other, even his hatred.

Just as they fixed on the stories Jesus told, African Americans also found themselves in the stories told about him. The Reverend Jesse Jackson takes the story of the woman caught in adultery in the Gospel of John as the text of an impromptu sermon about the scandal following the revelation that Jackson had fathered a child by a former staffer with whom he had had an extramarital affair. "In that story," writes *New Yorker* journalist Peter J. Boyer in his article on Jackson, "lay . . . the essence of Jackson's particular brand of faith."[48]

Jackson takes a controversial text. The story of Jesus and the woman accused of adultery appears in most modern Bibles as John 7:53–8:11 but is missing from several ancient biblical manuscripts as early as the fourth century: some early Christian scribes either ignored the story or refused to recopy it. In other ancient manuscripts of the Bible, the passage appears after John 21:25, an example of the "many other things Jesus did" mentioned in the Gospel. In a few manuscripts it shows up in the Gospel of Luke after 21:37–38 and 24:50–53, both of which report Jesus's activities in the Temple where the encounter with the woman takes place. Some ancient copyists who reproduced the manuscripts of the Bible had reservations about the story, and there was no consensus among them about where to put it in the greater narrative of the story of Jesus. Some included it in one place, some put it in another, and some did not include it at all.

Clearly later commentators as well as early manuscript copyists were uncomfortable with the lax morality of the tale. The woman, after all, was convicted of a capital offense, and after neither reviewing the evidence nor returning a judgment, Jesus merely releases her on her own recognizance with a warning. The sixteenth-century reformer John Calvin was worried that preachers would deduce from this—erroneously, by Calvin's lights—"that adultery should not be punished by death."[49]

Calvin, as it turned out, was justly worried about preachers like Jesse Jackson. Neither Jackson's compromising situation nor his easy sense of penance dispose him to consider the death penalty as just deserts for adulterers. He is more concerned to brake the rush to judgment—judgment returned against the woman and so against Jackson himself—and to highlight the hypocrisy that is so often only a stone's throw away from public morality. Jackson retells the story of Jesus, the woman, and her accusers with flourishes of vernacular language and imaginative embellishment characteristic of traditional African-American preaching.

> Jesus walking down the road and hears this loud, cheering crowd and a woman hollering and rocks thumping. He says, "What's happening, guys?" "We caught her in the act of prostitution. We saw the whole thing, no hearsay, we caught her cold. She broke religious law, she broke political law. She got to die." Jesus says, "Prostitution? You know, you can't prostitute by yourself. Where's her partner?" And the crowd got real still. "Where is he? And by the way, if there are any amongst you, you who are doing this rock throwing, who have not had sex with her, or wished you could have, then throw the rock." Then, all of a sudden, things got real quiet. And then one of the eldest of that crowd left first—I imagine he'd probably been doing it the longest. Then they all left. Now Jesus said to her, "You know, this is wrong. You stop whoring. Go and sin no more." We are all sinners, saved by mercy and grace."[50]

Jesus, explains Jackson, "brings to the agenda some mercy with justice, and some understanding. . . . He had to think, She was not born a prostitute. Was it that she grew up and saw her mother and father in the act of having sex? Was it that she saw her mama was a prostitute? Was she abused by some stepfather? Was she poor and had to sell her body for some money? Did she lose her self-esteem? What drove her there? That would be his concern." Jackson himself was born to an unwed teen-age mother and a father who shunned his paramour and his love child to protect his reputation in the community. "I can identify with Jesus," says Jackson, "I understand him. He was born with a controversy about who his daddy was."[51] In his commentary on the story of the adulteress, Jackson identifies one moment with the fallen woman and the next moment with Jesus, God's love child.

THE RELIGION OF JESUS

Jesus, as the enemy of hypocrisy, was the champion of African-American critics of American Christianity. African Americans appealed to Jesus's argument favoring "the weightier matters of the law" (Matt. 23:23) when confronted by legalistic arguments, even those based on scripture. David Walker protested that the Jesus of the Bible is at odds with the slaveholding religion in the United States that has expropriated his name.

> Have not the Americans the Bible in their hands? Do they be-lieve it? Surely they do not? See how they treat us in open viola-tion of the Bible!! They no doubt will be greatly offended with me, but if God does not awaken them, it will be, because they are superior to other men, as they have represented themselves to be. Our divine Lord and Master said, "All things whatsoever ye would that men should do unto you, do ye even so unto them." But an American minister, with the Bible in his hand, holds us and our children in the most abject slavery and wretchedness. Now, I ask them, would they like for us to hold them and their children in abject slavery and wretchedness?[52]

In Martin Delany's pan-Africanist novel *Blake*, Henry Blake explains to the Cuban poet Placido that the figure of Jesus is a controlling principle of biblical interpretation.

> "Ah, Placido, . . . I still believe in God, and have faith in His promises; but serving Him in the way that I was, I had only 'the shadow without the substance,' the religion of my oppres-sors. I thank God that He timely opened my eyes."
> "In this, Henry, I believe you are right; I long since saw it,

but you are clear on the subject. I had not thought so much as that."

"Then as we agree, let us at once drop the religion of our oppressors, and take the Scriptures for our guide and Christ as our example."

"What difference will that make to us? I merely ask for information, seeing you have matured the subject."

"The difference will be this, Placido—that we shall not be disciplined in our worship, obedience as slaves to our master, the slaveholders, by associating in our mind with that religion, submission to the oppressor's will."[53]

Frederick Douglass insisted more than a century and a half ago that America was possessed of two religions called Christianity, one the faith of the master and the other the faith of the slave, and that to call both by the same name was a crime of linguistic legerdemain. The religion of Jesus, what Douglass called "the Christianity of Christ," differed fundamentally from the faith of the master class that went by the same name.

For between the Christianity of this land [the United States] and the Christianity of Christ, I recognize the widest possible difference—so wide as to receive the one as good, pure, and holy, and of necessity to reject the other as bad, corrupt, and wicked. To be friend of one, is of necessity to be the enemy of the other. I love the pure, peaceable, and impartial Christianity of Christ: I therefore hate the corrupt, slave-holding, women-whipping, cradle-plundering, partial and hypocritical Christianity of this land. Indeed, I can see no reason, but the most deceitful one, for calling the religion of this land Christianity. I look upon it as the climax of all misnomers, the boldest of all frauds, and the grossest of all libels.[54]

Douglass argued that in creating two classes of people—one slave, the other free—American slavery had also created two species of Christianity, the religion of the master class and "the Christianity of Christ." The latter is the authentic faith of Jesus, the former, criminal hypocrisy. "Dark and terrible as is this picture, I hold it to be strictly true of the overwhelming mass of professed Christians in America. They strain at a gnat, and swallow a camel. . . . They attend with Pharisaical strictness to the outward forms of religion, and at the same time neglect the weightier matters of the law, judgment, mercy, and faith."[55] Douglass's condemnation echoes the biblical words of Jesus's outrage against the scribes and Pharisees, whom he excoriates as "hypocrites" because they "have omitted the weightier matters of the law, judgment, mercy, and faith. . . . Ye blind guides, which strain at a gnat, and swallow a camel" (Matt. 23:23–24).

At the end of the nineteenth century, African-American author, educator, and activist Anna Julia Cooper underscored the distinction between the victory of Christ and the failures of Christendom. In her essay "Womanhood a Vital Element in the Regeneration of the Race," she acknowledged that "individuals, organizations, whole sections of the Church . . . may offend the Christ whom they profess. They may ruthlessly trample both the spirit and the letter of his instructions." Cooper insisted, however, that "the source of the vitalizing principle of the development and amelioration of woman is the Christian Church, so far as it agrees with Christianity." According to Cooper, Jesus was the great prophet of every socially progressive impulse, especially the full emancipation of women: "Throughout his [Jesus's] life and in his death he has given to men a rule and guide for the estimation of woman as an equal." The abuses of contemporary society and even contemporary Christendom are a consequence of the failure of humanity to catch up with the radical humanity advocated by Jesus nineteen hundred years earlier. "Nineteen centuries of great advances in knowledge, arts, and sciences, in social and ethical principles have not been able to probe to the depth of these lessons or exhaust them in practice." Modern progress fell far behind Jesus of Nazareth's first-century moral revolution—especially in Christian congregations, black and white, where the dominance of man over woman was all but unquestioned.[56]

W. E. B. Du Bois called Jesus "the greatest of religious rebels." Socialist labor leader A. Philip Randolph, himself the son of a minister, on occasion tried to shame African-American churches and their leadership into embracing the workers' struggle by appeal to their proletarian Messiah. "If the church, white or black, is to express the true philosophy of Jesus Christ, Himself a worker," Randolph wrote, "it will not lend itself to the creed of oppressive capitalism which would deny to the servant his just hire."[57] African-American intellectuals in the twentieth century would have a revolutionary Jesus or no Jesus at all. When Jesus was identified with the white icon of American churches, he was likely to be rejected along with the triumphant Christianity preached and practiced in his name. This rejection, informed by Marxist rhetoric and expressed in the idiom of the working class, inspires Langston Hughes's "Goodbye, Christ."

> Listen, Christ,
> You did alright in your day, I reckon—
> But that day's gone now.
> They ghosted you up a swell story, too,
> Called the Bible—
> But it's dead now.
> The popes and the preachers've
> Made too much money from it.
> They've sold you to too many.
>
> Kings, generals, robbers, and killers—
> Even to the Tzar and the Cossacks,
> Even to Rockefeller's Church,
> Even to THE SATURDAY EVENING POST.
> You ain't no good no more.
> They've pawned you
> Till you've done wore out.
>
> Goodbye,
> Christ Jesus Lord God Jehova,
> Beat it on away from here now.
> Make way for the new guy with no religion at all—
> A real guy named
> Marx Communist Lenin Peasant Stalin Worker ME[58]

For some African-American intellectuals, Jesus becomes the merchandise bought and sold by a Christianity that coddles the wealthy and casts aspersions on the working classes. In his ascension Jesus deserts the wretched of the earth that he came to save. In Countee Cullen's poem "Black Magdalens" (1925), Jesus is no longer the justifier of prostitutes and publicans. Alluding to the biblical stories of the woman caught in adultery (John 7:53–8:11) and the "sinful woman" who tearfully anoints the feet of Jesus (Luke 7:37–39), Cullen laments that Jesus no longer stoops to defend the lowly against the shame of poverty and the arrogance of the well-to-do. These women of ill repute

> . . . have no Christ to spit and stoop
> To write upon the sand,
> Inviting him that has not sinned
> To raise the first rude hand.
>
> . . . .
>
> They fare full ill since Christ forsook
> The cross to mount a throne,
> And Virtue still is stooping down
> To cast the first hard stone.[59]

The Christ that disgusts Hughes's worker and deserts Cullen's working women has sold out to and been sold out by American Christians worshipping at the altars of race, caste, and class.

The late 1960s and early 1970s would witness a revival of anticlerical, antiecclesiastical, and anti-Christian sentiments among radical African-American intellectuals frustrated by the limits of the Civil Rights Movement. They rejected the doctrines of non-violence and redemptive suffering for which Jesus stood as quintessential symbol. In Amiri Baraka's sardonic "When We'll Worship Jesus," the poet laureate of the Black Arts Movement of the early 1970s flaunts a disdain laced with the politics of Black Power.

> we'll worship jesus when
> he get bad enough to at least scare
> somebody—cops not afraid
> of jesus
> pushers not afraid
> of jesus, capitalists racists
> imperialists not afraid
> of jesus shit they makin money
> off jesus
> we'll worship jesus when mao
> do, when toure does
> when the cross replaces Nkrumah's
> star
> Jesus need to hurt some a our

enemies, then we'll check him
out[60]

Conservative black clergy objected to the interpretation of Jesus as a revolutionary and forerunner of Black Power. Black Evangelical preacher Tom Skinner insisted that Jesus was indeed "radical," but radically nonviolent. The Good News that Jesus proclaimed transcended race: in his own time, Jesus did not "come to be on the Roman side or the Jewish side" but came "to establish a new Kingdom, a kingdom that starts by radically transforming the lives of people." The kingdom that he advocated was spiritual: "Revolutions," asserts Skinner, "cannot be effective if they are merely economic, if they are merely social, if they are merely political; they've got to be spiritual and moral, they've got to shape people from the inside, they've got to transform the very structure of a man."[61] The revolution of Jesus would properly take place in the hearts of individuals as a politics of personal conversion. Even though Jesus was a revolutionary, his politics and those of his church were not.

The Christ of orthodox religion, who promises heaven after death but does nothing for those living in hell, is the object of both veneration and scorn in August Wilson's play *Joe Turner's Come and Gone*. Herald Loomis's long-lost wife, Martha Pentecost, attempts to talk her estranged husband out of his armed rage using the words of the Twenty-third Psalm, long associated with the image of Jesus the gentle shepherd.

MARTHA: Herald . . . put down that knife. You got to look to Jesus. Even if you done fell away from the church you can be saved again. The Bible say, "The Lord is my shepherd I shall not want. He maketh me to lie down in green pastures. He leads me beside the still water. He restoreth my soul. He leads me in the path of righteousness for His name's sake. Even though I walk through the valley of death—"

LOOMIS: That's just where I be walking!

MARTHA: "I shall fear no evil. For Thou art with me. Thy rod and thy staff, they comfort me."

LOOMIS: You can't tell me nothing about no valleys. I done been all across the valleys and the hills and the mountains and the oceans.

MARTHA: "Thou preparest a table for me in the presence of my enemies."

LOOMIS: And all I see is a bunch of niggers dazed out of their woolly heads. And Mr. Jesus Christ standing there in the middle of them, grinning.

MARTHA: "Thou anointest my head with oil, my cup runneth over."

LOOMIS: He grin that big old grin . . . and niggers wallowing at his feet.

MARTHA: "Surely goodness and mercy shall follow me all the days of my life, and I shall dwell in the house of the Lord forever."

LOOMIS: Great big old white man . . . your Mr. Jesus Christ. Standing there with a whip in one hand and a tote board in another, and them niggers swimming in a sea of cotton.[62]

Loomis complains that the suffering of black people—"niggers swimming in a sea of cotton"—is merely glossed over in the celebration of Jesus's suffering on their behalf. The slavery of African Americans begins with—and in some perverse way continues to depend on—the claim that Jesus died to set them free: indeed, they came to be enslaved in Jesus's name. It is a contradiction to which slavery's children have never quite reconciled themselves. Reflecting on his encounter with Evangelical Christianity in West Africa in the early 1990s, hip-hop recording artist and culture critic Chuck D pondered the contradiction. "Christianity is running rampant . . . and all I could think about was the so-called 'Christians' who went to Africa over four hundred years ago, and we all know what that led to—the most dreadful account of human enslavement that the world has ever known. They even had the nerve to name one of the first slave ships Jesus. Now that's some shit to think about."[63]

Ultimately the Christ of American Christianity could not be the Jesus of African Americans. The Jesus of black people in the twentieth century bore the sins of the world: he was the Crucified One, brutalized, colonized, dehumanized. This was the Jesus that Howard Thurman rediscovered in his extended meditation on the biblical Christ and contemporary Christianity, *Jesus and the Disinherited*. Thurman insisted on the distinction between the faith of Christ and the faith of Christendom as the fundamental difference between the religion of the oppressor and the religion of the oppressed. Christendom, especially its Western European species, was irreconcilable with the social, political, and economic marginality of the historical Jesus.

Thurman's meditation on Jesus is all the more remarkable for its timing. Though *Jesus and the Disinherited* was published in 1949, the book is an expansion of an essay entitled "Good News for the Disinherited" that Thurman wrote while serving as dean of Howard University's Rankin Chapel in 1935. German biblical scholarship was teaching the world how to see Jesus wholly apart from his Jewish background—an immaculate lotus rising above the sullying mud pond of first-century Palestinian Judaism. For Thurman, however, Jesus was "a perfect flower of the brooding spirit of God in the soul of Israel . . . his roots . . . fed by the distilled elements accumulated from Israel's wrestling with God." Jesus spoke "to the House of Israel, a minority within the Graeco-Roman world, smarting under the loss of status, freedom, and autonomy, haunted by the dream of restoration of a lost glory and a former greatness."[64]

Thurman distinguishes Christianity, historically aligned with the imperial powers of the modern West, from what he calls "the religion of Jesus," the revelation that God stands with those "with their backs against the wall." "That it became, through the intervening years, a religion of the powerful and dominant, used sometimes as an instrument of oppression, must not tempt us to believe that it was thus in the mind and life of Jesus." For Thurman the religion of Jesus has always been and continues to be "a technique of survival for the oppressed" in the face of the racism, imperialism, and colonialism.[65]

The religion of Jesus was the faith of many African-American Christians involved in the Civil Rights Movement of the 1950s and 1960s. For Fannie Lou Hamer, the indomitable leader of the Freedom Movement in Mississippi in the early 1960s and founding organizer of the Mississippi Freedom Democratic Party, Jesus was the ultimate inspiration for resistance to the racist repression of the apartheid South. "Christ was a revolutionary person, out there where it was happening," she asserted during the most difficult and dangerous days of the struggle. "That's what God is all about, and that's where I get my strength." Martin Luther King, Jr., gave a revolutionary, nonviolent gloss to Jesus's warning that he had come to bring not peace but a sword: "I have not come to bring this old negative peace with its deadening passivity. I have come to lash out against such a peace. Whenever I come, a conflict is precipitated between the old and the new. Whenever I come, a division sets in between justice and injustice. I have come to bring a positive peace which is the presence of justice, love, yea, even the Kingdom of God."[66]

In the reactionary aftermath of the Civil Rights and Black Power Movements, many churches quietly closed their doors to the armed and dangerous man from Nazareth. The revolutionary Jesus of the 1970s, partially eclipsed by the radicalism and reaction of the decade, continued to shine on Black Theology. In the 1980s the figure of Jesus took to the streets, evoked among the black urban youth that were to become the cultural cadres of hip-hop. The angry son of an angry god became one of the most potent images in rap music. Poet Charlie Braxton's "Apocalypse" (1990) expects the Second Advent of a pistol-packing black Messiah:

> beware
> jesus is a big mean assed black man
> . . . .
> last seen kicking asses
> and calling names
> headed straight for the second
> coming.[67]

"Jesus," says hip-hop philosopher and rap artist KRS-One, "is the only revolutionary in the Bible."[68] In humorist Aaron McGruder's contemporary comic strip *The Boondocks*, Huey, the strip's pint-sized intellectual protagonist, tells his own counternarrative Christmas tale featuring "the original Santa." "The Santa you see today is an imposter," Huey insists. The real Santa, "a brotha named St. Nick Jenkins," went house to house on Christmas Eve with books and wisdom until he was unjustly arrested by police and consigned to death row. Huey's neighbor, a bourgeois black civil rights lawyer, challenges Huey's racially chauvinistic travesty of the American Christmas myth as "a ridiculous story." Huey replies, "Well, every year at Christmas my family remembers a certain famous revolutionary who was unjustly jailed and lost his life." The lawyer demands, "Who? Martin Luther King Jr.? . . . Steven Biko? Nat Turner? There's a lot of them, you know. But what does this have to do with Christmas?" Huey sighs, "C'mon, think really hard."[69]

"BACKSTABBERS DO THIS"

Though African Americans have seen themselves in what Jesus said and did, at least as clear and compelling has been the reflection of their collective condition in what was done to him. African Americans have seen

in the Crucifixion the treachery they themselves have suffered individu-
ally and collectively. Marcus Garvey likened the struggle of pan-African
emancipation to the early Jesus movement.

> As with Christianity, so with every great human Movement
> taught under similar circumstances. . . . May we not say to
> ourselves that the doctrine Jesus taught—that of redeeming
> mankind—is the doctrine we ourselves must teach in the
> redemption of our struggling race? . . . As Christ by His teach-
> ings, His sufferings and His death, triumphed over His foes,
> through the resurrection, so do we hope that out of our
> sufferings and persecution of today we will triumph in the
> resurrection of our newborn race.

Along with this collective identification of "the doctrine of Jesus" with
African redemption is the treachery and persecution that Garvey himself
experienced as leader of the United Negro Improvement Association.
The U.S. government and envious African-American leaders had Garvey
arrested on charges of mail fraud. Garvey protested that he was the victim
of "a mulatto conspiracy," a cabal of light-skinned Negroes who resented
his black skin and his black politics. The conspiracy, in fact, included the
Federal Bureau of Investigation, American and British diplomatic circles,
and the Firestone Rubber Company, which saw Garvey's attempts to establish his African base in Liberia as a threat to the company's exploitative
control of Liberian labor and natural resources. Explains Garvey,

> Christ came into the world centuries ago to redeem lost man-
> kind. . . . But His fellow Jews became jealous of His success
> and sought means to get rid of Him. They argued among
> themselves saying, "How can we do it? We have no power, no
> judges, and if we lay hands upon Him, He will have us appre-
> hended by the Roman authorities. The best thing we can do is
> frame him up." So they made certain statements to the Roman
> Government which had Jesus incarcerated . . . the Jews who
> were jealous of Christ said, "This man is preaching against
> Caesar and the State; He is preaching the doctrine of rebellion
> among peaceful Jews and citizens of the State; if you do not
> convict this man, you are not a friend of Caesar." Pilate being

thus forced against his will, was compelled to decide against Jesus, even though he knew that Jesus had done no wrong.[70]

Garvey draws the parallel between his troubles and the suffering of the crucified Messiah.

> So we have a relative position at this time. Selfish, jealous Negroes know they can do nothing to impede the progress of the Universal Negro Improvement Association, and if left alone we will go on organizing Negroes throughout the world, so they say: "We cannot handle Garvey and his Organization, as we have no power, let us go to the State and Federal authorities, and frame him up, let us say he is an anarchist, a seditionist and is speaking against the government." Like the Jews of old, they cry, "Crucify him," or rather, "Send him to prison, deport him."[71]

Jesus, the quintessential victim of treachery, becomes an icon of the pain of being betrayed by one's own people, even one's own kin. Rap artist Ja Rule uses the biblical language of Jesus's divine paternity in the song "Only Begotten Son" to express the anger and pain of being abandoned by his father:

> For he so feared the world
> He left his only begotten son
> To shed his blood
> Show that pain is love.

The chorus is a parody of one the Bible's best-known texts, John 3:16: "For God so loved the world that he gave his only-begotten son." In traditional Christian theology, the death and resurrection of Jesus the Son of God secures the forgiveness of God the Father and redemption of humanity. But in Ja Rule's parodic turn on the terms of the divine economy, there is neither redemption nor forgiveness: "You bitch nigga, left me 'lone / And parts of me never out grown / The fact that you left home."[72] The biblical text provides words for the rage of an abandoned son who has grown up to become an angry son of man.

African Americans have read the story of Jesus's betrayal as both political history and a personal story, sometimes at the same time. The hip-hop diva Lauryn Hill captures both individual and collective dimensions of this treachery on her solo album, *The Miseducation of Lauryn Hill*. *Miseducation*, a brilliant synthesis of soul, rhythm and blues, hip-hop, rap, and reggae, almost spontaneously moved beyond the hip-hop underground and into the contemporary cultural mainstream and enjoyed enormous commercial success as well as widespread critical acclaim. The track entitled "Forgive Them, Father" not only quotes Jesus's words of absolution from the cross but alludes to his teaching about the betrayal and deception that his followers are certain to experience in the world. The lyric echoes the petition of the Lord's Prayer: "Forgive us our trespasses as we forgive those that trespass against us / Although them again we will never, never, never trust." Betrayal touches the most intimate of relations even as it governs global politics. The treachery of the Passion is emblematic of the collective experience of people of African descent and the personal experience of a woman wounded by unfaithful lovers. Hill, rapper and vocalist, relates the two dimensions, the personal and the political, in two different registers of the song. In one stanza she sings of infidelity in romance: "It took me a while to discover / Wolves in sheep coats who pretend to be lovers." In another stanza Hill raps about postcolonial plots against African people: "March through the streets like Soweto / . . . Jesus and Judas / Back-stabbers do this." Hill sings of the Passion as a personal experience of betrayal, then raps about the Passion as a problem of pan-African geopolitics. In the figure of Jesus, international treachery and intimate pain—the personal and the political—take on biblical proportions.[73]

CALVARY

The drama of the treachery that Jesus suffers reaches its climax, of course, in his brutal death. Even before the account of his arrest and crucifixion, the words and deeds of Jesus in the Gospels anticipate his death. Jesus includes himself in a long and venerable list of Wisdom's ill-fated prophets (Matt. 23:33–37). He tells the parable of an obedient son who is sent to his father's vineyard only to meet with violence of its murderous tenants (Matt. 21:33–46), a story that portends Jesus's rejection and death. He teaches that commitment to the coming kingdom that he proclaims is proven in one's resolve to bear one's cross (Mk. 8:34–35), a gruesome figure of speech that points to the instrument of Jesus's public execution.

Holy Writ and collective experience have compelled African Americans to see Jesus and themselves in the shadow of the cross. The Ethiopian eunuch (Acts 8:26–40) looked forward to how African peoples would be invited to stretch forth their hands to God. In that passage in Acts, the Ethiopian official reads from the Servant Song in the book of the prophet Isaiah:

> He is despised and rejected of men; a man of sorrows, and acquainted with grief: and we hid as it were our faces from him; he was despised, and we esteemed him not. Surely he hath borne our griefs, and carried our sorrows: yet we did esteem him stricken, smitten of God, and afflicted. . . . He was oppressed and afflicted, yet he opened not his mouth: he is brought as a lamb to the slaughter, and as a sheep before her shearers is dumb, so he opened not his mouth. He was taken from prison and from judgment: and who shall declare his generation? For he was cut off out of the land of the living: for the transgression of my people was he stricken. (Isa. 53:3–4, 7–8)

The poem reads more as a lament than a paean. The silent, innocent victim is Jesus. Anonymous in Isaiah's oracle, he lends his name to all the nameless souls lost in betrayal, humiliation, and death and reclaimed in resurrection. His name has become theirs: Jesus is the John Doe of many thousands gone. He is the protagonist of the Passion crafted by the Evangelist in the light of the Isaian poem of the suffering servant: "And [Pilate] went again into the judgment hall, and saith unto Jesus, Whence art thou? But Jesus gave him no answer" (John 19:9). The Negro spirituals would celebrate this Jesus as the condemned savior who said nothing in his own defense.

> They crucified my Lord
> An' He never said a mumbalin' word
> They crucified my Lord
> An' He never said a mumbalin' word
> Not a word, not a word, not a word.[74]

Isaiah's dirge presaged the suffering of the silent, innocent Jesus. It also presaged the suffering that people of African descent would undergo as an imitation of Christ. The interpretative key of the passage, Edward

Blyden explains, is the figure of Jesus. He is not mentioned by name, but his presence simultaneously makes sense of the Old Testament oracle and the New Testament proclamation. Blyden identifies the unnamed Jesus by identifying him with people of African descent.

> And there was something symbolic, also, of the future sad experience of his race—and at the same time full of consolation—in the passage which he read. It was holding up Christ as the "man of sorrows and acquainted with grief," as if in anticipation of the great and unsurpassed trials of the African. These were to be the words of comfort and uplifting to these people in their exile and captivity. They were to remember that if they were despised and scorned, a far greater than themselves had had a similar experience. Christ was to be held up to the suffering African not only as the propitiation for sin, and as a Mediator between God and man, but as a blessed illustration of the glorious fact that persecution and suffering and contempt are no proof that God is not the loving Father of a people —but may be rather an evidence of nearness to God, seeing that they have been chosen to tread in the footsteps of the firstborn of the creation.[75]

The suffering of African peoples, suggests Blyden, is not merely their collective misfortune. It is their collective vocation. Black people have the dubious distinction of being sanctified, set apart by God, for sorrow.

The Negro spiritual "Cry Holy" laments, "O Mary was a woman, and she had a son / And the Jews and the Romans had him hung." Veneration for Mary as such is entirely absent in the Protestant Evangelical sensibility of the Negro spirituals, even those that were apparently sung in the overwhelmingly Catholic parishes of Louisiana. As early as 1894, Henry Hugh Proctor observed in his Yale dissertation on Negro spirituals that these folk songs were devoid of Marian devotion and bore no trace of Catholic doctrine. The mother of Jesus in spirituals is not the Mary of "Ave Maria"; she is the grieving matron of the Pietà, the suffering mother of the suffering Jesus. African-American Christianity, with its strong Protestant cast, nevertheless has its own version of the Sorrows of Mary.[76]

And so the language of crucifixion has always been apposite for the summary execution of black people in the United States. When asked shortly before his execution by his court-appointed attorney if he had been mistaken in leading his abortive revolt against slavery, Nat Turner responded, "Was not Christ crucified?"[77] Showing neither fear nor remorse, Turner was hanged November 11, 1831. His public execution took place at the county seat of Hampton, Virginia—the town of Jerusalem.

Jesus's execution "on a tree," as the Apostle Paul and other writers refer to the cross, too closely resembled the strange fruit of lynching that hung on trees throughout the South and elsewhere in the United States from the demise of Radical Reconstruction until the middle of the twentieth century. Lynching reached its gristly peak of 161 Negroes per year in 1892.[78] In this period more than 3,500 African Americans were tortured, dismembered, and hanged, their bodies transformed by vicious white mobs into human billboards of terror in black communities across the nation. Jesus is acquainted with the grief of African Americans because he too was found without fault but nevertheless was found guilty and condemned to a torturous public death. The body of Jesus, like thousands of black bodies in America, was not cursed by being hanged on a tree—the biblical curse of Deuteronomy 21:23—but hanged on a tree because it was cursed. And just as Paul declared that Jesus bore this curse (see Gal. 3:13), so black folks defined that curse as the reproach of rejected and despised people of African descent. They have identified with the cross of Jesus because they have seen themselves as bearing one like it.

In W. E. B. Du Bois's short story "Jesus Christ in Texas," the true identity of the mysterious, swarthy protagonist is revealed supernaturally after the lynching of a Black convict wrongfully accused of attacking a white woman. Staggering through the melee of the lynch mob, the woman searches for the stranger, Du Bois's Christ-figure, with whom she had had a cryptic conversation earlier that evening. Illumined by far-off flames, the suspended body of the convict is transformed into an epiphany of the Crucified.

> She shuddered as she heard the creaking of the limb where
> the body hung. But resolutely she crawled to the window and
> peered out into the moonlight; she saw the dead man writhe.
> He stretched his arms out like a cross, looking upward. She
> gasped and clung to the windowsill. Behind the swaying body,

and down where the little, half-ruined cabin lay, a single flame
flashed up amid the far-off shout and cry of the mob. A fierce
joy sobbed up through the terror in her soul and then sank
abashed as she watched the flame rise. Suddenly whirling into
one great crimson column it shot to the top of the sky and
threw great arms athwart the gloom until above the world and
behind the roped and swaying form below hung quivering and
burning a great crimson cross. . . . There, heaven-tall and earth-
wide, hung the stranger on the cross, riven and bloodstained,
with thorn-crowned head and pierced hands.[79]

At the climax of Du Bois's mystic tale, Christ the mysterious stranger is
revealed in the dangling body of a dying black man.

Countee Cullen's poem "The Black Christ" recounts the lynching of
a black man by a vicious mob. Spewing epithets, angry white men seek
and then destroy a black man who has expressed his affection for a white
woman. The poet speaks of the hapless victim in the words of Jesus's
passion.

Lynch him! Lynch him! O savage cry,
Why should you echo, "Crucify!"
One sought, sleek-tongued, to pacify
Them with slow talk of trial, law,
Established court; the dripping maw
Would not be wheedled from its prey.

The illustration by the poet's brother Charles that appears on the flyleaf
of The Black Christ and Other Poems renders graphically the identity of
lynched man and crucified Christ that Cullen renders poetically. The black-
and-white etching superimposes a black body hanging lifeless from a tree
over the elevated image of Christ hanging on the cross.[80]

Langston Hughes likewise turns to the Black Christ, Christ as "a
nigger" in his caustic poem "Jesus Christ of Alabama." The poem is a
bitter denunciation of lynching in the South and the Christian mythology
inextricably bound up with it:

Most holy bastard
Of the bleeding mouth,
Nigger Christ

On the cross
Of the South.[81]

In Hughes's poem the crossbars of hatred and cruelty intersect in the public crucifix of lynching. The Crucifixion was the biblical image of racial terrorism in America. The Crucified One, as the premier victim of that terror, bears the cross of vigilante violence as one like unto black people because he bore with them their peculiar reproach.

This brutal legacy of slavery and Jim Crow continues to tincture the lives of young black men in cities throughout the United States. Poet Frank Horne laments that it is virtually the destiny of black boys that they would grow up to become the targets of terror.

Look you on yonder crucifix
Where He hangs nailed and pierced
With head hung low
And eyes all blind with blood that drips
From a thorny crown

. . . .

Look you well,
You shall know this thing.[82]

In the 1990s, young African-American men found themselves once again in targets of repressive harassment and violent police action. The complaint of hip-hop rap artists Public Enemy, whose logo features a young man standing in the shadow of crosshairs, resonated with a genera-tion of young people born guilty of blackness: "Crucifixion ain't no fiction / So-called chosen frozen / Apology made to whoever pleases / Still they got me like Jesus."[83] Tupac Shakur complained of "fightin' Devil niggas daily, / Plus the media be crucifyin' brothas severely":[84] it is the problem of unmerited, unavoidable suffering of young black people caught up in urban violence that Michael Eric Dyson has called "a thug theodicy."[85] Shakur's last recording, released posthumously, features him on the cover art of the compact disc jewel case hanging lifeless on a cross.

Gangsta poets have fixed on a venerable identification of Jesus and criminals as old as the Gospels. All the Gospels and the earliest Chris-tian traditions agree that Jesus had been executed as a criminal and in the company of criminals. The Gospel of Luke says even more: in Luke's account of the Passion, Jesus promises paradise to a condemned thief dying on the cross next to his.

> And one of the malefactors which were hanged railed on him, saying, If thou be Christ, save thyself and us. But the other answering rebuked him, saying, Dost thou not fear God, seeing thou art in the same condemnation? And we indeed justly; for we receive the due reward of our deeds: but this man hath done nothing amiss. And he said unto Jesus, Lord, remember me when thou comest into thy kingdom. And Jesus said unto him, Verily I say unto thee, Today shalt thou be with me in paradise. (Luke 23:39–43)

Jesus's agonized conversation with a criminal informs the lyrics of Nasir (a.k.a. Nas) Jones's "God Love Us": "God love us hood niggas / Cuz next to Jesus on the cross wuz the crook niggas."[86] Jesus's generous promise to the thief on the cross is a poignant moment in the history of justice. With his last breath Jesus affirms his solidarity with "the crook niggas."[87] This solidarity is Tupac Shakur's confidence in the track "Blasphemy": "They say Jesus is a kind man / Well he should understand / Times in this crime land."[88] This is the confidence that "gansta" malefactors have as they stand before Jesus as a judge far more just than the judges before whom they are condemned to stand "in this crime land." Only those who can view others with empathy are qualified to judge them, and Jesus is the perfect judge because he is perfectly empathetic. Jesus has been arrested as they have been arrested, convicted as they have been convicted, executed as they have been executed. He has been with them and they have been with him: "next to Jesus on the cross wuz the crook niggas."

"THE STONE DONE ROLL AWAY"

Even as African Americans had suffered as Jesus had suffered—and even as Jesus had suffered as African Americans had suffered—so their mutual identification aspired to an immortality more certain than death. The Christian story of Jesus's death ends with his life: in the Resurrection God takes revenge on mortality itself. "Easter," writes contemporary philosopher Cornel West, "focuses our attention on the decisive victory of Jesus Christ and hence the possibility of our victory over . . . this old world, with its history of oppression and exploitation." Jesus's decisive victory over death inaugurates "a new age . . . in which death is conquered but not abolished." The New Testament proclamation is the declaration of this possibility "despite how tragic and hopeless present situations and circumstances appear to be."[89] In an Easter sermon delivered in New York in 1922, Marcus Garvey drew the spiritual analogy between Jesus's victory over death and the future, collective resurrection of African peoples all over the world: "As Christ triumphed nearly two thousand years ago over death and the grave, as he was risen from the dead, so do I hope that 400,000,000 Negroes of today will triumph over the slavishness of the past, intellectually, physically, morally and even religiously; that on this anniversary of our risen Lord, we ourselves will be risen from the slumber of the ages; risen in thought to higher ideals, to a loftier purpose, to a truer conception of life."[90]

Nevertheless, the celebration of the Resurrection is qualified by the horrific agony that precedes it. At the end of the Gospel of Matthew, Jesus appears to his disciples after the Crucifixion as the victorious risen Lord: "All power is given unto me in heaven and on earth." This is as close as the New Testament comes to a celebratory tone in its post-Resurrection accounts, and the African-American folk tradition is equally reticent at the empty tomb. The Negro spiritual "De Angel Roll the Stone Away" focuses on the obstacles of the Easter story: the stone at the mouth of the tomb, the missing body of Jesus, the security force around the sepulcher, the collusion of the Roman ruler and the ruling class of Jerusalem.

Sister Mary came a runnin'
At the break of day
Brought the news from heaven,
The stone done roll away.

I'm-a lookin' for my Savior,
Tell me where he lay
High up on the mountain,
The stone done roll away.

The soldiers there a-plenty
Standin' by the door
But they could not hinder
The stone done roll away.

Old Pilate and his wise men,
Didn't know what to say,
The miracle was on them,
The stone done roll away.[91]

There is no mention of the Resurrection itself. Its biblical features—the words and deeds of the Risen Jesus, the reports of those who saw him and spoke to him—are absent. The miracle of his triumph over death is signaled by repeated reference to the very thing poised to prevent it—the stone that the angel rolled away.

Romare Bearden's painting *He Is Risen* recalls that the Resurrection is first announced at the grave: the message of life comes from the mouth of mortality. A bright concentric chorus of witnesses, some speaking and some silent, join the central figure on either side. And commanding the right lower corner of the painting—its visual anchor—is the blackness of the empty tomb. The figure at center, arm uplifted, is the angel in white raiment who announces the first Easter, "He is not here: for he is risen, as he said" (Matt. 28:6). The figure in the white robe could also be construed as the risen Jesus: but if so, even in Resurrection life Jesus takes, in Bearden's cubist rendering, a cruciform pose. Though the Resurrection, or, more precisely, the report of Resurrection, takes the foreground, the shadow of death looms ever in the background, "conquered but not abolished."

Nas said of his slain colleague Tupac Shakur, "Tupac was Jesus Christ. Now they can take that and run with it if they want to. . . . He was a part of us."[92] Shakur was shot to death in Las Vegas while in an automobile with his producer, Suge Knight of Death Row Records. In the music video "Smile" featuring Shakur and rap recording artist Scarface, Shakur assumes a cruciform pose. The producer of Shakur's last recording is listed as "Simon," the name of the Cyrenian who carries Jesus's cross in the Gospels. All this has fueled speculation that Shakur is still alive and that a resurrected Tupac Shakur will return to public life. In his song "Blasphemy" Shakur had rapped of "Brothas getting' shot / comin' back resurrected."[93] These words, some have claimed, now apply to Shakur himself.

THE BLACK CHRIST

By the twentieth century, black people in the United States had become peculiar by virtue of their color, an enduring mark that reminded the world of their forebears' previous condition of servitude and now their own condition of second-class citizenship. The twentieth century, as Du Bois famously lamented, was marked by the color line. And so in that century, identification with Jesus became a matter of color as well: Jesus's blackness was not experiential but literal and historical. Jesus had to have a racial identity in the racist Christianity of the United States, and that racial identity, explicitly or implicitly, was white. And a white Jesus was unacceptable to some African-American Christians and had been for some time. The iconoclastic AME bishop Henry MacNeal Turner had demanded as early as 1895 that for black people God too must be black.

> We have as much right biblically and otherwise to believe
> that God is a Negro as you buckra or white people have to be-
> lieve that God is a fine looking, symmetrical and ornamented
> white man. For the bulk of you and all the fool Negroes of the
> country believe that God is white-skinned, blue-eyed, straight-
> haired, projecting nosed, compressed lipped and finely robed
> white gentleman, sitting upon a throne somewhere in the
> heavens. Every race of people since time began who have at-
> tempted to describe their God by words, or by paintings, or
> by carvings, or by any other form or figure, have conveyed the
> idea that the God who made them and shaped their destinies
> was symbolized in themselves, and why should not the Negro
> believe that he resembles God as much as other people?[94]

Turner's effort to rid his churches of the white Jesus met with limited success. The Aryan Jesus had already become the American norm and may still be found in some African-American churches today. In Alice Walker's novel *The Color Purple*, the protagonist, Celie, tells her friend Shug that she has heard that, "somewhere in the bible it say Jesus' hair was like lamb's wool." Shug replies, "If he came to any of these churches we talking bout he'd have to have it conked. . . . The last thing niggers want to think about they God is that his hair kinky."[95] Shug's church folk prefer a savior with "conked" hair, that is, hair that has been chemically straight-ened, to "kinky" hair. The preference itself is backhanded confirmation of the principle of mutual identity. Ambivalent about their own physical appearance, African Americans have availed themselves of cosmetic pro-cesses to make themselves look more like white people. They have also insisted that their God do the same, as the exchange between Shug and Celie attests. Some black folks have refused to embrace Jesus's blackness because they have refused to embrace their own.

And yet, it was often in the church that many African Americans learned to embrace their blackness. Holiness preacher William Christian founded the Church of the Living God (Christian Workers for Fellowship) in Wrightsville, Arkansas, in 1889, the only independent religious organization to endorse Marcus Garvey's United Negro Improvement Association officially. Meeting in New Haven, Connecticut at its annual convention, the church voted to support the UNIA spiritually and materially, sending a special offering to the UNIA International Convention to be held in New York the following week.[96] The Church of the Living God was pro-black in its theology and in its liturgy, and the church's official catechism propounded a black Jesus.

> Was Jesus a member of the black race?
> Yes. Matthew 1.
> How do you know?
> Because He was in the line of Abraham and David the king.
> Is this assertion sufficient proof that Christ came of the black generation?
> Yes.
> Why?
> Because David said he became like a bottle in the smoke.
> Ps. 119:83.[97]

Later in the second quarter of the twentieth century Elijah Muhammad of the Nation of Islam taught that God, "the original man," as well as the children of Israel and all the prophets of Allah, including Jesus, were physically black.

The Nation of Islam's doctrine of the black Jesus also came to influence the black Christian nationalism of United Church of Christ minister Albert Cleage. Founder of the Shrine of the Black Madonna in Detroit in the late 1960s as an ecclesiastical affirmation of Black Power, Cleage preached, "We know that Israel was a black nation and that the descendents of the original black Jews are in Israel, Africa, and the Mediterranean area today. The Bible was written by black Jews. . . . Jesus was a Black Messiah. He came to free Black people from the oppression of the white Gentiles." With cries of "Black Power" echoing outside and inside African-American churches, Cleage's Jesus was a black Messiah, God's agent of deliverance for black people: "When we go to the Bible, we must search for the religion of Jesus, the Black Messiah." But with an important caveat: the religion of Jesus is to be found not in the New Testament but in the Old. Cleage complained that the Apostle Paul's influence corrupts the entire New Testament and has effectively trumped "the teachings of Jesus." Cleage distinguished the religion of Jesus from "Pauline interpretations which tend to make us think that Jesus was something which he was not, and that he taught something that he did not teach." The faith of the cross and the Atonement "is not the religion of Jesus . . . not the religion of Israel."[98]

And in response to the theological challenge posed by Black Power, theologian James Cone emphasizes Jesus's poverty and political disenfranchisement. Jesus was poor, Cone insists, and proclaimed a kingdom of God for the poor. "The message of the Kingdom," Cone explains, "is a message about the ghetto, and all other injustices done in the name of democracy and religion for the further social, political, and economic interests of the oppressor. In Christ, God enters human affairs and takes sides with the oppressed." Cone insists that Jesus, in his perfect solidarity with black people, was himself black. "Christ is black . . . because and only because Christ really enters into our world where the poor, the despised, and the black are, disclosing that he is with them, enduring their humiliation and pain and transforming oppressed slaves into liberated servants." Just as oppression defined black existence, so blackness now defined oppression.[99]

The early 1990s Five Percenter rap group Poor Righteous Teachers asserted, "Pictures you show of the Son of God is like that of the slave masters . . . These just ain't the fact. Why, God is true and livin'. Listen, Jesus Christ was Black!"[100] "Once you start to develop your African mind," insists rapper Kool Moe Dee, "you will see, you will understand that you can't just know the story of Jesus, you have to understand the fact that he was black. The fact that it was white society that killed him."[101] KRS-One offers this polemical disclaimer:

Jesus Christ, Jesus Christ, Jesus Christ was BLACK
Read and study and know thyself because this too is a fact

Abraham, Noah and King Solomon and John the Baptist
was BLACK
The European rewrote the Bible and they use it as a fact.[102]

The Five Percent Nation of Islam vehemently opposes white representations of biblical figures and so has insisted that all biblical characters must be black. Five Percenters have been especially insistent that Jesus must have been black. The black Jesus has been conspicuous in the implicit theological consensus among hip-hop poets and performers, among whom Five Percenter doctrines have been influential. As Rakeem Allah says of the church experience of his early youth as he moved away from traditional Christian religion and toward the Five Percent Nation of Islam, "I felt like this [the doctrine of the Five Percent Nation] was real. I was a believer in shit, but I was always confused and shit. I would look at the picture of a white Jesus." Rakeem Allah asserts that his confusion abated after listening to a group of Five Percenter intellectuals expound on teaching about the black Jesus.[103]

With the wide popularity of so-called gangsta rap, themes of criminal life and urban violence crowded out the messages of political empowerment and racial consciousness featured in much of hip-hop culture. West Coast performers such as Ice-T and NWA (Niggaz With Attitude) pioneered a genre of popular music accompanied by driving rhythms and marked by expletives, sexually explicit language, and the street lore of drugs, guns, fast money, and early death. But the black Jesus thrives even in this unlikely ambient. In Tupac Shakur's song "Black Jesuz," released posthumously on the album *Still I Rise* (1999), the solidarity of Jesus with those who believe in him is so intense that identification with him is complete, even reciprocal: "Black Jesuz / I know He sees us / Only he can feed us." "Black Jesus" identifies with the gangsta and is identified with the gangsta even in the criminal's criminality. "I'm a thug," confesses Shakur, and "Thugs / We pray to Black Jesuz all day." The self-confessed street criminals of what Shakur calls "my thug nation" are "searching for Black Jesuz / It's like a Saint that we pray to in the ghetto to get us through / Somebody that understand our pain / . . . Somebody that hurt like we hurt." Tupac Shakur's "Black Jesuz" is "somebody raw" who can "rally the troops like a saint we can trust."[104]

In an interview he gave two weeks before he was shot to death, Shakur said, "I feel like Black Jesus is controlling me. He's our saint that we pray to; that we look up to. . . . How I got shot five times—only a saint, only Black Jesus, only a nigga that know where I'm coming from, could be, like, 'You know what? He gonna end up doing some good.'"[105] It is as criminals that "gangstas" see themselves in Jesus and Jesus in themselves.

He "was searching for his black Jesus," said Sonia Sanchez of the slain Shakur. "He is really at some point looking and trying to figure out: exactly how do you get back to yourself, to your black self?"[106]

IMITATION OF CHRIST

The signature work of choreographer Alvin Ailey, "Revelations," features the pas-de-deux entitled "Fix Me, Jesus." The work takes its inspiration from the Negro spiritual of the same title. A male and a female dancer lean upon each other, draw near and bound away, move face to face and in tandem. And yet do not embrace. The male dancer neither supports the female dancer with his hands nor lifts her at the waist. At moments the dancers trade cruciform poses. Together and by turns, they represent the suffering Jesus and the suffering believer who abjectly depends upon him even as she imitates him in suffering.

The singer of the Negro spiritual pleads to be "fixed." The word is reminiscent of the language of dying soldiers on both sides of the Civil War. The soldiers would plead with nurses to "fix me for my Jesus," that is, to arrange their bodies with arms folded across the chest, head positioned straight and upturned so that they would be in the proper posture to meet Jesus in their final hour.[107] *Fixed* may mean repaired, corrected, rehabilitated. But it may also mean to be set in place, attached and unmovable, to be "nailed down." In the suffering of Jesus, the singer hopes to be "fixed" by the Crucified One, and fixed as the Crucified One was fixed on the cross. In the choreography of mutual identification, the dancers move in a kinetic synthesis of Incarnation and *imitatio Christi*.

The Gospel according to Saint Matthew records the flight of the Holy Family to Egypt to escape King Herod's plot to kill the Christ child. There the babe and his parents remain until the monarch's death. Matthew claims that the family's Egyptian sojourn is a fulfillment of the words of the Old Testament prophecy: "Out of Egypt I have called my son" (Hos. 11:1). Modern biblical critics have accused the Evangelist of desperately grasping for a proof text here. Certainly Hosea's words in context have an eye to Israel's past, not Israel's future; Hosea refers to the Israelite Exodus from Egypt. The Exodus is the story of the origin of Israel as a people. It is not a story of an individual and certainly not an event of the prophetic future.

But Matthew's intention here is not to retrofit isolated Old Testament passages to shore up his claim that Jesus Christ is the fulfillment of God's promises to Israel, though his use of scripture is clearly informed by that concern. Matthew also wants to show that Jesus Christ is a figure of the historical experience of Israel, Israel personified. Jesus, like Israel, is called out of Egypt. Like Israel, Jesus's fidelity to God's law is tested in the wilderness: indeed Jesus's answers to satanic provocation are citations of the Law of Moses, Israel's divinely ordained national constitution. Israel's collective experience is signified in an exalted individual in whom that experience is rendered meaningful, in whom its contradictions are resolved.

African Americans read their own collective experience into the agony and exaltation of Jesus. The story of the Christ child, blessed by God yet born in the shadow of poverty and violence, was their story. Jesus's humble birth in antiquity signified the humble origins of African peoples in modernity. In his impoverished entry into the world, Jesus turned the tables on earthly valuations. Fulfilling the promise of the oracle that celebrates his advent in a stable, the hills of the privileged and the valleys of the humble are inverted, marking the beginning of a new era. Henry Ossawa Tanner captured this cosmic inversion in his painting *Angels Appearing to the Shepherds* (c. 1910). The stable is rude and diminutive, barely visible, and the celestial messengers dominate the foreground. The point of view that Tanner provides for us is not that of the shepherds or that of the Holy Family, nor is it the perspective of the various onlookers that traditionally have come to crowd the crèche. The glazed, layered pigments of the oil paints, experimentally prepared by Tanner himself, render the visual effect all the more distant and extraterrestrial. Tanner has caused us to see the birth of Jesus through the eyes of angels.

Howard Thurman once noted that few of the Negro spirituals treat the birth of Jesus and speculated that the paucity of nativity spirituals was due to the debauchery historically associated with Christmas during slavery: antebellum Christmastide in the South was notorious for liquor and license. Clearly, however, the nativity inspired a veritable subgenre of slave songs, and Thurman qualifies his suggestion: "Nevertheless there are a few Christmas spirituals that point to the centrality of the significant event that took place in Bethlehem."[108] In the Negro spirituals Black Christian poets sang of Jesus's birth as the signal event of a new order:

> Go tell it on the mountain,
> Over the hills and everywhere
> Go tell it on the mountain
> That Jesus Christ is born.

It is in the exalted places, "on the mountain / Over the hills and everywhere," that the world hears the proclamation. The lowly birth of an obscure child has been exalted to the highest heaven. The Negro spiritual "What Will You Name That Pretty Little Baby?" announces that this obscure child is the infant king of a glorious kingdom:

> Oh, Mary, what will you name
> That pretty little baby?
> Glory, glory, glory
> To the new born King!
> Some will call Him one thing,
> But I think I'll call him Jesus.
> Glory, glory, glory to the newborn King!
> Some will call him one thing,
> But I think I'll call him Emmanuel.
> Glory, glory, glory
> To the new born King!

Jesus is at once the child of poverty and the king of glory, He is "Emmanuel," literally "God with us," as the messianic child is called in Isaiah's oracle (Isa. 7:14): he is the very presence of God among the poor and the powerless. He is among them, nevertheless, as one of them. He shares their humility, even their humiliation. As one Negro spiritual put it,

> Poor little Jesus boy
> Made him to be born in a manger
> World treated him so mean
> Treat me mean, too.

Because Jesus, in the words of Second Isaiah, is the man of sorrows and acquainted with grief, his humiliation is ever the mark of his exaltation.

In the Bible Jesus is at simultaneously exalted and abased. He is the just judge who becomes a convicted criminal, the master who becomes a slave. He is a king, but a king of shreds and patches. African Americans have not seen Jesus without seeing at the same time the tension of this complex biblical image. Contemporary African-American theologian Jacqueline Grant reminds us that African-American women have related to the image of Jesus "who identified with them and empowered them" through his lowly birth, his ministry to the weak, his shameful and wrongful death, and his victorious resurrection.[109] Even Nat Turner, when he spoke of himself in the shadow of the hangman's noose, ultimately appealed neither to the blood-spattered judge nor to the victorious king but to the unjustly crucified Jesus.

There are few African-American images of the *Christus Victor,* Jesus resplendently crowned and palming an *orbis terrarum.* But then images of the triumphant Christ are rare in the Bible that testifies to him. Even the regal judge of the book of Revelation, head laden with crowns, rides a white horse into battle. He is not at ease; wrapped in a bloody robe, he stands at the head of a celestial army on red alert. Only once does the Bible depict Jesus as enthroned and recumbent. Such is the apocalyptic cartoon of the book of Revelation: "And I beheld, and, lo, in the midst of the throne and of the four beasts, and in the midst of the elders stood a Lamb as it had been slain, having seven horns and seven eyes, which are the seven spirits of God sent forth into all the earth" (Rev. 5:6). Here, Jesus the Lion of Judah has become the Lamb of God.

Jesus is "the lamb that was slain"—the "little lamb," for the Greek word for "lamb" here is diminutive—whose perennial wound signifies his suffering. That wound is the warrant for Jesus's elevation as the just judge at the end of the age. He has suffered as those who suffer judgment. He is, in the words of Tupac Shakur, "Somebody that hurt like we hurt. . . . That understand where we're coming from."[110] The world that had condemned slavery's children will be judged one day by one like unto them. His justice, a justice that not merely permits but demands immortality, would be greater than the sum of all injustices perpetrated against them. Jesus is the only judge fit to sit on the bench. The woman caught in adultery, the thief on the cross, and the "crook niggas" look to the bar of his justice as though looking in a mirror.

More than the Lord and God of slavery's children, Jesus is their peer:

he is as they are, for he has suffered as they have suffered. Even in his glory, African Americans have seen Jesus as Second Isaiah saw the lamb led silent to the slaughter, as the author of the book of Revelation saw the slaughtered lamb on the throne and on the rampage, and as the women of the Reverend Deal's church saw the slain mother's son—as "the truly innocent victim," and so as themselves. "The Lamb's eye," never far from his Passion, ever nigh unto them in theirs.

Postscript

IN THE FOUR COMPELLING images of Exile, Exodus, Ethiopia, and Emmanuel, slavery's children have called into question their history and their destiny, and all things human and divine—including themselves.

The effects of Ezekiel's exilic vision show that the question of exile remains alive in the African-American imagination. This is so because the issues of the Middle Passage and its aftermath are very much with us. Those who insist that we put slavery behind us, that "that was all in the past," close their eyes to the valley of dry bones that African Americans having been singing about, preaching about, writing about, and dreaming about for centuries. African Americans are still permanent exiles in their native land, and return to the land of their distant ancestors is impossible: as Kenyan historian Ali Mazrui has put it, African Americans have been denied the right to be homesick. The biblical image of exile is still robust because it still captures the devastation of modern slavery and its pernicious legacy. The image still poses the question Afro–Puerto Rican poet Guillermo Nuñez raises in his poem "Al Negro Norteamerico" (To the North American Negro): "¿Donde vas a poner / tus huesos y tu sangre, / si el yanki te aborrece?"—"Where will you put / your bones and your blood, / if the Yankee hates you?"

For the same reasons African Americans cannot be properly homesick, they cannot be properly at home in the land of their birth. The land that the Puritan founders called the Promised Land has been Pharaoh's Egypt for African Americans. For many in the blighted inner cities and forgotten rural backwaters, it still is. At best, African Americans are stalled at the "Deep River," as one Negro spiritual refers to the Jordan, languishing somewhere on the plains of Moab. The Promised Land beyond their collective grasp, they possess only questions. How would they find their own land of promise? How would God grant them title to it? And, without army or general, how would they take it? Ex-slave Charles Davenport put the question most poignantly: "De preachers 'ud exhort us dat us was de chillun o' Israel in de wilderness an' de Lawd done sont us to take dis lan' o' milk an' honey. But how us gwine a-take lan' what's already been took?"[1]

The biblical figure of Ethiopia has signified that slavery's children in the United States have more in common with slavery's children throughout the New World than they do with their fellow citizens. Their common slave past has forged historical and psychic bonds far stronger and truer than any nationalist claim. W. E. B. Du Bois described the sojourn of four centuries in the howling wilderness of America as a nightmarish inversion of the Ethiopian oracle. "For 400 years," wrote Du Bois, "the dark captives wound to the sea amid the bleaching bones of the dead; for 400 years the sharks followed the scurrying ships; for 400 years America was strewn with the living and dying millions of a transplanted race; for 400 years Ethiopia stretched forth her hands unto God."[2] In the United States, in Latin America, and in the Caribbean, slavery's children bear the greatest burdens of poverty, disease, and violence in the New World. Their common heritage has its roots in sub-Saharan Africa, which even now bears the greatest burdens of poverty, disease, and violence in the Old World. And both worlds, the New and the Old, are content to let Africans perish on both sides of the ocean. If there is any salvation for these Atlantic Africans, they must seek it themselves, and seek it together. In the words of the Ethiopian oracle, it is Ethiopia, not God, who stretches forth her hands. In the wake of recent disasters and instability in Liberia, Nigeria, and the Congo—all places to which the descendants of slaves in the United States trace their ancestry—pragmatic, pan-African solidarity may be all that stands between the present crisis and perpetual catastrophe. A revived "pan-Negroism," as Du Bois called it, with a transcendent vision of justice, would not allow African Americans to await the Second Coming of Christ before stretching forth their hands to near and distant kin.

The renewed resolve would be fitting, for in the collective imagination of African Americans, Christ is not in heaven, waiting in the wings for his curtain call at the end of time. He is present here, suffering along with black folks the slings and arrows of their outrageous fortune. And he is the arch revolutionary in whose name revolutionary African Americans have been praising the Lord and passing the ammunition since antebellum times. The militant Jesus of the Negro spirituals, of Nat Turner, and of Fannie Lou Hamer is profoundly true to the Jesus of scripture who gives the lie to smarmy Protestant hymnody and the schlock of Carl Bloch paintings: he is "a different Jesus," in the words of novelist David Bradley, a "Jesus who had a temper. A Jesus who could get fed up."³ This Jesus is at odds with an American Christianity whose devotees do not pray to God that his kingdom come but instead praise him that the kingdom, delivered by the market and wrapped in the American flag, has already arrived. Emmanuel's legacy makes the reign of "King Jesus," as the Negro spirituals call him, irreconcilable with the hard-hearted, tight-fisted religion of Mammon that is America's only real orthodoxy. Though American Evangelical Christianity has claimed that "Jesus is the answer," he remains for slavery's children the man of that impertinent question: "Suppose ye that I am come to give peace on earth?"

For African Americans, the Bible has not been a book that answered questions. Indeed, it was precisely biblical answers that the first African-American readers called into question. Their encounter with the Bible provoked the development of a critical sensibility, a penchant for interrogating themselves and others. The Bible has been their license for calling things into question.

The Bible authorized African Americans to question others. Abd Al-Rahman Ibrahima, a Muslim slave well versed in the Qur'an and literate in Arabic, heard the Bible read aloud and its texts treated in sermons when he attended services at the church of his Evangelical Presbyterian master. Manumitted at sixty-six years of age after forty years of involuntary servitude, he commented, "I tell you, the Testament is very good law, you no follow it; you no pray often enough; you greedy after money. You good man, you join religion. You want more land, more neegurs; you make neegurs work hard, make more cotton. Where you find that in you law?"⁴

In a celebrated sermon entitled "The Sun Do Move," nineteenth-century ex-slave preacher John Jasper argues against the heliocentric model of the solar system and against science itself. According to Jasper, the proponents of modern science are "on the wrong side of the Bible—that's on the outside of the Bible, and there's where the trouble comes in with them."

> A man talked with me last week about the laws of nature and he say they can't possibly be upset and I had to laugh right in his face. As if the laws of anything were greater than the God who is the lawgiver for everything. My Lord is great! He rules in the heavens, in the earth and down under the ground. He is great and greatly to be praised. Let all the people bow down and worship before Him! There you are! Ain't that the movement of the sun? Bless my soul! Hezekiah's case beat Joshua. Joshua stop the sun, but here the Lord make the sun walk back ten degrees; and yet they say that the sun stand stone still and never move a peg. It look to me he move around mighty brisk and is ready to go any way that the Lord orders him to go. I wonder if any of them philosophers is round here this afternoon?[5]

The knowledge of the truth is informed, not by nature and nature's God, but by God and God's nature. The record of the mighty acts of God—the Bible—overrules the mere record of the courses of the heavenly bodies that Almighty God has hung in the sky. The Bible is Jasper's "arsenal" against hostile knowledge: "The Word of the Lord is my defense and bulwark, and I fears not what men can say nor do—my God gives me the victory."[6] It is the Bible that emboldens Jasper to assault modern science itself with a salvo of questions.

The Bible even authorized African Americans to question God. Olaudah Equiano waxed poetic as he wrote in his autobiography in 1789,

> Unhappy more than some on earth,
> I thought the place that gave me birth—
> Strange thoughts oppress'd—while I replied
> "Why not an Ethiop died?"[7]

Would not death have been better? The question was Job's, Jeremiah's, and Jonah's. In the Bible, those closest to God are most probing in their inquiry into his inscrutable ways. With a relentlessness as extraordinary as his tact, Abraham questions the justice of God's impending destruction of Sodom and Gomorrah. Moses questions God's choice in calling him to lead the children of Israel out of Egypt, going so far as to demand that God state his name and present some form of identification. Job's attempt to put God in the dock, and his failure to do so, is famous. And of Jesus's anguished query from the cross, "My God, my God, why hast Thou forsaken me?" itself a borrowed question from the Psalter, critic Stanley Crouch once quipped that it is "perhaps the greatest blues line of all time."[8]

The question of evil, especially in the egregious form of the slave regime and the American apartheid that followed it, did not admit of a satisfying answer. The Bible ultimately failed to furnish an answer because the Bible itself resisted the question. God's classic response to Job is "Don't ask." On the Fourth of July, 1827, Emancipation Day in the state of New York, the Reverend Nathaniel Paul of the Hamilton Street Baptist Church posed the question in his commemorative address only to retreat from it or, rather, only to allow God to retreat into his inscrutable sovereignty. On an occasion celebrating freedom while so many remained enslaved, Paul was constrained to ask, "Why it was that thou didst look with calm indifference of an unconcerned spectator, when thy holy law was violated, thy divine authority despised and a portion of thine own creatures reduced to a state of mere vassalage and misery?" But God "answers from on high," says Paul, "proclaiming from the skies—Be still, and know that I am God! Clouds and darkness are round about me; yet righteousness and judgment are the habitation of my throne. I do my will and pleasure in the heavens above, and in the earth beneath; it is my sovereign prerogative to bring good out of evil, and to cause the wrath of man to praise me, and the remainder of that wrath I will restrain."[9] African-American Christians found the existential pressure of the inquiry irresistible, even though the God they rhetorically place on the witness stand is always allowed, in accordance with biblical precedent, to plead the Fifth.

Howard Thurman begins his *Jesus and the Disinherited* with an account of his visit to Ceylon and his conversation with a Hindu who did not understand how Thurman, a black man, could be a Christian given the history of Christianity, slavery, and racism in the United States.

> More than three hundred years ago your forefathers were taken
> from the western coast of Africa as slaves. The people who

dealt in the slave traffic were Christians. . . . The name of one
of the famous British slave vessels was "Jesus." The men who
bought slaves were Christian ministers, quoting the Christian
apostle Paul, gave the sanction of religion to the system of slavery. Some seventy years or more ago you were freed by a man
who was not a professing Christian. . . . During all the period
since then you have lived in a Christian nation in which you
are segregated, lynched, and burned. . . . I am a Hindu. I do
not understand. Here you are in my country, standing deep
within the Christian faith and tradition. I do not wish to seem
rude to you. But sir, I think you are a traitor to all the darker
people of the earth. I am wondering what you, an intelligent
man, can say in defense of your position.

Thurman's book is a Christian response to a Hindu question. "The clue
to my own discussion with this probing, honest, sympathetic Hindu,"
Thurman writes, "is found in my interpretation of the meaning of the
religion of Jesus."[10]

Thurman did not choose the rutted roads in the history of Christian
encounters with those who do not share their view. His response was
neither dogmatic nor apologetical. Both dogmatics and apologetics have
the effect of placing claims of faith above criticism. Thurman eschewed
both. He returned to the story of Jesus in the Bible and, in seeking to
answer for himself the pointed question of his Hindu interlocutor, found
profounder meaning in his own faith.

Their acquaintance with the Bible has afforded African Americans
a knack for criticism in both directions, a capacity to question and be
questioned. This disposition to critical consciousness is not a property
of the Bible itself, of course; certainly many have claimed the Bible as an
exemption from criticism. Many still do. But to arrogate such exemption
requires a prior claim to privilege that comes with membership in a ruling
class, a chosen people, a master race. African Americans enter modernity
quintessentially bereft of privilege, and so have had no collective basis for
avoiding the questions of others or evading the disconsolation of their
own. History has denied them such hubris.

This gift of questioning, an accident of history if not an act of Providence, is, like grace, the gift of God in which African Americans cannot

boast. It is not a virtue; it is a birthright—a gift, but not an inalienable one. It is theirs, and theirs to lose.

As Esau sold his birthright for a bowl of stew, African Americans may forego asking the tough questions of our time and instead choose to savor the hand-me-down emoluments of wealth and power acquired at their ancestors' expense. They would close this deal with the Devil as second-class citizens of an imperial, imperious nation. Such is the present lot of slavery's children in the land of their birth. The electoral process illegally disenfranchises them. Both major political parties regularly neglect them. The criminal justice system unjustly arrests, incarcerates, and executes them. The military disproportionately dispatches them to the front in its many and unjust wars. The executive branch of the federal government refuses to hear them, the judiciary branch refuses to protect them, and the legislative branch refuses to represent them. African Americans may choose to sell their birthright to the descendants of a master class that has proven itself as crafty and unscrupulous as the young Jacob. A century and a half after the fall of the slave regime, these heirs to ill-gotten gains still rule the United States as did their forebears—with scripture and injustice.

Or, with the collective critical consciousness that is their heritage, slavery's children may call both scripture and injustice into question. At sundry times and in diverse manners, they have done so before. Might they yet do so again?

NOTES

CHAPTER 1. THE TALKING BOOK

Epigraph: Frances Harper, "Learning to Read" (1872), in Henry Louis Gates, Jr., and Nellie Y. McKay, eds., *The Norton Anthology of African American Literature* (New York: W. W. Norton, 1997), 419.

1. William Brown Hodgson, "The Gospel, Written in the Negro Patois of English with Arabic Characters by a Mandingo Slave in Georgia" (New York: American Ethnological Society, 1957), 5, 10, quoted in Richard Brent Turner, "African Muslim Slaves, the Nation of Islam, and the Bible," in Vincent Wimbush, ed., *African Americans and the Bible: Sacred Texts and Social Textures* (New York: Continuum, 2000), 297.

2. Cotton Mather, *The Negro Christianized: An Essay to Excite and Assist the Good Work, the Instruction of Negro-Servants in Christianity* . . . (Boston: B. Green, 1706), 42–43.

3. I follow the analysis of Mark Noll, "Revolution and the Rise of Evangelical Social Influence in North Atlantic Societies," in Noll, David W. Bebbington, and George A. Rawlyk, eds., *Evangelicalism: Comparative Studies of Popular Protestantism in North America, the British Isles, and Beyond, 1700–1990* (New York: Oxford University Press, 1994), 113–136, esp. 128–130.

4. See Harvey Graff, *The Literacy Myth: Literacy and Social Structure in the Nineteenth-Century City* (New York: Academic Press, 1979), 28, quoted in Janet Cornelius, *When I Can Read My Title Clear: Literacy, Slavery, and Religion in the Antebellum South* (Columbia: University of South Carolina Press, 1991), 4, n. 10. I am thankful to the late Richard Newman of the Du Bois Institute at Harvard University for bringing Cornelius's fine monograph to my attention.

5. Cited in Albert J. Raboteau, *Slave Religion: The "Invisible Institution" in the Antebellum South* (New York: Oxford University Press, 1978), 129–130.

6. See Albert J. Raboteau, "African-Americans, Exodus, and the American Israel," in Paul E. Johnson, ed., *African-American Christianity: Essays in History* (Berkeley: University of California Press, 1994), 4.

7. Sterling Stuckey, "'My Burden Lightened': Frederick Douglass, the Bible, and Slave Culture," in Wimbush, ed., *African Americans and the Bible*, 264.

8. Cornelius, *When I Can Read*, 100, n. 34; John Boles, ed., *Masters and Slaves in the House of the Lord: Race and Religion in the American South, 1740–1870* (Lexington: University Press of Kentucky, 1988), 135.

9. Raboteau, "Exodus," 6.

10. Cornelius, *When I Can Read*, 20.

11. Charles F. James, ed., *Documentary History of the Struggle for Religious Liberty in Virginia* (Lynchburg, VA: J. P. Bell, 1900), 84–85, cited in Raboteau, "Exodus," 5, n. 7.

12. Cited in Raboteau, "Exodus," 5, n. 9.

13. See ibid., 5–7.

14. Cornelius, *When I Can Read*, 4, 23–24, 94.

15. Raboteau, "Exodus," 8.

16. Cited in Vincent Harding, "Religion and Resistance among Antebellum Slaves, 1800–1860," in Timothy E. Fulop and Albert J. Raboteau, eds., *African-American Religion: Interpretive Essays in History and Culture* (New York: Routledge, 1997), 112, n. 15.

17. "Confessions of Ben, alias Ben Woolfolk," in Willie Lee Rose, ed., *A Documentary History of Slavery in North America* (New York: Oxford University Press, 1976), 113–114.

18. Charleston Corporation, *An Account of the Late Intended Insurrection* (N.p.: 1822), 34 (italics in the original), quoted in Harding, "Religion and Resistance," 113.

19. "The Vesey Conspiracy," in Herbert Aptheker, ed., *A Documentary History of the Negro People in the United States*, 3 vols. (New York: Citadel Press, 1951), 1:75–76.

20. Urich B. Phillips, *American Negro Slavery* (Baton Rouge: Louisiana State University Press, 1966), 421, cited in Harding, "Religion and Resistance," 115.

21. See Margaret Washington, "The Meanings of Scripture in Gullah Concepts of Liberation and Group Identity," in Wimbush, ed., *African Americans and the Bible*, 326–327.

22. See S. L. Greenslade, ed., *The Cambridge History of the Bible*, vol. 3: *The West, from the Reformation to the Present Day* (Cambridge: Cambridge University Press, 1963), 209.

23. Quoted in Haven P. Perkins, "Religion for Slaves: Difficulties and Methods," *Church History*, 10, no. 3 (1941): 232, cited in Harding, "Religion and Resistance," 116.

24. John B. Cade, "Out of the Mouths of Ex-Slaves," *Journal of Negro History* 20 (1935): 318, reprinted in Paul Finkelman, ed., *Articles on American Slavery,* vol. 1 (New York: Garland, 1989), 82. All subsequent citations to this article follow the pagination in Finkelman's edition.

25. Frederick Douglass, *Life and Times of Frederick Douglass: His Early Life as a Slave, His Escape from Bondage, and His Complete History; Written by Himself,* introduction by Rayford W. Logan (New York: Collier Books, 1962), 78–79.

26. Ibid., 153.

27. Cornelius, *When I Can Read,* 32–33.

28. Quoted in William W. Freehling, *Prelude to Civil War: The Nullification Controversy in South Carolina, 1816–1836* (New York: Harper and Row, 1966), and Whitemarsh Seabrook, *Essay on the Management of Slaves* (Charleston, SC, 1834), 15, 28–30, both cited in Charles Joyner, *Down by the Riverside: A South Carolina Slave Community* (Urbana: University of Illinois Press, 1984), 157–158.

29. George P. Rawick, ed., *The American Slave: A Composite Autobiography,* 12 vols. (Westport, CT: Greenwood Press, 1977), 7:24; John W. Roberts, *From Trickster to Badman: The Black Folk Hero in Slavery and Freedom* (Philadelphia: University of Pennsylvania Press, 1989), 145.

30. Zephaniah Kingsley, *Treatise on the Patriarchal or Co-operative System of Society as It Exists in Some Governments, and Colonies in America, and in the United States, under the Name of Slavery, with Its Necessities and Advantages, by an Inhabitant of Florida,* 2nd ed. (1829), excerpted in Dena J. Epstein, *Sinful Tunes and Spirituals: Black Folk Music to the Civil War* (Urbana: University of Illinois Press, 1977), 194, and cited in Roberts, *Trickster,* 142.

31. John Mason Peck, *Forty Years of Pioneer Life,* ed. Rufus Babcock (Philadelphia: American Baptist Publication Society, 1864), cited in Roberts, *Trickster,* 143.

32. Cited in Joyner, *Down by the Riverside,* 154–155.

33. Ibid., 114–115.

34. Ibid., 162–163.

35. Elizabeth Botume, *First Days amongst the Contrabands* (1893; reprint ed., New York: Arno Press, 1968), 74–75, quoted in Margaret Washington, "The Meanings of Scripture," in Wimbush, ed., *African Americans and the Bible,* 335.

36. Elizabeth Ware Pearson, ed., *Letters from Port Royal Written at the Time of the Civil War* (Boston: W. B. Clarke, 1906), 27.

37. See Raboteau, *Slave Religion,* 242; Norman Yetman, ed., *Voices from Slavery* (New York: Holt, Rinehart and Winston, 1970), 177; Cade, "Out of the Mouths of Ex-Slaves," 91.

38. In Henry Louis Gates, Jr., *The Signifying Monkey: A Theory of Afro-American Literary Criticism* (New York: Oxford University Press, 1988), 131–132.

39. Henry Louis Gates, Jr., and William L. Andrews, eds., *Pioneers of the Black*

Atlantic: Five Slave Narratives from the Enlightenment, 1772–1815 (Washington, DC: Civitas, 1998), 40–41.

40. John Jea, "John Jea: The Life, History, and Unparalleled Suffering of John Jea, the African Preacher: Compiled and Written by Himself," in ibid., 391–392.

41. See Gates's introduction in ibid., 21.

42. In B. A. Botkin, ed., *Lay My Burden Down: A Folk History of Slavery* (New York: Delta, 1994), 50.

43. Quoted in Cornelius, *When I Can Read*, 89.

44. In Gates and Andrews, eds., *Pioneers*, 392–393.

45. Ibid., 393.

46. Gates, *Signifying Monkey*, 163.

47. Cornelius, *When I Can Read*, 94.

48. Rebecca Cox Jackson, *Gifts of Power: The Writings of Rebecca Cox Jackson, Black Visionary, Shaker Eldress*, ed. Jean McMahon Humez (Amherst: University of Massachusetts Press, 1981), 108, quoted in Gates, *Signifying Monkey*, 242.

49. Gates and Andrews, eds., *Pioneers*, 28–29.

50. In Rawick, ed., *American Slave*, 8, pt. 3:940.

51. Cade, "Out of the Mouths of Ex-Slaves," 94.

52. Booker T. Washington, *Up from Slavery* (1901; reprint ed., New York: Doubleday, 1998), 63, 95, 63.

53. In Rawick, ed., *American Slave*, 12, pt. 1:180.

54. Octavia V. Rogers Albert, *The House of Bondage or, Charlotte Brooks and Other Slaves* (New York: Hunt and Eaton, 1890), 10–11, quoted in Cornelius, *When I Can Read*, 91.

55. Mary Mann-Page Newton, "Aunt Deborah Goes Visiting," *Journal of American Folklore* 4, no. 15 (1891): 354–356.

56. Ralph Ellison, "A Very Stern Discipline," in John Callahan, ed., *The Collected Works of Ralph Ellison* (New York: Modern Library, 1995), 728.

57. Toni Morrison, *Song of Solomon* (New York: Alfred A. Knopf, 1977), 18–19.

58. Toni Morrison, *Beloved: A Novel* (New York: Penguin, 1987), 218.

59. Jupiter Hammond, *An Address to the Negroes of the City of New York* (Long Island, NY: Carroll and Patterson, 1786), reprinted in Milton C. Sernett, ed., *Afro-American Religious History: A Documentary Witness* (Durham, NC: Duke University Press, 1985), 40.

60. Washington, *Up from Slavery*, 26.

CHAPTER 2. THE POISON BOOK

Epigraph: Elijah Muhammad, *Message to the Blackman in America* (Chicago: Muhammad Mosque of Islam No. 2, 1965), 95.

1. Quoted in Sterling Stuckey, *Slave Culture: Nationalist Theory and the Foundations of Black America* (New York: Oxford University Press, 1987), 165.

2. *North Star*, Aug. 17, 1849, cited in Sterling Stuckey, "'My Burden Lightened':

Frederick Douglass, the Bible, and Slave Culture," in Vincent Wimbush, ed., *African Americans and the Bible: Sacred Texts and Social Textures* (New York: Continuum, 2000), 262.

3. Stuckey, "'My Burden Lightened,'" 251–265.

4. In Charles H. Nichols, *Many Thousands Gone: The Ex-Slaves' Account of Their Bondage and Freedom* (Leiden: Brill, 1963), 82.

5. William Wells Brown, *The Narrative of William W. Brown, a Fugitive Slave* (Chapel Hill: University of North Carolina Press, 1996), 82.

6. John Jea, "John Jea: The Life, History, and Unparalleled Suffering of John Jea, the African Preacher: Compiled and Written by Himself," in Henry Louis Gates, Jr., and William L. Andrews, eds., *Pioneers of the Black Atlantic: Five Slave Narratives from the Enlightenment, 1772–1815* (Washington, DC: Civitas, 1998), 391.

7. Phillis Wheatley, "On Being Brought from Africa to America," in William H. Robinson, ed., *Phillis Wheatley and Her Writings* (New York: Garland, 1984), 160.

8. *Midrash Rabba-Genesis,* 22:5–6.

9. James W. C. Pennington, *A Textbook of the Origin and History, etc., etc., of the Colored People* (Hartford, CT: L. Skinner, 1841), 7–8.

10. "De Ways of de Wimmens," in Langston Hughes and Arna Bontemps, eds., *The Book of Negro Folklore* (New York: Fleming H. Revell, 1958), 130–135.

11. "Origin of Races," in ibid., 155.

12. *Babylonian Talmud,* Sanh. 108b; *Midrash Rabba-Genesis,* 36:7–8.

13. Quoted in William Sumner Jenkins, *Pro-Slavery Thought in the Old South* (Chapel Hill: University of North Carolina Press, 1935), 205–206.

14. George R. Price and James Brewer Stewart, eds., *To Heal the Scourge of Prejudice: The Life and Writings of Hosea Easton* (Amherst: University of Massachusetts Press, 1999), 70, 80–81, 83.

15. Quoted in Anthony B. Pinn, ed., *Moral Evil and Redemptive Suffering: A History of Theodicy in African-American Religious Thought* (Gainesville: University Press of Florida, 2002), 138.

16. Alonzo Potter Burgess Holly, *God and the Negro: Synopsis of God of the Negro or the Biblical Record of the Race of Ham* (Nashville, TN: National Baptist Publishing Board, 1937), 122.

17. Sondra A. O'Neale, *Jupiter Hammon and the Biblical Beginnings of African-American Literature* (Metuchen, NJ: Scarecrow Press, and [Philadelphia]: American Theological Library Association, 1993), 2.

18. Milton C. Sernett, ed., *Afro-American Religious History: A Documentary Witness* (Durham, NC: Duke University Press, 1985), 35, 41.

19. Cited in Raboteau, *Slave Religion,* 294.

20. William M. Manross, *A History of the American Episcopal Church,* 3rd ed. (New York: Morehouse-Gorham, 1959), 148–150. Neau's catechism quoted in Wood, *Arrogance of Faith,* 72.

21. Cotton Mather, *The Negro Christianized: An Essay to Excite and Assist the Good Work, the Instruction of Negro-Servants in Christianity*. . . (Boston: B. Green, 1706), 42–43.

22. In Paul D. Escott, *Slavery Remembered: A Record of Twentieth-Century Slave Narratives* (Chapel Hill: University of North Carolina Press, 1979), 113–114.

23. John W. Blassingame, ed., *The Frederick Douglass Papers*, ser. 1: *Speeches, Debates, and Interviews*, vol. 1: *1841–1846* (New Haven and London: Yale University Press, 1979), 404–405.

24. Alexander Glennie, *Sermons Preached on Plantations to Congregations of Slaves* (Charleston, SC, 1844), 22–26, cited in Charles Joyner, *Down by the Riverside: A South Carolina Slave Community* (Urbana: University of Illinois Press, 1984), 156.

25. Mariah Heywood in *Slave Narratives: A Folk History of Slavery in the United States from Interviews with Former Slaves*, 17 vols. (Washington, DC: Library of Congress, 1941), 14, pt. 1:285, cited in Joyner, *Down by the Riverside*, 156.

26. John W. Blassingame, ed., *Slave Testimony: Two Centuries of Letters, Speeches, Interviews, and Autobiographies* (Baton Rouge, LA: Louisiana State University Press, 1976), 642–643, 538.

27. Howard Thurman, *Jesus and the Disinherited* (Richmond, IN: Friends United Press, 1981), 30–35.

28. William Wells Brown, *Clotel* (New York: Arno Press, 1969), 100.

29. Herbert Aptheker, ed., *A Documentary History of the Negro People in the United States*, 3 vols. (New York: Citadel Press, 1951), 1:8–9.

30. Wood, *Arrogance of Faith*, 43.

31. Ibid., 62–65.

32. Anthony Benezet and John Wesley, *Views of American Slavery, Taken a Century Ago* (Philadelphia: Association of Friends for the Diffusion of Religious and Useful Knowledge, 1858), 47–48.

33. Olaudah Equiano, *The Interesting Narrative of the Life of Olaudah Equiano, or Gustavus Vassa, the African, Written by Himself*, 2 vols. (1789), in Gates and Andrews, eds., *Pioneers of the Black Atlantic*, 223.

34. *Minutes of Several Conversations between the Rev. Thomas Coke, L.L.D., the Rev. Francis Asbury, and Others, at a Conference, Begun in Baltimore, in the State of Maryland, on Monday, the 27th of December, in the Year 1784* (Philadelphia, 1785), 15, quoted in H. Shelton Smith, *In His Image, But . . . : Racism in Southern Religion, 1780–1910* (Durham, NC: Duke University Press, 1972), 103.

35. Quoted in Wood, *Arrogance of Faith*, 64.

36. James Henley Thornwell, "Slavery and the Religious Instruction of the Coloured Population," *Southern Presbyterian Review* (July 1850): 135, quoted ibid.

37. Robert L. Dabney, *A Defense of Virginia, and through Her, of the South, in Recent Contests against the Sectional Party* (New York, 1867), 197, quoted ibid.

38. Richard Fuller and Francis Wayland, *Domestic Slavery Considered as a Scriptural Institution* (New York: Lewis Colby, 1847), 202, quoted ibid.

39. Ibid.

40. Sernett, ed., *Afro-American Religious History*, 169.

41. Ibid., 178.

42. Marilyn Richardson, ed., *Maria W. Stewart, America's First Black Woman Political Writer: Essays and Speeches* (Bloomington: Indiana University Press, 1987), 66.

43. Ibid., 68.

44. James Baldwin, *The Fire Next Time . . .* (New York: Dial Press, 1963), 50.

45. Alice Walker, *The Color Purple* (New York: Washington Square Press, 1982), 177.

46. "Balm in Gilead," in Verolga Nix and J. Jefferson Cleveland, eds., *Songs of Zion*, Supplemental Worship Resources 12 (Nashville, TN: Abingdon, 1981), 123.

47. Theophus H. Smith, *Conjuring Culture: Biblical Formations of Black America* (New York: Oxford University Press, 1994), 169.

CHAPTER 3. THE GOOD BOOK

Epigraph: Dorothy Scarborough, *On the Trail of Negro Folk Songs* (Cambridge, MA: Harvard University Press, 1925), 71–72.

1. In Lawrence W. Levine, *Black Culture and Black Consciousness: Afro-American Folk Thought from Slavery to Freedom* (New York: Oxford University Press, 1977), 34.

2. In Albert J. Raboteau, *Slave Religion: The "Invisible Institution" in the Antebellum South* (New York: Oxford University Press, 1978), 291–292.

3. Moses Roper, *A Narrative of the Adventures and Escape of Moses Roper from American Slavery* (London, 1840), 62, cited in John W. Roberts, *From Trickster to Badman: The Black Folk Hero in Slavery and Freedom* (Philadelphia: University of Pennsylvania Press, 1989), 146.

4. Charlotte Forten, "Life on the Sea Islands," pt. 2, *Atlantic Monthly*, June 1864, 672, quoted in Margaret Washington, "The Meanings of Scripture," in Vincent Wimbush, ed., *African Americans and the Bible: Sacred Texts and Social Textures* (New York: Continuum, 2000), 336.

5. In V. P. Franklin, *Black Self-Determination: A Cultural History of African-American Resistance* (Brooklyn, NY: Lawrence Hill Books, 1992), 60.

6. Douglass Strange, "Document: Bishop Alexander Payne's Protestation of American Slavery," *Journal of Negro History* 52 (January 1967): 63, quoted in Raboteau, *Slave Religion*, 313.

7. "Walk in Jerusalem Jus' Like John," in James Weldon and J. Rosamond Johnson, *The Books of American Negro Spirituals: Including the Book of American Negro Spirituals and The Second Book of Negro Spirituals*, 2 vols. (New York: Viking Press, 1925–1926; reprint ed., New York: Da Capo Press, 1989), 2:58–59.

8. Mary A. Livermore, *My Story of the War: A Woman's Narrative of Four Years*

Personal Experience as Nurse in the Union Army . . . (Hartford, CT: A. D. Worthington, 1889), quoted in Raboteau, *Slave Religion*, 313.

9. Quoted in Sterling Brown, "Negro Folk Expression: Spirituals, Seculars, Ballads and Work Songs," *Phylon* 14 (Winter 1953): 45–61.

10. "Joshua Fit the Battle of Jericho," in Weldon and Johnson, *Books of American Negro Spirituals*, 1:56–58.

11. W. E. B. Du Bois, *The Souls of Black Folk* (1903; reprint ed., New York: Penguin, 1989), 163.

12. "A Secret Organization for Freedom, 1856," in Herbert Aptheker, ed., *A Documentary History of the Negro People in the United States*, 3 vols. (New York: Citadel Press, 1951), 1:379.

13. Ibid., 380.

14. Quoted in Charles Joyner, *Down by the Riverside: A South Carolina Slave Community* (Urbana: University of Illinois Press, 1984), 168.

15. Ibid.

16. Cited in Roberts, *Trickster*, 154.

17. Thomas L. Johnson, *Twenty-Eight Years a Slave: Or, The Story of My Life in Three Continents*, 7th ed. (Bournemouth, Eng.: W. Mate, 1909), 29–30, quoted in Raboteau, *Slave Religion*, 312.

18. Martin R. Delany, *Blake, or The Huts of America, a Novel* (Boston: Beacon Press, 1970), 258.

CHAPTER 4. EXILE

Epigraph: Howard Thurman, "On Viewing the Coast of Africa," in *For the Inward Journey* (Richmond, IN: Friends United Press, 1984), 60.

1. "Babel's Streams," in George Pullen Jackson, ed., *Down-East Spirituals and Others: Three Hundred Songs Supplementary to the Author's Spiritual Folk-Songs of Early America* (New York: J. J. Augustin, [1943]), 186.

2. See http://www.africanamericans.com/FrederickDouglassJuly4th.htm.

3. Robert Hayden, "Frederick Douglass," in Henry Louis Gates, Jr., and Nellie Y. McKay, eds., *The Norton Anthology of African American Literature* (New York: W. W. Norton, 1997), 1508–9.

4. See http://www.africanamericans.com/FrederickDouglassJuly4th.htm.

5. Thomas Sowell, *Conquests and Cultures: An International History* (New York: Basic Books, 1998), 110.

6. Ibid., 153–157.

7. See Michael Crowder, *West African Resistance: The Military Response to Colonial Occupation* (New York: Africana, 1971).

8. Hugh Thomas, *The Slave Trade: The Story of the Atlantic Slave Trade, 1440–1870* (New York: Simon and Schuster, 1997), 119–121.

9. Ibid., 123, nn. 10, 11.

10. See Ronald Takaki, *A Different Mirror: A History of Multicultural America* (Boston: Little, Brown, 1993), 58–66.

11. See Ira Berlin, *Generations of Captivity: A History of African-American Slaves* (Cambridge, MA: Belknap Press of Harvard University Press, 2003).

12. Toni Morrison, *Beloved: A Novel* (New York: Penguin, 1987), 221–222.

13. Ibid., 257.

14. William Wells Brown, *The Narrative of William W. Brown, a Fugitive Slave*, in Gates and McKay, eds., *Norton Anthology of African American Literature*, 253.

15. Charles H. Long, *Significations: Signs, Symbols, and Images in the Interpretation of Religion* (Philadelphia: Fortress Press, 1986), 177.

16. Cheryl J. Sanders, *Saints in Exile: The Holiness-Pentecostal Experience in African American Religion and Culture* (New York: Oxford University Press, 1996), 129, 128.

17. Jeanette Robinson Murphy, "The Survival of African Music in America," *Popular Science Monthly* 55 (1899): 660–672, quoted in James Abbington, "Biblical Themes in the R. Nathaniel Dett Collection," in Vincent Wimbush, ed., *African Americans and the Bible: Sacred Texts and Social Textures* (New York: Continuum, 2000), 282.

18. Cornel West, *Keeping Faith: Philosophy and Race in America* (New York: Routledge, 1993), xiii.

19. Andrew Fede, "Legitimized Violent Slave Abuse in the American South, 1619–1865: A Case Study of Law and Social Change in Six Southern States," *American Journal of Legal History* 29 (1985): 94.

20. Catherine Clinton, "'With a Whip in His Hand': Rape, Memory, and African American Women," in Genevieve Fabre and Robert O'Meally, eds., *History and Memory in African-American Culture* (New York: Oxford University Press, 1994), 208.

21. W. E. B. Du Bois, *The Souls of Black Folk* (1903; reprint ed., New York: Penguin, 1989), 156.

22. Albert J. Raboteau, "The Black Experience in American Evangelicalism: The Meaning of Slavery," in Timothy E. Fulop and Albert J. Raboteau, eds., *African-American Religion: Interpretive Essays in History and Culture* (New York: Routledge, 1997), 97.

23. Ibid., 97–98; *American Missionary*, January 1868, 9, September 1870, 194, 221.

24. B. A. Botkin, ed., *Lay My Burden Down: A Folk History of Slavery* (New York: Delta, 1994), 27.

25. Albert J. Raboteau, "African-Americans, Exodus, and the American Israel," in Paul E. Johnson, ed., *African-American Christianity: Essays in History* (Berkeley: University of California Press, 1994), 4.

26. Michael Gomez, "The Preacher Kings," in Wimbush, ed., *African Americans and the Bible*, 510.

27. Ibid.

28. In John W. Roberts, *From Trickster to Badman: The Black Folk Hero in Slavery and Freedom* (Philadelphia: University of Pennsylvania Press, 1989), 124.

29. James Weldon and J. Rosamond Johnson, *The Books of American Negro*

Spirituals: Including the Book of American Negro Spirituals and the Second Book of Negro Spirituals, 2 vols. (New York: Viking Press, 1925–1926; reprint ed., New York: Da Capo Press, 1989), 1:20.

30. Marion A. Haskell, "Negro Spirituals," _Century Magazine_ 36 (1899): 578.
31. R. Nathaniel Dett, ed., _Religious Folk-Songs of the Negro as Sung at Hampton Institute_ (Hampton, VA: Hampton Institute Press, 1927), xlii.
32. Frederick Law Olmstead, _A Journey in the Seaboard Slave States_ (1856), cited in Albert J. Raboteau, _Slave Religion: The "Invisible Institution" in the Antebellum South_ (New York: Oxford University Press, 1978), 69.
33. Elizabeth Ware Pearson, ed., _Letters from Port Royal Written at the Time of the Civil War_ (Boston: W. B. Clarke, 1906), 27.
34. H. G. Spaulding quoted in Walter F. Pitts, _Old Ship of Zion: The Afro-Baptist Ritual in the African Diaspora_ (New York: Oxford University Press, 1993), 93–94.
35. Pearson, ed., _Letters from Port Royal,_ 27.
36. Pitts, _Old Ship of Zion,_ 93; Sterling Stuckey, _Slave Culture: Nationalist Theory and the Foundations of Black America_ (New York: Oxford University Press, 1987), 10–17.
37. Daniel Alexander Payne, _Recollections of Seventy Years_ (Nashville, TN: AME Sunday School Union, 1888), 253–256.
38. Clifton Joseph Furness, "Communal Music among Arabians and Negroes," _Musical Quarterly_ 16 (1930): 49–51, cited in Lawrence W. Levine, _Black Culture and Black Consciousness: Afro-American Folk Thought from Slavery to Freedom_ (New York: Oxford University Press, 1977), 27.
39. Pitts, _Old Ship of Zion,_ 95.
40. Lomax and Parrish cited in Raboteau, _Slave Religion,_ 70.
41. Dorothy Scarborough, assisted by Ola Lee Gulledge, _On the Trail of Negro Folk-Songs_ (Hatboro, PA: Folklore Associates, 1963), 14–16; Frederick Douglass, _My Bondage and My Freedom_ (1855; reprint ed., New York: Dover, 1969), 99, 104.
42. Mahalia Jackson with Evan McLeod Wylie, _Movin' on Up_ (New York: Hawthorn Books, 1966), 32, 63; Miles Davis with Quincy Troupe, _Miles, the Autobiography_ (New York: Simon and Schuster, 1989), 7.
43. _New York Times,_ Aug. 18, 2002.
44. Judith Weisenfeld, "'For the Cause of Mankind': The Bible, Racial Uplift, and Early Race Movies," in Wimbush, ed., _African Americans and the Bible,_ 736–738.
45. August Wilson, _Joe Turner's Come and Gone: A Play in Two Acts_ (New York: Penguin Books, 1988), "The Play" [unpaginated].
46. Ibid., 52–55, 73.
47. Cited in Jaqueline L. Tobin and Raymond G. Dobard, _Hidden in Plain View: The Secret Story of Quilts and the Underground Railroad_ (New York: Doubleday, 1999), 133.
48. Murphy, _Working the Spirit,_ 162.

49. James Baldwin, *Go Tell It on the Mountain* (New York: Dial Press, 1953), 200–201.

50. G. A. Cooke, *A Critical and Exegetical Commentary on the Book of Ezekiel* (Edinburgh: T. and T. Clark, 1960), 397.

51. "Great Day," in Weldon and Johnson, *Books of Spirituals,* 2:56–57.

52. Carl J. Anderson, "Ezekiel and the Vision of Dry Bones," in Linda Goss and Marian E. Barnes, eds., *Talk That Talk: An Anthology of African American Storytelling* (New York: Simon and Schuster/Touchstone, 1989), 199.

53. Ibid., 205.

54. Douglass, *My Bondage and My Freedom,* 104.

55. See Steven S. Tuell, "Divine Presence and Absence in Ezekiel's Prophecy," in Margaret S. Odell and John T. Strong, eds., *The Book of Ezekiel: Theological and Anthropological Perspectives* (Atlanta, GA: Society of Biblical Literature, 2000), 97–116, esp. 109–113; Carol Newsome, *Songs of the Sabbath Sacrifice: A Critical Edition* (Atlanta, GA: Scholars Press, 1985), esp. 52–56, 226, 303.

56. W. E. B. Du Bois, *The Souls of Black Folk* (1903; reprint ed., New York: Penguin, 1989), 208. See Stephen Breck Reid, "The Theology of the Book of Daniel and the Political Theory of W. E. B. Du Bois," in Randall C. Bailey and Jacquelyn Grant, eds., *The Recovery of Black Presence: An Interdisciplinary Exploration; Essays in Honor of Dr. Charles B. Copher* (Nashville, TN: Abingdon Press, 1995), 37–49.

CHAPTER 5. EXODUS

Epigraph: Diary entry, Dec. 12, 1857, by her mistress: Barbara Leigh Smith Bodichon, *An American Diary, 1857–8,* ed. Joseph W. Reed, Jr. (London: Routledge and K. Paul, 1972), 65, cited in Albert J. Raboteau, "African-Americans, Exodus, and the American Israel," in Paul E. Johnson, ed., *African-American Christianity: Essays in History* (Berkeley: University of California Press, 1994), 13.

1. Exod. 5:1, 7:16, 8:1, 8:20, 9:1, 9:13, 10:3.

2. Iveson L. Brookes, *A Defense of Southern Slavery, against the Attacks of Henry Clay and Alex'r Campbell . . .* (Hamburg, SC, 1851), 5, quoted in Forrest G. Wood, *The Arrogance of Faith: Christianity and Race in America from the Colonial Era to the Twentieth Century* (New York: Alfred A. Knopf, 1990), 86.

3. "Go Down, Moses," in James Weldon and J. Rosamond Johnson, *The Books of American Negro Spirituals: Including the Book of American Negro Spirituals and the Second Book of Negro Spirituals, 2 vols.* (New York: Viking Press, 1925–26; reprint ed., New York: Da Capo Press, 1989), 1:51–53.

4. "Didn't Ol' Pharoah Get Lost?" in ibid., 60–61.

5. Edwin Williams to the Rev. S. S. Jocelyn of the American Missionary Association, Jan. 28, 1863, quoted in Margaret Washington, "The Meanings of Scripture in Gullah Concepts of Liberation and Group Identity," in Vincent Wimbush, ed., *African Americans and the Bible: Sacred Texts and Social Textures* (New York: Continuum, 2000), 337.

6. Abel McGee Chreitzberg, *Early Methodism in the Carolinas* (Nashville, TN: Publishing House of the M[ethodist] E[piscopal] C[hurch], South, 1897), 158–159, quoted in Albert J. Raboteau, *Slave Religion: The "Invisible Institution" in the Antebellum South* (New York: Oxford University Press, 1978), 8–9.

7. Paul Laurence Dunbar, "An Antebellum Sermon," in Henry Louis Gates, Jr., and Nellie Y. McKay, eds., *The Norton Anthology of African American Literature* (New York: W. W. Norton, 1997), 892.

8. Ibid.

9. B. A. Botkin, *Lay My Burden Down: A Folk History of Slavery* (New York: Delta, 1989), 27.

10. Paul Laurence Dunbar, "We Wear the Mask," in Gates and McKay, eds., *Norton Anthology of African American Literature,* 896.

11. Dunbar, "Antebellum Sermon," 893.

12. In Richard M. Dorson, *American Negro Folktales* (Greenwich, CT: Fawcett, 1967), 256–257.

13. Cited in John W. Roberts, *From Trickster to Badman: The Black Folk Hero in Slavery and Freedom* (Philadelphia: University of Pennsylvania Press, 1989), 155.

14. Gerhard Von Rad, *Old Testament Theology,* trans. D. M. G. Stalker, 2 vols. (New York: Harper, 1962), 1:35.

15. Harry Middleton Hyatt, *Hoodoo—Conjuration—Witchcraft—Rootwork: Beliefs Accepted by Many Negroes and White Persons, These Being Orally Recorded among Blacks and Whites,* 5 vols. (Hannibal, MO: Western, 1970–1978), 2:1758, quoted in Kevin J. Hayes, *Folklore and Book Culture* (Knoxville: University of Tennessee Press, 1997), 14–27.

16. Works Project Administration, *Drums and Shadows: Survival Studies among the Georgia Coastal Negroes* (Garden City, NY: Anchor Books, 1972), 25.

17. Charles Joyner, *Down by the Riverside: A South Carolina Slave Community* (Urbana: University of Illinois Press, 1984), 143.

18. Ibid., 145.

19. Zora Neale Hurston, "Hoodoo in America," *Journal of American Folklore* 44 (October–December 1931): 414.

20. Zora Neale Hurston, *Tell My Horse,* in Cheryl A. Wall, ed., *Zora Neale Hurston: Novels and Stories* (New York: Library of America, 1995), 378.

21. Zora Neale Hurston, *Moses, Man of the Mountain,* in Wall, ed., *Hurston: Novels and Stories,* 443.

22. Quoted in Joyner, *Down by the Riverside,* 164.

23. Frances Harper, "Our Greatest Want," in Gates and McKay, eds., *Norton Anthology,* 431–432.

24. Quoted in Raboteau, "Exodus," 13.

25. In Charles L. Perdue, Jr., Thomas E. Barden, and Robert K. Phillips, *Weevils in the Wheat: Interviews with Virginia Ex-Slaves* (Charlottesville: University of Virginia Press, 1976), 10, quoted in Roberts, *Trickster,* 161.

26. Quoted in Jaqueline L. Tobin and Raymond G. Dobard, *Hidden in Plain View: The Secret Story of Quilts and the Underground Railroad* (New York: Doubleday, 1999), 147.

27. James Weldon Johnson, "Let My People Go," in Johnson, *God's Trombones: Seven Negro Songs in Verse* (New York: Viking Press, 1927), 45–52.

28. Beauford Delaney, *The Burning Bush*, 1941, reproduced in Gary A. Reynolds and Beryl J. Wright, *Against the Odds: African-American Artists and the Harmon Foundation* (Newark, NJ: Newark Museum, 1989), 127, pl. 7.

29. Hurston, *Moses, Man of the Mountain*, 501.

30. Charlotta Bass, "I Accept This Call," *National Guardian* Apr. 2, 1952, reprinted in Gerda Lerner, ed., *Black Women in White America: A Documentary History* (New York: Vintage Books, 1973), 345.

31. Martin Luther King, Jr., *Where Do We Go from Here: Chaos or Community?* (New York: Harper and Row, 1967), 124; King, "Out of the Long Night of Segregation," *Presbyterian Outlook*, Feb. 10, 1958, 6.

32. Martin Luther King, Jr., "I See the Promised Land," in James Melvin Washington, ed., *A Testament of Hope: The Essential Writings and Speeches of Martin Luther King, Jr.* (San Francisco: Harper and Row, 1986), 279.

33. Ibid., 280.

34. Ibid., 286.

35. Jesse L. Jackson, "Protecting the Legacy: The Challenge of Martin Luther King, Jr.," in Jackson, *Straight from the Heart*, ed. Roger D. Hatch and Frank E. Watkins (Philadelphia: Fortress Press, 1987), 127.

36. Mattias Gardell, "The Sun of Islam Will Rise in the West: Minister Farrakhan and the Nation of Islam in the Latter Days," in Yvonne Yazbeck Haddad and Jane Idleman Smith, eds., *Muslim Communities in North America* (Albany: State University of New York Press, 1994), 17.

37. See Taylor Branch, *Pillar of Fire: America in the King Years, 1963–65* (New York: Simon and Schuster, 1998), 34.

38. Louis Farrakhan, "Remarks at the Million Man March," http://www.africawithin.com/mmm/transcript.htm.

39. Ibid.

40. "Didn't Ol' Pharaoh Get Lost?" in Weldon and Johnson, *Books of American Negro Spirituals*, 1:61.

41. Eddie S. Glaude, Jr., *Exodus! Religion, Race, and Nation in Early Nineteenth-Century Black America* (Chicago: University of Chicago Press, 2002), 46. See David Lyle Jeffrey, "The Bible and the American Myth," in Jeffrey, *People of the Book: Christian Identity and Literary Culture* (Grand Rapids, MI: William B. Eerdmans, 1996), 317–352.

42. *Winthrop Papers*, vol. 2 (Boston: Massachusetts Historical Society, 1931), 282–284, 292–295, reprinted in Conrad Cherry, ed., *God's New Israel: Religious Interpretations of American Destiny* (Englewood Cliffs, NJ: Prentice-Hall, 1971), 43, cited in Raboteau, "Exodus," 10.

43. Werner Sollors, *Beyond Ethnicity: Consent and Descent in American Culture*

(New York: Oxford University Press, 1986), 42–44; Herman Melville, *White Jacket: or, The World in a Man-of-War* (New York: Oxford University Press, 1967), 152–153; James Russell Lowell, "Oration Ode," in William Michael Rossetti, ed., *The Poetical Works of James Russell Lowell* (New York, 1889), 298.

44. Martin R. Delany, *Blake, or The Huts of America, a Novel* (Boston: Beacon Press, 1970), 315, n. 3.

45. Ibid., 43.

46. See Gilbert Osofsky, ed., *Puttin' on Ole Massa: The Slave Narratives of Henry Bibb, William Wells Brown, and Solomon Northup* (New York: Harper and Row, 1969), 147, 166, 215.

47. Von Rad, *Old Testament Theology,* 2:133.

48. "Didn't Ol' Pharaoh Get Lost?" in Weldon and Johnson, *Books of American Negro Spirituals,* 1:60.

49. *The New National Baptist Hymnal* (Nashville, TN: National Baptist Publishing Board, 1977), 512.

50. Cheryl Townsend Gilkes, "The Virtues of Brotherhood and Sisterhood: African American Fraternal Organizations and Their Bibles," in Wimbush, ed., *African Americans and the Bible,* 401, n. 1.

51. Cited in Roberts, *Trickster,* 152.

52. Albert Murray, *The Hero and the Blues* (New York: Vintage, 1995), 61.

53. Ibid., 62.

54. In Louis Ruchames, ed., *Racial Thought in America,* vol. 1: *From the Puritans to Abraham Lincoln* (Amherst: University of Massachusetts Press, 1969), 47, 58.

55. Francis Grimké, "A Resemblance and a Contrast between the American Negro and the Children of Israel, in Egypt, or the Duty of the Negro to Contend Earnestly for His Rights Guaranteed under the Constitution," in Carter Woodson, ed., *The Works of Francis L. Grimké,* 4 vols. (Washington, DC: Associated Publishers, 1942), 1:352.

56. Glaude, *Exodus!* 54.

57. Henry Highland Garnet, "An Address to the Slaves of the United States of America," in John H. Bracey, Jr., August Meier, and Elliott Rudwick, eds., *Black Nationalism in America* (Indianapolis, IN: Bobbs-Merrill, 1990), 74.

58. Ibid., 72.

59. See Glaude, *Exodus!* 147–149.

60. G. K. Chesterton, "On Leisure," in *Selected Essays,* chosen by Dorothy Collins (London: Methuen, 1955), 269.

61. Cited in Timothy B. Tyson, *Radio Free Dixie: Robert F. Williams and the Roots of Black Power* (Chapel Hill: University of North Carolina Press, 1999), 97.

62. Cited in ibid., 98.

63. Samuel Sewall, "The Selling of Joseph: A Memorial," in Ruchames, *Racial Thought,* 1:47.

64. In Henry Louis Gates, Jr., and William L. Andrews, eds., *Pioneers of the Black*

Atlantic: Five Slave Narratives from the Enlightenment, 1772–1815 (Washington, DC: Civitas, 1998), 210.

65. Vincent Harding, "The Anointed Ones: Hamer, King, and the Bible in the Southern Freedom Movement," in Wimbush, ed., *African Americans and the Bible*, 544.

66. Glaude, *Exodus!* 54.

67. *American Missionary* 6, no. 2 (February 1862): 33, cited in Raboteau, "Exodus," 14.

68. "I Wish I Had Died in Egypt Land," in John Wesley Work, ed., *American Negro Songs* (New York: Howell, Soskin, 1940), 157.

69. "Go Down, Moses," in Weldon and Johnson, *Books of American Negro Spirituals*, 1:51–53; "Walk Together Children," in Gates and McKay, eds., *Norton Anthology of African American Literature*, 9.

70. Martin Luther King, Jr., "I See the Promised Land," in Washington, ed., *Testament of Hope*, 279–286.

71. At the 1963 Chicago Conference on Religion and Race, quoted in Branch, *Pillar of Fire*, 24.

72. "God's A-Gwinter Trouble de Water," in Weldon and Johnson, *Books of American Negro Spirituals*, 2:85.

73. Elizabeth Hyde Botume, *First Days amongst the Contrabands* (1893; New York: Arno Press, 1968), 204, quoted in Margaret Washington, "The Meanings of Scripture," in Wimbush, ed., *African Americans and the Bible*, 336.

74. In George P. Rawick, ed., *The American Slave: A Composite Autobiography*, suppl. ser. 2, vol. 16 (Westport, CT: Greenwood Press, 1972), 89.

75. Frederick Douglass, *Life and Times of Frederick Douglass: His Early Life as a Slave, His Escape from Bondage, and His Complete History; Written by Himself*, introduction by Rayford W. Logan (New York: Collier Books, 1969), 159–160, cited in Raboteau, "Exodus," 14.

76. Joseph M. Murphy, *Working the Spirit: Ceremonies of the African Diaspora* (Boston: Beacon Press, 1994), 153. See also Lawrence W. Levine, *Black Culture and Black Consciousness: Afro-American Folk Thought from Slavery to Freedom* (New York: Oxford University Press, 1977), 37–38.

77. Quoted in Joyner, *Down by the Riverside*, 167–168.

78. Sarah H. Bradford, *Scenes from the Life of Harriet Tubman* (Salem, NH: Ayer, 1992), 18–19.

79. Arthur H. Fauset, *Sojourner Truth, God's Faithful Pilgrim* (1938; reprint ed., New York: Russell and Russell, 1971), 175.

80. George M. Fredrickson, *Black Liberation: A Comparative History of Black Ideologies in the United States and South Africa* (New York: Oxford University Press, 1995), 66, n. 18.

81. Delany, *Blake*, 21.

82. Ibid., 29.

83. Fredrickson, *Black Liberation*, 67.

84. Herbert Aptheker, ed., *A Documentary History of the Negro People in the United States*, 3 vols. (New York: Citadel Press, 1951), 2:713.

85. Ibid.

86. Moses Moore, "'Behold the Dreamer Cometh': Orishatukeh Fadama and Pan-African Biblical Hermeneutics," in Wimbush, ed., *African Americans and the Bible*, 423.

87. In *Africa's Offering* (New York: John A. Gray, 1862), republished in Anthony B. Pinn, ed., *Moral Evil and Redemptive Suffering: A History of Theodicy in African-American Religious Thought* (Gainesville: University Press of Florida, 2002), 87–88.

88. Quoted in Fredrickson, *Black Liberation*, 77, n. 39.

89. Orishatukeh Fadama, "What the African Movement Stands For," *African Mail*, Sept. 25, 1914, cited in Moore, "'Behold the Dreamer Cometh,'" 422, 430, n. 26.

90. Fadama, "The A.M.E. Church and Kittrell Normal Institute," *Christian Recorder*, Apr. 16, 1890, 289, cited in Moore, "'Behold the Dreamer Cometh,'" 430, n. 27.

91. "The Afro-Americans at Victoria Park," *Sierra Leone Weekly News*, Jan. 23, 1915, cited in Moore, "'Behold the Dreamer Cometh,'" 430.

92. Milton Sernett, "Rereadings: The Great Migration and the Bible," in Wimbush, ed., *African Americans and the Bible*, 449.

93. Ibid., 449, nn. 5–7.

94. David Walker, *Appeal to the Colored Citizens of the World*, in Charles M. Wiltse, ed., *David Walker's Appeal, in Four Articles, Together with a Preamble, to the Coloured Citizens of the World, but in Particular, and Very Expressly, to Those of the United States of America* (New York: Hill and Wang, 1965).

95. Ibid., 7, 10, 14.

96. Garnet, "Address to the Slaves," 72–73.

97. Ibid., 74.

98. Grimké, "Resemblance and Contrast," 350–351.

99. Address in Carter Godwin Woodson, *Negro Orators and Their Orations* (1925; reprint ed., New York: Russell and Russell, 1969), 64, cited in Raboteau, "African-Americans, Exodus, and American Israel," 14.

100. Henry MacNeal Turner, *AME Recorder*, Jan. 25, 1883, in Milton C. Sernett, ed., *Afro-American Religious History: A Documentary Witness* (Durham, NC: Duke University Press, 1985), 261–262.

101. W. E. B. Du Bois, "The Migration of Negroes," *Crisis* (June 1917): 66, quoted in Sernett, "Rereadings," 449.

102. Nannie Helen Burroughs, "Unload Your Uncle Toms," *Louisiana Weekly*, Dec. 23, 1933, reprinted in Lerner, *Black Women in White America*, 551–553.

103. Arna Bontemps, *Black Thunder* (New York: Macmillan, 1936), 50–53.

104. Ibid., 166–168.

105. Cited in Tobin and Dobard, *Hidden in Plain View*, 143–144.

106. Orishatukeh Fadama, "The African Movement: The Perils of Pioneering—

A Parallel," *Sierra Leone Weekly News*, Sept. 11, 1915, cited in Moore, "'Behold the Dreamer Cometh,'" 426.

CHAPTER 6. ETHIOPIA

Epigraph: W. E. B. Du Bois, *The Souls of Black Folk* (1903; reprint ed., New York: Penguin, 1989), 6.

1. Albert J. Raboteau, "'Ethiopia Shall Soon Stretch Forth Her Hands': Black Destiny in Nineteenth-Century America," in Raboteau, *A Fire in the Bones: Reflections on African-American Religious History* (Boston: Beacon Press, 1995), 42.

2. George M. Fredrickson, *Black Liberation: A Comparative History of Black Ideologies in the United States and South Africa* (New York: Oxford University Press, 1995), 62.

3. William Scott, "'And Ethiopia Shall Stretch Forth Its Hands': The Origins of Ethiopianism in Afro-American Thought, 1767–1896," *Umoja*, n.s., 2 (Spring 1978): 3.

4. Cotton Mather, *The Negro Christianized: An Essay to Excite and Assist the Good Work, the Instruction of Negro-Servants in Christianity . . .* (Boston: B. Green, 1706).

5. Cotton Mather, *Rules for the Society of Negroes, 1693* (New York: Lenox Library, 1888), 3–4.

6. Cited in Albert J. Raboteau, *Slave Religion: The "Invisible Institution" in the Antibellum South* (New York: Oxford University Press, 1978), 129–130.

7. George Shepperson, "Ethiopianism Past and Present," in C. G. Baëta, ed., *Christianity in Tropical Africa: Studies Presented and Discussed at the Seventh International African Seminar, University of Ghana, April 1965* (London: Oxford University Press for the International African Institute, 1968), 249. Carol V. R. George, *Segregated Sabbaths: Richard Allen and the Emergence of Independent Black Churches, 1760–1840* (New York: Oxford University Press, 1973), 165.

8. Phillis Wheatley to the Rev. Samuel Hopkins, Boston, Feb. 9, 1774, in Julian D. Mason, Jr., *The Poems of Phillis Wheatley* (Chapel Hill: University of North Carolina Press, 1966), 110.

9. Jupiter Hammond, "An Address to Miss Phillis Wheatley, Ethiopian Poetess (1778)," in Richard Barksdale and Kenneth Kinnamon, eds., *Black Writers of America: A Comprehensive Anthology* (New York: Macmillan, 1972), 47–48.

10. Cited in Scott, "'And Ethiopia Shall Stretch Forth,'" 2.

11. Phillis Wheatley, "To the University of Cambridge in New England (1767)," in Mason, ed., *Poems of Phillis Wheatley*, 5–6, cited ibid., 3.

12. Richard Allen, *The Life, Experience, and Gospel Labours of the Rt. Rev. Richard Allen* (Philadelphia: Martin and Boden, 1833; reprint ed., New York: Abingdon, 1960), 76.

13. Prince Hall, "A Charge, Delivered to the African Lodge, June 24, 1797, at

Menotonomy," in Dorothy Porter, ed., *Early Negro Writing, 1760–1837* (Boston: Beacon Press, 1971), 72.

14. Robert A. Young, *The Ethiopian Manifesto*, in Sterling Stuckey, ed., *The Ideological Origins of Black Nationalism* (Boston: Beacon Press, 1972), 30–38.

15. David Walker, *Appeal to the Colored Citizens of the World*, in Charles M. Wiltse, ed., *David Walker's Appeal, in Four Articles, Together with a Preamble, to the Coloured Citizens of the World, but in Particular, and Very Expressly, to Those of the United States of America* (New York: Hill and Wang, 1965), 18.

16. Fredrickson, *Black Liberation*, 64–65, 65, n. 15.

17. Ibid., 62.

18. Josiah Nott, *Two Lectures, on the Natural History of the Caucasian and Negro Races* (Mobile, AL, 1844), 30–34, quoted in Forrest G. Wood, *The Arrogance of Faith: Christianity and Race in America from the Colonial Era to the Twentieth Century* (New York: Alfred A. Knopf, 1990), 99.

19. Louis Agassiz, "The Diversity of the Origin of the Human Race," *Christian Examiner and Religious Miscellany* 49 (July 1850): 181–204.

20. Frederick Douglass, "The Claims of the Negro Ethnologically Considered (1854)," in Philip S. Foner, ed., *The Voice of Black America: Major Speeches by Negroes in the United States, 1797–1971* (New York: Simon and Schuster, 1972), 144.

21. Frederick Douglass, "The Abilities and Possibilities of Our Race (1865)," in Foner, *Voice of Black America*, 331.

22. Henry Highland Garnet, *The Past and the Present Condition, and the Destiny, of the Colored Race* (1848; reprint ed., Miami, FL: Mnemosyne, 1969), 6–12.

23. Frances E. W. Harper, "Ethiopia," in Henry Louis Gates, Jr., and Nellie Y. McKay, eds., *The Norton Anthology of African American Literature* (New York: W. W. Norton, 1997), 412.

24. See John Saillant, "Origins of African American Biblical Hermeneutics in Eighteenth-Century Black Opposition to the Slave Trade and Slavery," in Vincent Wimbush, ed., *African Americans and the Bible: Sacred Texts and Social Textures* (New York: Continuum, 2000), 237–250.

25. John Marrant, "A Sermon Preached on the 24th Day of June 1789, Being the Festival of Saint John the Baptist, at the Request of the Right Worshipful the Grand Master Prince Hall, and the Rest of the Brethren of the African Lodge of the Honorable Society of Free and Accepted Masons in Boston," in Adam Potkay and Sandra Burr, eds., *Black Atlantic Writers of the Eighteenth Century: Living the New Exodus in England and the Americas* (New York: St. Martin's Press, 1995), 106–122, quotation on 115.

26. Paul Cuffe, "Address to My Scattered Brethren and Fellow Countrymen at Sierra Leone," cited in Sheldon H. Harris, ed., *Paul Cuffe: Black America and the Africa Return* (New York: Simon and Schuster, 1972), 56.

27. Lott Carey to friends in Virginia, Apr. 24, 1826, in Adelaide Cromwell Hill and Martin Kilson, eds., *Apropos of Africa: Sentiments of Negro American Leaders on Africa from the 1800s to the 1950s* (London: Cass, 1969), 94–95.

28. Silvia M. Jacobs, "Pan-African Consciousness among African Americans," in Talmadge Anderson, ed., *Black Studies: Theory, Method, and Cultural Perspective* (Pullman: Washington State University Press, 1990), 70.

29. W. E. B. Du Bois, "Of Alexander Crummell," in Du Bois, *Souls of Black Folk,* 177.

30. Alexander Crummell, *The Future of Africa: Being Addresses, Sermons, etc., Delivered in the Republic of Liberia* (New York: Schlein, 1862), 107, 108.

31. Ibid., 125–126, 122–123.

32. Ibid., 125–126, 129.

33. In *Africa's Offering* (New York: John A. Gray, 1862), republished in Anthony B. Pinn, ed., *Moral Evil and Redemptive Suffering: A History of Theodicy in African-American Religious Thought* (Gainesville: University Press of Florida, 2002), 91.

34. Ibid., 92.

35. "Blyden's Letter," *New York Age,* Jan. 21, 1895; "Blyden's Letter," *Sierra Leone Weekly News,* Mar. 9, 1895; both quoted in Moses Moore, "'Behold the Dreamer Cometh': Orishatukeh Fadama and Pan-African Biblical Hermeneutics," in Wimbush, ed., *African Americans and the Bible,* 420, 428, n. 12.

36. Edward Wilmot Blyden, "The Ethiopian Eunuch," in Blyden, *Christianity, Islam, and the Negro Race* (London: W. B. Whittingham, 1887; reprint ed., Chesapeake, VA: ECA Associates, 1990), 152–172, quotation on 162.

37. Cited in Howard Brotz, ed., *Negro Social and Political Thought, 1850–1920: Representative Texts* (New York: Basic Books, 1966), 191.

38. Fredrickson, *Black Liberation,* 65, n. 15.

39. Martin R. Delany, *Blake, or The Huts of America, a Novel* (Boston: Beacon Press, 1970), 172.

40. Ibid., 247, 259–260.

41. Fredrickson, *Black Liberation,* 66, n. 18, 60, n. 17.

42. Lawrence S. Little, *Disciples of Liberty: The African Methodist Episcopal Church in the Age of Imperialism, 1884–1916* (Knoxville: University of Tennessee Press, 2000), 70.

43. Cited in Fredrickson, *Black Liberation,* 75, n. 34.

44. Scott, "'And Ethiopia Shall Stretch Forth,'" 11.

45. Fredrickson, *Black Liberation,* 75.

46. *AME Church Review* 1, no. 6 (October 1884): 79–85, reprinted in Pinn, *Moral Evil,* 131–140, quotations on 133–134, 134, 135, 136.

47. Ibid., 137, 137–138.

48. James A. Handy, "An Exposition on Psalm 68:31," in Theophilus Gould Steward, *The End of the World, or, Clearing the Way for the Fullness of the Gentiles* (Philadelphia: A.M.E. Church Book Rooms, 1888), 137–151, quotation on 150.

49. Ibid., 149–150.

50. *Cleveland Gazette,* Mar. 28, 1896, 2.

51. *Savannah Tribune,* Mar. 21, 1896, 2, 4.

52. In Chris Prouty, *Empress Taytu and Menilek II: Ethiopia, 1883–1910* (Trenton, NJ: Red Sea Press, 1986), 270, cited in Clarence E. Walker, *We Can't Go Home Again: An Argument about Afrocentrism* (New York: Oxford University Press, 2001), 47.

53. See Fredrickson, *Black Liberation*, 80–85.

54. Quoted ibid., 83.

55. Ibid., 84.

56. See J. Mutero Chirenje, *Ethiopianism and Afro-Americans in Southern Africa, 1883–1916* (Baton Rouge: Louisiana State University Press, 1987), 164–165.

57. Paul Lawrence Dunbar, "Ode to Ethiopia," in Gates and McKay, eds., *Norton Anthology*, 887.

58. Pauline Hopkins, *Of One Blood, or, The Hidden Self*, cited in Hopkins, *The Magazine Novels of Pauline Hopkins* (New York: Oxford University Press, 1988), 590, 531, 533, 570.

59. Du Bois, "Of Our Spiritual Strivings," 6.

60. Marcus Garvey, "The Future as I See It," in Gates and McKay, eds., *Norton Anthology*, 979–980.

61. Amy Jacques-Garvey, ed., *Philosophy and Opinions of Marcus Garvey*, 2 vols. in 1 (New York: Atheneum, 1969), 2:37–38.

62. Ibid., 1:44.

63. See Randall K. Burkett, *Garveyism as a Religious Movement: The Institutionalization of a Black Civil Religion* (Metuchen, NJ: Scarecrow Press, 1978), 34–36, 44.

64. Jacques-Garvey, ed., *Philosophy of Garvey*, 2:140–141.

65. On Diggs, see Burkett, *Garveyism*, 122–126.

66. *New York World*, Aug. 15, 1922, 3, quoted in Burkett, *Garveyism*, 126.

67. Amy Jacques Garvey, *Garvey and Garveyism* (Kingston, Jamaica: United Printers, 1963), 104.

68. Jacques-Garvey, ed., *Philosophy of Garvey*, 1:46, 60.

69. Ibid., 1:82.

70. See the Chicago Commission on Race Relations, *The Negro in Chicago: A Study of Race Relations and a Race Riot* (Chicago: University of Chicago Press, 1922), 59–64.

71. Universal Hagar's Spiritual Church documents are accessible on the Web site of the Rev. George H. Latimer-Knight, "The History of Father George William Hurley and the Universal Hagar's Spiritual Church," at http://fatherhurley.com.

72. See http://www.fatherhurley.com/tc.htm.

73. Nathaniel Samuel Murrell, "Turning Hebrew Psalms into Reggae Rhythms: Rastas' Revolutionary Lamentations for Social Change," at http://www.crosscurrents.org/murrell.htm, p. 2.

74. George Schuyler, "Views and Reviews," *Pittsburgh Courier*, Nov. 23, 1935.

75. Langston Hughes, "Call of Ethiopia," *Opportunity, Journal of Negro Life* 13, no. 9 (September 1935): 276.

76. See John Cullen Gruesser, *Black on Black: Twentieth-Century African American Writing about Africa* (Lexington: University Press of Kentucky, 2000), 4, 176–177.

77. Alain Locke, "Apropos of Africa," in Hill and Kilson, eds., *Apropos of Africa*, 352–355.

78. Funkadelic, "Mothership Connection (Star Child)," *Mothership Connection*, Casablanca Records 824502.

79. Alice Walker, *The Color Purple* (New York: Washington Square Press, 1982), 209–210.

80. Alexander Crummell, "The Destined Superiority of the Negro," in J. R. Oldfield, ed., *Civilization and Black Progress: Selected Writings of Alexander Crummell on the South* (Charlottesville: University Press of Virginia, 1995), 48; W. E. B. Du Bois, "The Conservation of Races," *American Negro Academy Occasional Papers* 2 (1897): 12.

81. Adam Hochschild, *King Leopold's Ghost: A Story of Greed, Terror, and Heroism in Colonial Africa* (New York: Houghton Mifflin, 1998), 111–112; Georges Nzongola-Ntalaja, *The Congo from Leopold to Kabila: A People's History* (London: Zed Books, 2002), 23, n. 44, 25.

82. Quoted in Hochschild, *King Leopold's Ghost*, 264.

83. Locke, "Apropos of Africa," 352.

84. Walker, *Color Purple*, 126.

85. W. E. B. Du Bois, *The Negro* (1915; reprint ed., Philadelphia: University of Pennsylvania Press, 2001), 9.

86. Walker, *Color Purple*, 125–126.

CHAPTER 7. EMMANUEL

Epigraph: Howard Thurman, *Jesus and the Disinherited* (Richmond, IN: Friends United Press, 1981), 112.

1. Toni Morrison, *Sula* (New York: New American Library, 1973), 65.

2. Ronald Steiner, "'Seeking Jesus': A Religious Rite of Negroes in Georgia," *Journal of American Folklore* 14, no. 54 (1901): 172.

3. David Macrae, *The Americans at Home: Pen-and-Ink Sketches of American Men, Manners, and Morals*, 2 vols. (Edinburgh: Edmonston and Douglas, 1870), 2:112–113.

4. Quoted in Albert J. Raboteau, *Slave Religion: The "Invisible Institution" in the Antebellum South* (New York: Oxford University Press, 1978), 242.

5. Aaron McGruder and Reginald Hudlin, illustrated by Kyle Baker, *Birth of a Nation: A Comic Novel* (New York: Crown, 2004), 65.

6. Lawrence W. Levine, *Black Culture and Black Consciousness: Afro-American Folk Thought from Slavery to Freedom* (New York: Oxford University Press, 1977), 50.

7. Quoted in Margaret Washington, "The Meanings of Scripture in Gullah Concepts of Liberation and Group Identity," in Vincent Wimbush, ed.,

African Americans and the Bible: Sacred Texts and Social Textures (New York: Continuum, 2000), 334.

8. Cited in Jaqueline L. Tobin and Raymond G. Dobard, *Hidden in Plain View: The Secret Story of Quilts and the Underground Railroad* (New York: Doubleday, 1999), 146.

9. Cited in ibid., 152.

10. See the version of this Negro spiritual recorded by the contemporary African American a cappella group Take Six, "O Mary," *Take Six*, Warner Bros/ Wea, 25892. See also Cheryl Townsend Gilkes, "'Go and Tell Mary and Martha': The Spirituals, Biblical Options for Women, and Cultural Tensions in the African-American Religious Experience," *Social Compass* 43, no. 4 (1996): 570–573.

11. Charles White, *O Mary, Don't You Weep*, reproduced in Richard J. Powell, *Black Art and Culture in the Twentieth Century* (London: Thames and Hudson, 1997), 77, no. 117.

12. "Daniel Saw the Stone," in James Weldon and J. Rosamond Johnson, *The Books of American Negro Spirituals: Including the Book of American Negro Spirituals and the Second Book of Negro Spirituals*, 2 vols. (New York: Viking Press, 1925–1926; reprint ed., New York: Da Capo Press, 1989), 1:162–163.

13. See David Emmanuel Goatley, *Were You There? Godforsakenness in Slave Religion* (Maryknoll, NY: Orbis Books, 1996), 49, n. 39.

14. In Harold Courlander, *Negro Folk Music U.S.A.* (New York: Columbia University Press, 1963), 61.

15. In R. Nathaniel Dett, ed., *Religious Folk-Songs of the Negro as Sung at Hampton Institute* (Hampton, VA: Hampton Institute Press, 1927), 145.

16. "He Is King of Kings," in ibid., 146–147.

17. David Walker, *Appeal to the Colored Citizens of the World*, in Charles M. Wiltse, ed., *David Walker's Appeal*, in *Four Articles, Together with a Preamble, to the Coloured Citizens of the World, but in Particular, and Very Expressly, to Those of the United States of America* (New York: Hill and Wang, 1965), 11–12.

18. W. E. B. Du Bois, "Of the Faith of the Fathers," in Du Bois, *The Souls of Black Folk* (1903; reprint ed., New York: Penguin, 1989), 163.

19. See the summary of the story and the sources in Gayraud Wilmore, *Black Religion and Black Radicalism*, 2nd ed. (Maryknoll, NY: Orbis Books, 1983), 62–71.

20. Thomas Wentworth Higginson, *Army Life in a Black Regiment* (1870; reprint ed., New York: Collier Books, 1962), 48.

21. Thomas Wentworth Higginson, "Negro Spirituals," *Atlantic Monthly*, June 1867, 695.

22. "Judgment," in Dett, ed., *Religious Folk-Songs*, 158.

23. "My Lord, What a Mourning," in ibid., 157.

24. Ice Cube, "When I Get to Heaven," *The Predator*, Priority Records, 57185.

25. Richard M. Dorson, *American Negro Folktales* (Greenwich, CT: Fawcett, 1967), 255–256.

26. James Baldwin, *The Amen Corner: A Play* (New York: Dial Press, 1968), 6–7.

27. Cited in John W. Roberts, *From Trickster to Badman: The Black Folk Hero in Slavery and Freedom* (Philadelphia: University of Pennsylvania Press, 1989), 153.

28. Cited in ibid., 155.

29. In Dett, ed., *Religious Folk-Songs*, 180–181, 146–147.

30. W. B. Allen, interviewed by J. R. Jones at *American Slavery: A Composite Autobiography*, http://greenwood.scbbs.com/servlet/sdssfile/gwsn_03s _all_w.pdf.

31. Jerry Eubanks, interviewed by J. R. Jones at ibid.

32. In Washington, "Meanings of Scripture," 337.

33. See Timothy B. Tyson, *Radio Free Dixie: Robert F. Williams and the Roots of Black Power* (Chapel Hill: University of North Carolina Press, 1999), 216–218.

34. In ibid., 230.

35. Ibid.

36. Quoted in Neal Robinson, *Christ in Islam and Christianity* (Albany: State University of New York Press, 1991), 168–170.

37. Yvonne Yazbeck Haddad and Jane Idelman Smith, *Mission to America: Five Islamic Sectarian Communities in North America* (Gainesville: University Press of Florida, 1993), 96–97.

38. James G. Spady and Joseph D. Eure, eds., *Nation Conscious Rap* (New York: PC International Press, 1991), 268–269.

39. Kelly Brown Douglas, *The Black Christ* (Maryknoll, NY: Orbis Books, 1994), 111–112; James H. Cone, *The Spirituals and the Blues: An Interpretation* (Maryknoll, NY: Orbis Books, 1991), 43–44.

40. Joseph R. Washington, Jr., *Black Religion: The Negro and Christianity in the United States* (Boston: Beacon Press, 1964), 147.

41. Mahalia Jackson and Doris Akers, "Lord, Don't Move This Mountain," in Verolga Nix and J. Jefferson Cleveland, eds., *Songs of Zion*, Supplemental Worship Resources 12 (Nashville, TN: Abingdon Press, 1981), 173.

42. Muhammad, *Message to the Blackman*, 95.

43. James Weldon Johnson, "The Prodigal Son," in Johnson, *God's Trombones: Seven Negro Songs in Verse* (New York: Viking Press, 1927), 25.

44. Prince Hall, *A Charge Delivered to the Brethren of the African Lodge on the 25th of June, 1792* . . . (Boston: Bible and Heart, 1792), 4.

45. Martin Luther King, Jr., "On Being a Good Samaritan," in King, *Strength to Love* (New York: Harper and Row, 1963), 17.

46. Ibid., 23.

47. James L. Wells, *The Good Samaritan*, c. 1932–1933, in Gary Reynolds and Beryl J. Wright, *Against the Odds: African-American Artists and the Harmon Foundation* (Newark, NJ: Newark Museum, 1989), 270, pl. 94.

48. Peter J. Boyer, "Man of Faith," *New Yorker*, Oct. 22, 2001, 50.

49. John Calvin, *The Gospel According to Saint John*, ed. D. W. Torrance and T. F. Torrance, trans. T. H. L. Parker (Grand Rapids, MI: Eerdmans, 1959), 209.

50. Boyer, "Man of Faith," 52.

51. Ibid., 50, 52.

52. Walker, *Appeal*, 37–38.

53. Martin R. Delany, *Blake, or The Huts of America, a Novel* (Boston: Beacon), 197.

54. Frederick Douglass, *Narrative of the Life of Frederick Douglass* (New York: Signet, 1968), 120.

55. Ibid., 123.

56. Anna Julia Cooper, "Womanhood a Vital Element in the Regeneration of the Race," in Mary Helen Washington, ed., *A Voice from the South* (New York: Oxford University Press, 1988), 16, 18.

57. W. E. B. Du Bois, "Darrow," *Crisis* 35 (June 1928): 203, reprinted in *Writings by W.E.B. Du Bois in Periodicals Edited by Others*, vol. 2: *1910–1934*, ed. Herbert Aptheker (Millwood, NY: Kraus-Thomson Organization, 1982), 516.
A. Philip Randolph, "Negro Labor and the Church," reprinted in *A Documentary History of the Negro People of the United States*, vol. 2: *1910–1932*, ed. Herbert Aptheker (Secaucus, NJ: Citadel Press, 1969), 630–636.

58. Langston Hughes, "Goodbye, Christ" (1932), in Nathan Irvin Huggins, ed., *Voices from the Harlem Renaissance* (New York: Oxford University Press, 1976), 419–420.

59. Countee Cullen, "Black Magdalens" (1925), in Huggins, ed., *Voices*, 347.

60. Amiri Baraka, "When We'll Worship Jesus" (1972), in Paul Vangelisti, ed., *Transbluesency: The Selected Poems of Amiri Baraka/Leroi Jones (1961–1995)* (New York: Marsilio, 1995), 158–161.

61. Tom Skinner, *How Black Is the Gospel?* (Philadelphia: J. B. Lippincott, 1970), 96, 104.

62. August Wilson, *Joe Turner's Come and Gone* (New York: Penguin Books, 1988), 91–93.

63. Chuck D with Yusuf Jah, *Fight the Power: Rap, Race, and Reality* (New York: Delacorte Press, 1997), 156–157.

64. Thurman, *Jesus and the Disinherited*, 17.

65. Ibid., 21.

66. Fannie Lou Hamer, in Edwin King, "Go Tell It on the Mountain: A Prophet from the Delta," *Sojourners*, December 1982, 20; Martin Luther King, Jr., *Stride toward Freedom: The Montgomery Story* (New York: Harper and Row, 1958), 40.

67. Charlie Braxton, "Apocalypse" (1990), in Kevin Powell and Ras Baraka, eds., *In the Tradition: An Anthology of Young Black Writers* (New York: Harlem River Press, 1992), 112.

68. KRS-One in Spady and Eure, eds., *Nation Conscious Rap*, 184.

69. Aaron McGruder, *A Right to Be Hostile: The Boondocks Treasury* (New York: Three River Press, 2003), 43.

70. In Amy Jacques-Garvey, ed., *Philosophy and Opinions of Marcus Garvey*, 2 vols. in 1 (New York: Atheneum, 1969), 1:62, 60–61.

71. Ibid., 1:61.

72. Ja Rule, "Only Begotten Son," *Venni, Vetti, Vecci*, Def Jam, 538920.

73. Lauryn Hill, "Forgive Them Father," *The Miseducation of Lauryn Hill*, Ruffhouse/ Columbia, 69035.

74. "Crucifixion," in Weldon and Johnson, *Books of American Negro Spirituals*, 1:174.

75. Edward Wilmot Blyden, "The Ethiopian Eunuch," in Blyden, *Christianity, Islam, and the Negro Race* (London: W. B. Whittingham, 1887; reprint ed., Chesapeake, VA: ECA Associates, 1990), 162.

76. See Goatley, *Were You There?* 46. The text of the Negro spiritual appears in ibid., 60.

77. Thomas C. Gray, *The Confessions of Nat Turner: Leader of the Late Insurrection in Southampton, Va* (1861; reprint ed., Salem, NH: Ayer, 1991), 5.

78. U.S. Bureau of the Census, *Historical Statistics of the United States: Colonial Times to 1970* (Washington, DC: U.S. Government Printing Office, 1976), 422, cited in Thomas Sowell, *Conquests and Cultures: An International History* (New York: Basic Books, 1998), 168.

79. W. E. B. Du Bois, "Jesus Christ in Texas," from *Darkwater: Voices from within the Veil* (1920), reprinted in David Levering Lewis, ed., *W. E. B. Du Bois: A Reader* (New York: Henry Holt, 1995), 501–502.

80. Countee Cullen, *The Black Christ and Other Poems* (New York: Harper and Brothers, 1929), 96, and flyleaf illustration by the poet's brother Charles.

81. Langston Hughes, *The Panther and the Lash: Poems of Our Times* (New York: Alfred A. Knopf, 1967), 37.

82. Frank Horne, "On Seeing Two Brown Boys in a Catholic Church," in Arnold Adolff, ed., *The Poetry of Black America: Anthology of the Twentieth Century* (New York: Harper and Row, 1973), 55.

83. Public Enemy, "Welcome to Terrordome," *Fear of a Black Planet*, Def Jam Records, 23446.

84. Tupac Shakur as Makaveli, "Blasphemy," *The Don Killuminati: The Seven Day Theory*, Interscope, 90039.

85. Michael Eric Dyson, *Holler If You Hear Me: Searching for Tupac Shakur* (New York: Basic Civitas Books, 2001), 230.

86. NAS, "God Love Us," *Nastradamus*, Sony, 63930.

87. Erik J. Williams, "Thugology: Carving Out Explosive Biblical and Theological Space in a Hip-Hop Universe," *BMa: The Sonia Sanchez Literary Review* 6, no. 1 (Fall 2000): 79.

88. Makaveli, "Blasphemy."

89. Cornel West, "A Philosophical View of Easter," in West, *Prophetic Fragments*

(Grand Rapids, MI: William B. Eerdmans; Trenton, NJ: Africa World Press, 1988), 265–266.

90. Marcus Garvey, "The Resurrection of the Negro," in Jacques-Garvey, ed., *Philosophy and Opinions of Marcus Garvey*, 1:88.

91. "De Angel Roll De Stone Away," in Weldon and Johnson, *Books of American Negro Spirituals*, 2:118–120.

92. Nas speaking in an interview in AllHipHop.com, as reported in http://www.rapnewsdirect.com/Artists/2Pac/News/0-202-1100-00.html.

93. Tupac Shakur as Makaveli, "Blasphemy," *The Don Killuminati: The Seven Day Theory*, Interscope, 90039.

94. Turner, writing in *The Voice of Missions*, Feb. 1, 1898, quoted in Wilmore, *Black Religion and Black Radicalism*, 125.

95. Alice Walker, *The Color Purple* (New York: Washington Square Press, 1982), 177.

96. Randall K. Burkett, *Garveyism as a Religious Movement: The Institutionalization of a Black Civil Religion* (Metuchen, NJ: Scarecrow, 1978), 183.

97. Quoted in Wilmore, *Black Religion and Black Radicalism*, 182.

98. Albert B. Cleage, Jr., *The Black Messiah* (New York: Sheed and Ward, 1968), 3, 92–93.

99. James H. Cone, *Black Theology and Black Power* (New York: Seabury Press, 1969), 36.

100. Poor Righteous Teachers, *Pure Poverty*, Profile, 1415.

101. Spady and Eure, eds., *Nation Conscious Rap*, 230.

102. KRS-One, "The Eye Opener," Boogie Down Productions, on *Live Hardcore Worldwide*, Jive, 1425.

103. Darrell Dawsey, *Living to Tell about It: Young Black Men in America Speak Their Piece* (New York: Doubleday, 1996), 243.

104. Tupac Shakur, "Black Jesuz," *Still I Rise*, Interscope Records, 490413.

105. *Tupac Shakur, 1971–1996*, by the editors of *Vibe* (New York: Crown, 1997), 126.

106. Sonia Sanchez quoted in Dyson, *Holler If You Hear Me*, 209–210.

107. I am grateful to Professor Harvey Cox of Harvard Divinity School for bringing this grim gesture of Evangelical piety to my attention.

108. Howard Thurman, *Deep River and the Negro Spiritual Speaks of Life and Death* (Richmond, IN: Friends United Press, 1990), 4, 17; Goatley, *Were You There?* 46.

109. See Jacquelyn Grant, *White Women's Christ and Black Women's Jesus: Feminist Christology and Womanist Response* (Atlanta, GA: Scholar's Press, 1989), 209–216.

110. Shakur, "Black Jesuz."

POSTSCRIPT

1. Norman R. Yetman, *Voices from Slavery* (New York: Holt, Rinehart, and Winston, 1970), 75.

2. W. E. B. Du Bois, *The Souls of Black Folk* (1903; reprint ed., New York: Penguin, 1989), 144.

3. David Bradley, "Passion Play at Mount Pisgah," *Pennsylvania Gazette* (March 1997), 29.

4. *Southern Galaxy* (Natchez), June 12, 1828, quoted in Terry Alford, *Prince among Slaves* (New York: Harcourt Brace Jovanovich, 1977), 81–82.

5. John Jasper, "The Sun Do Move," in Langston Hughes and Arna Bontemps, eds., *The Book of Negro Folklore* (New York: Fleming H. Revell, 1958), 228–229.

6. Ibid., 228.

7. In Henry Louis Gates, Jr., and William L. Andrews, eds., *Pioneers of the Black Atlantic: Five Slave Narratives from the Enlightenment, 1772–1815* (Washington, DC: Civitas, 1998), 331.

8. Stanley Crouch, "Do the Afrocentric Hustle," *The All-American Skin Game, or, The Decoy of Race: The Long and the Short of It, 1990–1994* (New York: Pantheon Books, 1995), 44.

9. Nathaniel Paul, "An Address, Delivered on the Celebration of the Abolition of Slavery, in the State of New York, July 5, 1827," in Milton C. Sernett, ed., *Afro-American Religious History: A Documentary Witness* (Durham, NC: Duke University Press, 1985), 85.

10. Howard Thurman, *Jesus and the Disinherited* (Richmond, IN: Friends United Press, 1981), 14–15.

SCRIPTURE INDEX